BLACKS IN THE NEW WORLD

AUGUST MEIER, *Series Editor*

A list of titles in the series appears at the end of this book.

Slaves and Missionaries

✝

SLAVES AND MISSIONARIES

The Disintegration of
Jamaican Slave Society,
1787–1834

MARY TURNER

UNIVERSITY OF ILLINOIS PRESS
Urbana   Chicago   London

© 1982 by the Board of Trustees of the University of Illinois
Manufactured in the United States of America

This book is printed on acid-free paper.

Library of Congress Cataloging in Publication Data

Turner, Mary, 1931–
Slaves and missionaries.

(Blacks in the New World)
Bibliography: p.
Includes index.
1. Slavery—Jamaica.   2. Missionaries—Jamaica—History.
3. Slavery and the church.   4. Church and race relations—
Jamaica—History   I. Title.   II. Series.
HT1096.T87   305.5'67'097292   82-6983
ISBN 0-252-00961-4   AACR2

The maps in this volume are based on
original work prepared by J. D. Parson.

*For Sam Sharpe, his
supporters and successors*

Contents

Abbreviations

P.A.	*Periodical Accounts*
S.M.R.	*Scottish Missionary and Philanthropic Register*
W.M.M.S. Letters	Letters from missionaries in Jamaica to the Wesleyan Methodist Missionary Committee in London
B.M.S.	Baptist Missionary Society
C.O.	Colonial Office records

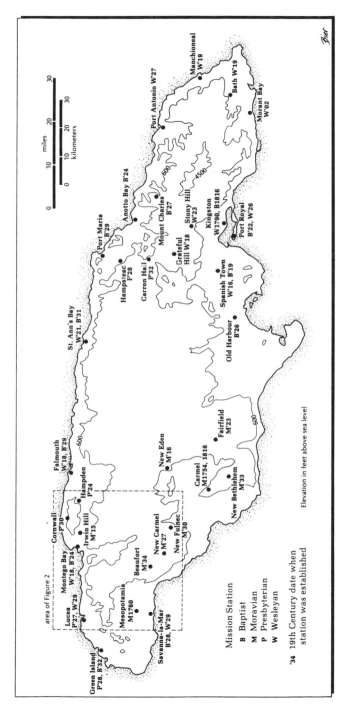

Green Island
P'28, B'32

Lucea
P'27, W'29

Montego Bay
W'18, B'24

area of Figure 2

Cornwall
P'30

Irwin Hill
M'15

Hampden
P'24

Falmouth
W'18, B'29

600

St. Ann's Bay
W'21, B'31

Port Maria
B'29

Anotto Bay B'24

Port Antonio W'27

Manchioneal
W'19

Bath W'19

Morant Bay
W'02

600

4500

Hampstead
P'28

Carron Hall
P'32

Mount Charles
B'27

Stony Hill
W'23

Grateful
Hill W'18

Kingston
W1790, B1816

Port Royal
B'22, W'26

Mesopotamia
M1760

Beaufort
M'34

New Carmel
M'27

New Eden
M'16

New Fulnec
M'30

Spanish Town
W'16, B'19

Savanna-la-Mar
B'28, W'29

Carmel
M1754, 1816

New Bethlehem
M'33

Fairfield
M'23

600

Old Harbour
B'26

Mission Station

B   Baptist
M   Moravian
P   Presbyterian
w   Wesleyan

'34   19th Century date when
      station was established

Elevation in feet above sea level

Mission Stations in Jamaica, 1834

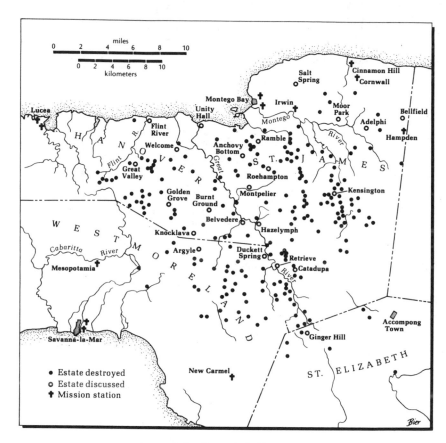

miles

| 0 | 2 | 4 | 6 | 8 | 10 |

kilometers

| 0 | 2 | 4 | 6 | 8 | 10 |

Lucea

H A N O V E R

Flint River

Flint River

Welcome

Great Valley

Golden Grove

Burnt Ground

Knocklava

Argyle

W E S T M O R E L A N D

Cabaritta River

Mesopotamia

Savanna-la-Mar

New Carmel

Montego Bay

Unity Hall

Anchovy Bottom

Belvedere

Duckett Spring

Irwin

Montego River

Ramble

Roehampton

Montpelier

Hazelymph

Retrieve

Catadupa

River

Ginger Hill

Salt Spring

Cinnamon Hill

Cornwall

Moor Park

Adelphi

Bellfield

Hampden

River

S T . J A M E S

Kensington

Accompong Town

S T . E L I Z A B E T H

• Estate destroyed
○ Estate discussed
✝ Mission station

Bier

Area of the Slave Rebellion, 1831

The Planters and
the Missionaries

JAMAICA IN THE eighteenth century was England's most important asset in the Caribbean. It was the largest island in the British West Indies, 140 miles long and forty miles at its widest part. The eastern parishes were overhung by mountains that rose to 7,000 feet over the Liguanea plain, dominated the magnificent harbor of Kingston, and subsided into ranges of rugged hills in the western parishes. Skirting the mountains and in the valleys wedged between their ranges were the two million acres of rich earth worked by slave labor that were the basis of Jamaican wealth. By 1763 Jamaica produced more sugar than all the other British West Indian islands put together.

The development of Jamaica added to the worldwide trade network that stimulated British commercial expansion. In the early eighteenth century the island was a component in the great triangular trade, "one of the most nearly perfect commercial systems of modern times,"[1] which brought British manufactures into Africa, African laborers into the land masses of the Americas, and tropical products into the markets of Europe. When this trade pattern shifted, Jamaica retained links with Africa and Britain and added links with Britain's North American colonies, where saltfish, lumber, and plantation supplies were purchased.

Participation in this intercontinental trade gave Jamaica's ruling class opportunities to make immense personal fortunes. They adorned their plantations with domestic palaces and dazzled London society with displays of conspicuous consumption.

Within the island, planters dominated every branch of government. They were members of the Jamaica Assembly,[2] which claimed constitutional parity with the House of Commons and, in fact, enjoyed real bargaining power through its control of taxes and supplies. Twelve Assembly members were chosen to serve on the governor's advisory council. In their parishes they served as magistrates of the petty session courts and as chief magistrates (called custodes). They also sat as judges in the assize courts; the island had only one professional judge, the chief justice, appointed by the crown, who presided over the grand courts held quarterly in each of the three counties, Middlesex, Surrey, and Cornwall. Two nonprofessional assistants recruited from the white ruling class shared the bench with him in the grand court, and three nonprofessionals presided in the quarterly assize courts. This concentration of authority put the island's internal affairs effectively into the hands of a small, white squirearchy comprising about fifty families.

Within this structure the planters enjoyed virtually unlimited power over the slave population. Officially their power was limited by the slave codes formulated by the Assembly. But no provisions were made to administer those clauses designed to protect the slaves, which defined hours of work, appropriate punishments, leisure time, or rations. The planters' primary interest was simply to keep the slaves under control, so living standards were low, work hours long, and punishment (usually flogging with a cart whip) harsh and arbitrary. The free colored and black population was also kept strictly subordinate to the whites and enjoyed no legal or civil rights.

In the imperial framework, however, the Jamaican planters were ultimately at the mercy of the British government, which determined their terms of trade, reviewed their legislation, and sanctioned the supply and use of slave labor. The planters, consequently, made every effort to protect their interests by exerting influence at Westminster. From 1682 the Jamaica Assembly, like its counterparts throughout the British Caribbean and in North America, employed agents in London to keep it informed of political trends in the capital, to provide British ministers with information and opinions independently of the island governor, and to organize lobbies on particular issues. As their wealth increased, some of the Jamaican planters established themselves in England as absentee landlords and acquired seats in Parliament.

The West India interest, which included both planters and merchants, emerged early in the eighteenth century; by 1761 they formed a considerable lobby composed of an "inner ring" of thirteen West Indians, including seven Jamaicans, and an "outer ring" of eight or nine associates.[3] The parliamentary lobby was supported by associations of West India planters and merchants formed in the principal West Indian trade centers, Bristol, Glasgow, and London. Through these associations and particularly through the London-based associations which formed the joint Committee of West India Planters and Merchants[4] in 1775, the absentees were able to exert considerable influence on their fellows in the West Indies and, at the same time, establish strong personal relations with influential members of the British government.

Until the last decades of the eighteenth century the West Indians' chief problem was to maintain and extend their sugar marketing privileges within the British empire and in Europe. The British West Indies supplied Britain and its North American colonies with sugar, but both markets limited their profits. In Britain the government charged high customs duties and insisted on British merchants handling the re-export of sugar to the Continent. In North America illegal trade with the French islands, which supplied duty-free sugar and molasses in return for food and lumber, created competition. The West India interest successfully tackled both these problems; in 1733 they secured the passage of the Sugar, or Molasses, Act, intended to suppress North American trade with the French islands through the introduction of prohibitive duties on the import of foreign sugar and molasses into the British American colonies. The act was never successfully enforced and had to be revised in 1766, but this initial West Indian triumph over the North American interests was followed in 1739 by a victory over the British sugar interests, when permission was given to export sugar directly to the European continent on the sole proviso that ships trading north of Cape Finisterre must touch at a British port. Little sugar was in fact exported because the British internal market was expanding, but the threat of a rival market boosted sugar prices in England and increased the planters' profits.

The British West Indian sugar planters maintained some marketing privileges in Britain until 1854, though their pre-eminence as world sugar producers was lost during the Napoleonic wars.[5] In the last decades of the eighteenth century, however, the British West Indians found that their relationship with the mother country could no longer be conducted on a straightforward commercial basis. British society was itself undergoing transformation and its West Indian colonies were, willy-nilly, involved in this process.

The industrial revolution altered Britain's economic base; in the course of two generations manufacturing became a mainstay of the national economy and industrialists a key element in the ruling class. This upheaval, which affected every class in the society, together with the wars and revolutions of the period, forced both secular and religious thinkers to review the newly emerging economic and social order and to formulate critiques. It was these ideological developments, characteristic of Britain's industrial take-off period, which first touched the West Indian planter interest by making slavery a political issue. The attack on slavery was formulated in religious terms and, from first to last, practicing Christians provided leadership for the cause. Slavery was also condemned, however, by political radicals across a wide spectrum, ranging from Tom Paine to the Whig politician Charles James Fox, and by political economists, most notably Adam Smith.

The social and moral dislocation attendant on the economic transformation of society prompted a religious revival characterized by an emphasis on the fundamentals of the Christian message, the imperatives of sin and salvation. This emphasis provided the dynamic for a reassertion of Christian values both among the growing conglomerations of heathen urban poor, removed from the traditional supervision of squire and establishment parson, and among the nominally Christian wealthy. The results were seen in the revival of existing sects, the formation of the Wesleyan Methodist church, and the multiplication of charitable trusts and charitable causes that comprised the humanitarian movement. It was the reinterpretation in eighteenth-century terms of the concept of sin that, for the first time, designated slavery as sinful.

The radicals arrived at the same conclusion by a different route. Their ideas derived not from evangelical Christianity but from the religious radicals of the seventeenth century, whose conflict with the state had prompted the acute critiques of government developed and secularized by the philosophers of the Enlightenment. For the radicals, chattel slavery symbolized the political slavery of citizens chained to a state structure that embalmed privilege and functioned by corruption, that denied political office to Dissenters and Catholics and representation to developing sectors of propertied citizens. Their minimum demand was constitutional reform, their maximum universal suffrage; but all radicals perceived in slavery the ultimate in human and political degradation and considered freedom for the slaves a necessary assertion of the rights of man.

A new edge was added to these condemnations by the political economist Adam Smith, whose analysis reflected the developing interests of the expanding commercial and industrial sectors. In his view slavery was part of a mercantilist system, characterized by monopolies and special privileges, inimical to the natural development of wealth and morality. The master-slave relationship, which denied the slave any share in the fruits of his labor and encouraged him to do as little work as possible, represented, in its most extreme form, the disincentives to production and social harmony consequent on arbitrary restaints on trade.[6]

The condemnation of slavery marked a significant step forward in the concept of human rights. Slavery had been justified by John Locke on the ground that it did not interfere with the fundamentals of intellectual freedom. If the slave found the hardship of slavery greater than the value of his life, he was free to resist the will of his master and "draw on himself the death he desires." Locke proved to be the last major philosopher to argue this case.[7]

The Quakers, who led the attack on slavery, embodied all the intellectual currents that condemned it. Prosperous Quakers, such as brewers, bankers, iron masters, and mineowners, were in the spearhead of the industrial revolution and were conscious of the interests that gave rise to Smith's analysis. As Dissenters they were excluded from political office, and their stance on nonviolence, which dictated that they refuse military service and the payment of war taxes, involved them in recurrent conflict with the government. It also compelled intermittent discussion of the ethics of slavery; it was this discussion which, in 1761, led the London Yearly Meeting to declare on theological grounds that participation by any Friend in the slave trade merited disownment.

The West Indians found that Quaker opposition created profound reverberations; within a decade it was the received wisdom of the educated, including the political nation, that slavery was morally and philosophically condemned.[8] Moral condemnation was strengthened in 1772 by the Mansfield ruling on the Somerset case that no positive English law allowed slave ownership in England. And in the immediate aftermath of England's defeat in the American Revolution, when the government's corruption and inefficiency in general were brought into question, a political attack took shape.

A Quaker petition for the abolition of the slave trade, presented to Parliament in 1783, led rapidly to a spate of antislavery propaganda. No less than one hundred petitions were sent to Parliament in 1787, and by that time a predominantly Quaker committee had launched the Society for the Abolition of the Slave Trade, and a parliamentary spokesman, the evangelical Anglican William Wilberforce, a rising young Tory politician and friend of Prime Minister Pitt, had been recruited to promote the cause in the House of Commons. Early in 1788 a special committee of the Privy Council was appointed to conduct an inquiry and, that summer, the antislavery movement won its first parliamentary success, a provisional measure to regulate the conduct of the trade.[9]

The antislavery movement did not confine its criticism to the slave trade; both in Parliament and in propaganda pamphlets slavery itself was condemned as a degrading institution, the Africans praised for their civilized accomplishments, and the blacks embraced as brothers. Particular emphasis was put on the fact that, having imposed slavery on the heathen blacks, the slave owners had made no attempt to provide them with religious instruction. Much attention was focused on the Jamaican planters, who owned most of the slaves in the West Indies.

The attack on slavery threatened both the planters' livelihood and the very structure of West Indian society. Throughout the slave colonies the small white minority which controlled the vast black majority assumed that slavery, a system which gave them unlimited power over the black population, was the only method whereby they could maintain law and order. The assumption was based on their definition of the blacks as inferiors. The human nature of the slaves was essentially denied by the masters, who considered them ultimately unresponsive to the social sanctions customary in white society. Abolition therefore threatened the continued existence of any civilized society in the West Indies, and the defense of the slave system necessarily became the planters' primary political concern.

Confronted by the abolitionists' attack and its initial achievements, the West India interest brought all its political experience to bear and organized for defense. Defense involved two tactics: protest against abolition of the trade, and a substantial counterattack of proslavery propaganda, backed up by some politic adjustments, on paper, of the island slave codes. Proslavery pamphlet writers, like their opponents, ransacked the Bible for texts to justify their cause, and countered information about the brutalities of the slave system with tales of the planters' essentially humanitarian interest in their slave property. The Jamaica Assembly, which represented the largest slave owners and the biggest sugar producers in the British West Indies, cooperated with this scheme. It passed a formal remonstrance against the abolition of the trade, but approved the Slave Trade Regulation Act and made successive revisions of the island slave code in 1787, 1789, and 1792. The 1792 slave code was officially intended to "obviate the causes which impeded the natural increase of the negroes; gradually to diminish the necessity of the slave trade; and ultimately, to lead to its complete termination." Under the planters' benign administration the slave trade would dwindle away. No provisions were made to administer the innovations, but they were well publicized in London and deprived the abolitionists of useful propaganda derived from the old slave laws.[10] Thus in the prolonged struggle for the abolition of slavery the West India interest, in cooperation with the Jamaica Assembly, repeatedly undermined parliamentary criticism by reforming the slave system on paper.

The demand for reforms, however, was not limited to legislative battles in Parliament. Antislavery propaganda stressed the importance of religious instruction for the slaves, and this particular reform was demanded by men prepared to implement it. In 1789 a Wesleyan preacher, first of a contingent of missionaries dedicated to teaching the slaves Christianity, began preaching in Kingston.

The Protestant churches before the religious revival had largely ignored the Christian obligation to carry the gospel to the heathen. This work was pioneered by the German Moravian church; their first missionaries were sent to the Danish West Indies, and in 1754 a mission was established in Jamaica on an estate in St. Elizabeth belonging to absentee English Moravian proprietors.[11] Missionary work became an established feature of church activity only when the triumphant progress of religion among the English working class stimulated visions of worldwide conquests for Christianity. Appropriately, it was a close associate of John Wesley who took the lead. Thomas Coke was a prominent preacher and widely regarded as a possible successor to Wesley himself. He demonstrated an intellectual interest in mission work by planning, in 1784, a nondenominational missionary society.[12] Missions became his life work, however, only after he had actually seen, on a chance visit to Antigua, a Methodist society flourishing among the slaves under the guidance of a converted planter.[13] All his energies were then thrown into promoting overseas missions. He became a one-man missionary society, preaching for funds, selecting missionaries, and visiting the West Indian mission field. When he died in 1814, on his way to India to inaugurate the Methodist conquest of the subcontinent, he left as legacy missions in Sierra Leone, Newfoundland, Nova Scotia, and no less than fifteen West Indian islands.[14]

The Moravian and Wesleyan example influenced the Particular Baptists. It was William Carey of the Northamptonshire Association, inspired by the vision of a Christian India, who first proposed a mission there in 1786. When Coke's early successes demonstrated that Carey was not an impractical zealot, the Baptist Missionary Society was founded in 1792, a society separate from the church and not financially dependent on it.[15] Church organizations were chary of mission work, fearful of the financial responsibility and doubtful that Christianity could be taught to naked savages.[16] But Coke and Carey tapped the enthusiasm of a church-going public attuned to good causes and aware of the needs of the heathen worldwide. Contemporary travel books, antislavery tracts, and the trial of Warren Hastings all demonstrated the extent of heathen darkness outside Europe, and after 1789 the French Revolution threatened Europe itself with triumphant godlessness. In Britain, which had become an embattled outpost of Christendom in western Europe, news of converted heathens made compelling propaganda and enlivened church magazines with heartening tales of sacrifice and success. Enthusiasts had no difficulty in forming committees and raising subscriptions, and between 1795 and 1799 the London, Scottish, and Church missionary societies were founded.[17]

The missionary challenge caused the slave owners a many-faceted political problem. At a practical level the whites in Jamaica were a small minority, barely 10 percent of the total population, ruling a slave force augmented yearly by Africans who had to be absorbed into the routine of estate work. They faced a slave rebellion of some dimension about every five years.[18] Any innovation in the system was regarded as a threat to security, and church attendance in itself meant a substantial innovation in the life of a people traditionally bound by the demands of estate labor. More disturbing was the fact that, even in England, the Wesleyan church was regarded by elements in the ruling class as yet another disruptive Dissenting sect. A church which raised up workingmen as preachers appeared to threaten the social order, and on this account English magistrates interfered with preaching and mobs were organized to drive preachers from the marketplace. The planters had reason to fear that the missionaries would teach the slaves not only the Christian virtues of industry and obedience but also that God made all men equal.

The most provocative element in the challenge was the relationship between missionary societies and the antislavery movement. In principle there was a vital division between these two. The antislavery movement, while it aimed only at abolishing the slave trade, condemned slavery. The missionary societies did not. They regarded slavery as a manifestation of the mysterious workings of God. Dr. Thomas Coke defined their viewpoint; he considered the status of the Negro to be anomalous and compared it with the anomaly of the tornado in the natural world, but concluded, "In both cases we are assured that justice must mark the footsteps of God, in what he does and in what he suffers, though we are unable to trace it in either case."[19]

At a practical level, however, the missionary societies and the antislavery movement shared a common conviction: that the most important single benefit to bestow upon the slaves within the framework of the slave system was Christianity. It followed, therefore, that individual leaders of the antislavery movement were closely associated with mission work. Wilberforce himself was a founding member of the Church Missionary Society and an honored guest and patron of other societies.[20] The situation was further complicated by the fact that some leading churchmen joined in the principled condemnation of slavery, including Coke's mentor, John Wesley. Wesley proclaimed, "Liberty is the right of every human creature as soon as he breathes the vital air. And no human law can deprive him of that right which he derived from a law of nature." He condemned "men buyers" equally with "men stealers." "The blood of thy brother," he warned the planters, "crieth against thee from the earth. . . . Instantly, at any price, were it half thy goods, deliver thyself from blood guiltiness."[21]

The missionary societies, however, did everything they could to preserve a political distinction between themselves and the antislavery movement; they carefully distinguished between Wilberforce the politician and Wilberforce the philanthropist and elevated the need to save souls above all civil and political questions. Particular care was taken to instruct prospective missionaries to this effect. Moravian recruits were told, in biblical terms, to avoid disputes about the rights of kings and princes. The Presbyterians were directed to take a lofty view of social circumstances: "Study to view them as matters of history. . . . Never converse with the natives on political subjects. Such conversation, you may be almost certain, will be misrepresented and turned as an engine against you." And Baptist missionaries were warned, "Do not intermeddle with politics. . . . Remember that the object is not to teach the principles and laws of an earthly Kingdom, however important a right understanding of these may be, but the principles and laws of the Kingdom of Christ. Maintain toward all in authority a respectful demeanor. Treat them with the honour to which their office entitles them. Political and party discussion avoid as beneath your office." Wesleyan instructions for missionaries to the West Indies were even more specific: ". . . your sole business is to promote the moral and religious improvement of the slaves to which you have access, without, in the least degree, in public or in private, interfering in their civil condition."[22]

The planters' fears were not allayed by the missions' attempt to disassociate themselves from the political dimensions of the slavery question. They correctly perceived that the attack on the slave trade and the appearance of the missionaries were inextricably connected. They were always alive to the suspicion that the missionaries, by deed or by default, were subversives, agents of the antislavery party. Their suspicions were well founded. Missions to the slaves were an innovation; no precedents established what the effects would be. The questions of what the missionaries would teach and, even more important, what the slaves would learn were real ones that could only be answered by events.

The missions gained an initial foothold in Jamaica because outright opposition to them would have been impolitic. The planters could not, at one and the same time, advertize their benevolence and hound preachers to the slaves out of the island. In formal terms the planters traditionally had some respect for religion as such, whatever their suspicions of the "sectarians." The Anglican church was established by the first white settlers in Jamaica, who endowed it with glebe land and made churches a customary feature of most parish capitals. Its staff included English gentlemen with university education but no property to inherit at home, who were made welcome at King's House, adventurers with virtually no education, as well as relatives and associates of the planters. They were appointed by the governor and were under the nominal supervision, from 1748, of the bishop of London. As clergy they shared all the shortcomings of their English contemporaries and were derisively categorized as "better qualified to be retailers of saltfish or boatswains to privateers" than ministers of the gospel.[23] But they provided the planters with the formalities required at birth, marriage, and death, and were generally regarded as a necessary appendage to white society.

Anglican clergy in Jamaica, however, did not regard the slaves as potential church-goers; they ignored their "home heathen" just as their English counterparts did. More than this, they were actively engaged in slave management and the majority remained so until emancipation.[24] An Anglican clergyman, the Reverend George W. Bridges, in fact emerged in the 1820s as the chief propagandist for the Jamaican planters.[25] Their only professional contact with the slaves was to conduct a mass baptism service occasionally, at the request of the planters.[26]

Some planters, however, demonstrated that they were not altogether opposed to serious efforts to convert the slaves. Black and colored emigré American Baptists, who arrived in Jamaica after the American Revolution, were allowed to set up as preachers. The founder of these Black Baptist churches was George Leile, born a slave in Savannah, Georgia, but freed by a religious master to work among his fellows. Leile left Georgia after his ex-master was killed in the Revolution and the family disputed his claim to freedom. He settled in Kingston, where he worked at first as an indentured servant and later set up in business as a wagoner.[27] He began preaching in 1784 at open-air meetings, built up a substantial, predominantly slave congregation of more than 800, and in 1793 opened a chapel where reading as well as Christianity were taught. By 1802 one of Leile's free converts, Thomas Nicholas Swigle, established a second Kingston congregation of some 500 members. Outside Kingston an American associate, Moses Baker, was employed by a Quaker planter to teach his slaves in Trelawney, and another, George Gibb, estabished a congregation in St. Mary.[28]

The Black Baptists looked on their church as a black church, a church of Ethiopia, but accounted themselves orthodox Baptists. They corresponded with American and British Baptists and received financial aid from the New Connection Baptists in Bristol.[29]

Leile and his colleagues provided the only experience the planters had of preachers who served the lower orders, since the Moravians, who lived on the estates, were not in the public eye. The black preachers excited some animosity and contempt; Leile on one occasion, for example, was challenged by a white to serve communion to his horse. Their work, however, enjoyed an uneasy tolerance. Leile was careful to admit no slaves as church members unless their owners testified to their good behavior and gave them permission to join. He was himself characterized by sympathetic whites as "decent, industrious and humble,"[30] every quality appreciated in a black. The missionaries, by contrast, were "renegade" whites, serving the slaves in a society where white was master. They were supported by British funds, British public opinion, British politicians, and, worse, recruited from a church accustomed to claim the protection not of patronage but of law.

Politic considerations, nevertheless, suggested that the planters' best

move was simply to keep the missionaries, as they kept the black preachers, under vigilant supervision. The wars and slave rebellions engendered
by the French Revolution, however, together with the success of the
attack on the slave trade, made preachers to the slaves the focus of the
full force of the planters' antagonism. In the upshot the Black Baptist
preachers were silenced, but a basis for the expansion of mission work
was established by the tenacity of the missionaries, the cooperation of
individual planters, and, not least important, the intervention of the
imperial government.

The Wesleyan-Methodist mission in Jamaica was an outcome of
Coke's pioneer missionary tour of the West Indies in 1789. Two hundred
blacks and coloreds and 400 whites, the largest number of whites he ever
preached to in the West Indies, attended his first service. Although the
service was interrupted by a "company of gentlemen inflamed by liquor"
who provided a foretaste of the antagonism the mission was to meet
with, Coke was very impressed both by the whites' "civilities" to him
and by the serious religious interest of some of the congregation. He
decided that "the island . . . was too populous to give sanction to neglect,
and too wicked to leave us any room to conclude that the inhabitants
were in the road to heaven." A mission bridgehead in Kingston was
established, and by 1790 a chapel accommodating 1,500 people had
proudly taken its place on the main square between the barracks and the
Anglican church.[31]

The Kingston mission was strongly supported by the free coloreds
and blacks, who in 1803 formed almost half the congregation. Some
1,200 free coloreds and blacks of the total island population of 10,000
lived in Kingston.[32] They were not a wealthy group; even in 1823, when
they had increased in prosperity and numbers, they contributed only one
thirty-fourth of the island's tax revenue. Most earned their living in the
towns as skilled workers, small traders, and clerks, and in the country as
small cultivators. With the exception of a wealthy, well-educated minority who were granted, individually, citizen status by special privilege acts
in the Assembly, they were firmly consigned by the whites to noncitizen
status and denied full legal rights until 1813 and civil rights until 1830.
Social segregation was almost complete and extended to the Anglican
church, where the free coloreds and blacks could sit only in the back
pews or in the organ loft with the slaves, the better to preserve, as the
Kingston Common Council so clearly expressed it, "the dominion of the

few over the many."[33] Accordingly, a number became active and devoted members of the Wesleyan mission and enabled the mission to sustain the vicissitudes of the next decades.

No sooner were the Wesleyans established than the slave system and the military power that sustained it seemed threatened with collapse. The Haitian revolution of 1791 drove panic-stricken white French colonists, together with their slaves and some free blacks and coloreds, to take refuge in Jamaica. The failure of the British invasion attempt launched from Jamaica and the triumph of Toussaint L'Ouverture, leader of the revolution, left Jamaica with a black republic as neighbor just ninety miles away. In St. Lucia the British were defeated by an army of freed slaves, and insurrections followed in the islands of Dominica, St. Vincent, and Grenada, where substantial French minorities had been under British rule for twenty-five years. In Jamaica itself the Trelawney Town Maroons, one of four communities of ex-slaves who had established a territorial base for themselves as the result of a prolonged struggle in the early eighteenth century, rebelled. They were forced to treat for peace only after a severe campaign in which a hundred man-hunting bloodhounds were imported from Cuba for use against them.[34]

All preachers to the slaves and the free blacks and coloreds were immediately seen, in these circumstances, as a threat to the island's security. In Kingston riots led by respectable whites prevented church services from being held after dark, and an attempt was made in 1791 to destroy the Wesleyan chapel. The magistrates restored order, but the rioters were acquitted in court. The Wesleyan missionaries lived in the midst of threats and newspaper scandals and their more prominent members were stoned. The Black Baptists suffered worse. Leile and his free colored co-worker, Moses Baker, were charged with preaching sedition and kept in irons while awaiting trial, although they were eventually acquitted.[35]

Once the Maroons were defeated, both the Wesleyans and the Black Baptists were allowed to resume work, and the Jamaica Assembly, in response to suggestions from the Committee of West India Planters and Merchants, for the first time admitted the utility of encouraging the Anglican church to undertake slave instruction. The impetus for this move derived initially from Beilby Porteus, who, as bishop of London (1787–1808), was nominally responsible for supervision of the Anglican churches in the British West Indies. Porteus was an evangelical and an early supporter of the plan propounded by the Reverend James Ramsay in his pioneer antislavery work published in 1784, *An Essay on the Treatment and Conversion of African Slaves in the British Sugar Colonies*. Its first priority was the establishment of a body of clergy, paid by the imperial government, who would set up free schools to educate the slaves in both Christianity and literacy.

Porteus at first appealed to the governors of the West Indian islands to set up Sunday schools along these lines, without success[36]; but he enlisted the support of several absentee planters, including the Jamaican Charles Ellis, in founding the Incorporated Society for the Instruction and Religious Conversion of the Negroes. Based on funds intended originally for the education of Indian children,[37] the society was to recruit and partially finance additional curates for work among the slaves. At the same time Porteus did all he could to improve the quality of clergy sent out to the islands and to encourage resident clergy to practice self-discipline. This led to the estabishment in Jamaica of an ecclesiastical commission, consisting of five rectors, to apply ecclesiastical law.[38]

The West India Committee was quick to take its cue from Porteus and urged the West Indian assemblies, in particular the Jamaica Assembly, to assist his efforts. As a result, the Anglican clergy in Jamaica was instructed to set aside time every Sunday to teach the slaves the meaning of baptism and the catechism. The provisions were nominal; the rectors were put in charge of slave populations ranging from 3,000 in St. Dorothy to more than 20,000 in St. Thomas in the East. The clergy, of course, was not about to turn the church into an evangelical force, as the Assembly members knew very well. Even after the appointment by the imperial government in 1824, as part of a program to reform the slave system, of a bishop specifically charged to promote slave instruction, the clergy engaged in this work was always a small minority. The bishop himself, Christopher Lipscomb, regarded such work at best with suspicion, and, partly as a result of his influence, the Anglican church in its official capacity never played a significant role among the slaves.[39] It was used more than once, however, by the planters and the West India Committee to brighten the slave owners' image.

The pattern established in the first decade of mission work, uneasy tolerance by the authorities giving way in times of political stress to overt hostility, was repeated in 1802 and in 1807. On each occasion opposition to slave instructors deepened.

In 1802, when a large French fleet was sent to the Caribbean to reconquer St. Domingue, and Jamaica feared invasion, the Assembly, as one of a number of security measures, passed a law to curtail mission work. The initiative was taken by Sir Simon Taylor, custos of St. Thomas in the East, one of the largest slave owners in the island, who was particularly hostile to the missionaries, suspicious of their growing numbers, and incensed by the formation of a Wesleyan society in the parish capital of Morant Bay. At his instigation an act was passed to prevent preaching by persons not "duly qualified by law." In traditional antisectarian terms the act condemned the preaching of "ill-disposed, illiterate, or ignorant enthusiasts" who were perverting the minds of the slaves and affording them opportunities for concerting mischief. "Unqualified" persons found preaching were to be charged as rogues and vagabonds and sentenced to a month's hard labor for the first offense and six months for the second.[40] The act struck directly both at the Black Baptists and at the use made by the Wesleyans of lay preachers recruited from the free colored and black population, who were playing an increasingly important role in developing mission work. But it was also brought to bear, by the magistrates in St. Thomas in the East, against the missionaries themselves, whose legal position had yet to be defined.

The rights of Dissenting preachers in England had been defined originally in the 1689 Toleration Act and during the eighteenth century, in response to pressure from Dissenters themselves, extended by the Toleration Acts of 1711 and 1779. The Jamaica Assembly had never passed such an act, but it had, in 1728, incorporated into island law all English laws and statutes in effect on October 1 that year, thereby, arguably, making the acts of 1689 and 1711 applicable. Until Sir Simon Taylor instigated the 1802 law, Jamaican magistrates, however, followed current English practice as established by the 1779 act; the missionaries appeared before them, took the oaths of allegiance and supremacy (to guarantee their fidelity to the king and constitution), and subscribed to a scriptural declaration that was accepted, in law, as equivalent to the Thirty-nine Articles of the Church of England. After that they were licensed to preach anywhere in Jamaica.[41] The 1802 act, however, threw the whole question into the melting pot; it prevented preaching by persons not "duly qualified by law" but did not define what constituted due qualification.

The imperial government considered that the law infringed on the principle of religious toleration; the law was disallowed and, in an effort to resolve the question, the Assembly was invited to consider the draft of a toleration act for the island. The Assembly, however, incensed by the disallowance as "an interference with the appropriate functions of the House," refused to do so.[42] It was left to the magistrates to respond informally to imperial pressure; the Wesleyans and the Black Baptists were allowed to resume work.

The planters made a second, more determined attack on preachers to the slaves in 1807. In the wake of a slave conspiracy came news of the victory of the antislave trade campaign. Rage and resentment against Wilberforce and his associates rose to a new pitch, and in July, 1807, the Wesleyan church itself added fuel to the flames: it aligned itself publicly with the antislavery cause by forbidding the missionaries either to hold slaves or to marry a slave owner. The missionaries were, consequently, defined in Jamaica as "the instrument of Fanatics and Enthusiasts in Great Britain for the purpose of effecting political mischief, and with it the destruction of life and property, to His Majesty's white subjects in this island."[43] When the Assembly met in October, 1807, it passed a new consolidated slave code which made missionary work illegal but attempted to silence potential criticism on this score by promoting Anglican instruction for the slaves. Clause one stated that slave owners and overseers should give their slaves religious instruction, and clause two specifically limited such instruction to Anglican doctrine; Methodists and all other sectarians were prohibited from preaching. One of the Methodist missionaries was immediately imprisoned for a month for defying the law, and all were persistently denied licenses.[44]

The missions were once more saved from annihilation by the imperial government; the 1807 code was disallowed and a different method of protecting the missionaries was attempted. An additional instruction was issued to the governor: "that you do not, on any pretence whatever, give your assent to any law or laws to be passed concerning religion, until you shall have first transmitted unto us . . . the draught of such bill or bills . . . unless you take care . . . that a clause or clauses be inserted therein suspending . . . the execution thereof until our will and pleasure shall be known thereupon."[45] The Assembly contested these provisions and refused to vote supplies until the governor, the Duke of Manchester, assented to yet another antimission act that designedly nullified the governor's power of suspension by being valid for only one year.[46]

The missionaries were left in an unenviable position: their activities could not be made illegal, but at the same time the legal base of their work was undefined. In this situation a practice developed of allowing the missionaries to work in each parish at the discretion of the magistrates. The precedent for this practice was established by a case arising from the 1802 law. The magistrates in St. Thomas in the East, guided by the custos, Sir Simon Taylor, used the law to charge the Kingston missionary who founded the Morant Bay mission, the Reverend Daniel Campbell, with illegal preaching. Campbell was tried at the Kingston assize and, as a missionary licensed by the Kingston magistrates to preach in Kingston, found guilty under the act, of not being "duly qualified" to preach in the adjacent parish of St. Thomas in the East.[47]

The missionaries were prepared to dispute the ruling, but on seeking legal advice they were told there was no toleration law operative in the island to which they could appeal. Though the 1802 act under which Campbell was tried was disallowed, the judgment in his case was used as a precedent. It had upheld the right of the magistrates in St. Thomas in the East to judge, independently of the Kingston magistrates, a preacher's credentials. From this time until 1828 missionaries applying for a license continued to take the oaths of allegiance and supremacy and subscribe to a scriptural declaration, but the magistrates decided whether their credentials as ordained ministers qualified them to preach in that parish.[48] These powers enabled the Kingston magistrates to keep the Wesleyan chapel closed from 1807 to 1814 simply by refusing to license any missionary. The one missionary who challenged their right spent a month in jail for holding one Sunday service.[49]

The impact of the ruling on the Black Baptists was more far-reaching. Their Kingston churches were closed. Baker's chapel became a hospital, and from this time forward the Black Baptist church ceased to develop, though some preachers were subsequently allowed by planter patrons to resume work on the estates; Moses Baker and George Gibb held congregations together until they died in the 1820s. Once the magistrates had established the right to insist on "due qualification" before licensing preachers, there was no place in the system for the Black Baptists. Preachers needed credentials which identified them as accredited ministers of a recognized church before they could hope to be awarded a license to preach. The congregations they established, however, were taken over in some instances by missionaries from the Baptist Missionary Society.

The B.M.S. proposed originally to send missionaries to assist Leile and Swigle, a scheme to which the Black Baptists had responded with enthusiasm.[50] When all preachers to the slaves were silenced, however, the B.M.S. shelved the proposal; it was not until 1814 that a man was sent to assist Moses Baker and eventually a missionary took over from him,[51] a pattern followed with other Black Baptist congregations.[52] In other cases the congregations broke up, though some of them, no doubt, became independent sects under their own leaders and merged with the Native Baptist groups discussed below, which both the Black Baptist and the mission churches engendered.

The Wesleyan missionaries, in the circumstances, addressed themselves to allaying planter hostility. They were not unfamiliar with the techniques required. Confronted by hostility in Britain, the church made every effort to be, in John Wesley's words, "friends of all and enemies of none." The annual conference of the church regularly exhorted members to "submit to magistrates for conscience sake" and not to "speak evil of dignitaries." Deference to authority was the guiding principle which the W.M.M.S. adopted to obtain a license for their Kingston chapel.

The society suggested to the imperial government that the governor should settle the issue by choosing for Kingston the most suitable man among the three Wesleyan missionaries on the island; if he found all three objectionable, the society undertook to send out another candidate.[53] The missionaries themselves approached the Jamaican authorities in this spirit; they petitioned the Kingston magistrates to re-open their chapel in 1809 but laid no claim to toleration. Instead they emphasized their qualifications: ordination by Dr. Coke and previous experience in Antigua.[54] Their efforts, nevertheless, were at this stage unsuccessful.

It was not until the second decade of the nineteenth century that conditions for mission work became more favorable. The considerations that had led the planters to extend a degree of toleration to the first missionaries carried even greater weight in the years following the end of the Napoleonic wars in 1815. The planters became increasingly the clients of the imperial government; alternative sources of cheap sugar for both the British and the continental markets developed in Cuba, Brazil, and the East Indies, making West Indian sugar producers dependent on the protection they were accorded in the British sugar market. And it was clear, by the 1820s, that there were powerful forces in Britain pressing for free trade.

The antislavery party, encouraged by its success in abolishing the slave trade, also remained active and influential. It pressured the government to end the international slave trade by treaties with the European governments involved, and prompted efforts to prevent illegal slave trading among British colonies in the West Indies. Slave registration was imposed on the crown colonies in 1814, and registration laws were requested from the island assemblies two years later.[55] There seemed every possibility that the party would move to a direct attack on slave property holding. The erosion of their economic importance, plus the political battering by the antislavery party, threatened to overwhelm the planters.

Under these circumstances the West India interest had to pay particular attention to its relationship with the imperial government. As clients they enjoyed some special advantages. They continued to comprise a substantial lobby in Parliament that, from the abolition of the slave trade until 1832, constituted a core group of at least twenty-two members in the House of Commons. In the House of Lords there were no less than eight Jamaican planters and the West Indian body totaled about eighteen. To the antislavery party, which never numbered more than twelve in the Commons, their numbers were formidable enough, but "their weight with the government," as Henry Brougham put it, "is far more to be dreaded."[56] Their weight derived, in part, from personal friendships (between, for example, the Jamaican planter Charles Ellis and the prominent Tory politician George Canning), but more significantly from their recognition that, increasingly, political influence was their only strength; willing cooperation with imperial policy became the West India Committee's main line of defense.

By 1815 the imperial government had defined two areas of interest requiring cooperation: religious instruction for the slaves and religious toleration for the missionaries. The British government's commitment to the principle of religious toleration was underlined by the 1812 Toleration Act, popularly known as the Grand Charter of the Dissenters. It represented a hard-won victory for Dissent; it established the right of any person who swore the oaths of supremacy and the scriptural declaration before one magistrate to become a preacher. It set a standard that made Jamaican efforts to deny the ministers sent out by the missionary societies an opportunity to preach completely anomalous. The West India Committee, therefore, used its influence with the island legislatures to promote religious instruction for the slaves and to allow mission work.

The Jamaica Assembly included a group of substantial resident planters who recognized the wisdom of the cooperation policy and exerted their influence accordingly. One of their chief spokesmen was Richard Barrett, who became custos of St. James, speaker of the Assembly, and editor and proprietor of the *Jamaica Journal and Kingston Chronicle*, the one liberal newspaper in the island. Their attitude toward religious instruction for the slaves was urbane and instrumental. As Barrett told a Presbyterian

missionary who wanted permission to teach on one of his estates, "I have
a bad set of people: they steal enormously, run away, get drunk, fight
. . . the women take no care of their children and there is no increase on
the property. Now, if you can bring them under fear of God, or a judgment to come, or something of that sort, you may be doing both them
and me a service."[57] As magistrates they dispensed licenses to such missionaries as appeared before them and demonstrated their confidence
that the slave system could absorb mission influence. This group was also
supported by a few members, like Stephen Drew of St. Ann's parish, who
were seriously committed to Christianity and exerted themselves inside
and outside the Assembly to help the missionaries and cooperate with
the imperial government.

The "cooperators" in the Assembly were by no means always successful; Sir Simon Taylor died in 1813, but his spirit went marching on.
Strenuous battles were fought throughout the period of slavery over the
implementation of many aspects of imperial policy, in particular, over
the program for the reform of slavery proposed in 1823. Opposition
focused then precisely on the issue of religious toleration for the missionaries. In the immediate aftermath of the Napoleonic wars, however, the
cooperators were in a position to promote the exercise of religious toleration.

The emergence of this group was greatly facilitated by the strength-
ening of British influence in the island through visits by Jamaican planters
to England and by absentees normally resident in England to Jamaica.
These exchanges established the extent to which charitable works had
become part of the pattern of English ruling-class behavior. Innumerable
charities—for foundlings, for the destitute, for lying-in hospitals, for
religious education—had boards of directors recruited from the aristoc-
racy and occasionally graced by members of the royal family. Such examples were calculated to inspire colonial emulation among both the
fashion-conscious and the religious-minded. It was in this context that
Jamaica's ruling class began to manifest a more liberal attitude toward
religious enterprises in general and religious instruction for the slaves in
particular.

The formation in 1812 of a branch of the British and Foreign Bible
Society, which collected £250 in a few weeks from both whites and free
coloreds,[58] was symptomatic of this change. In 1816 the Assembly itself
made a significant move. Its new slave code took cognizance of the
imperial government's stand on religious toleration to the extent that,

while it explicitly denied slave converts the right, customary in Dissenting churches, to preach and teach or attend night meetings, it imposed no restrictions on the missionaries themselves. At the same time the Assembly provided salaries for Anglican curates to be especially recruited to teach the slaves, and encouraged slave baptism by replacing customary charges, which ranged from more than £1 to six shillings and sixpence for each slave, to a standard fee of two shillings and sixpence.[59]

It was the Assembly's acceptance of the need for religious instruction that allowed individual planters and attorneys, in their capacities as magistrates, to license the missionaries and encourage their work. With their assistance the missionaries gained countenance and the societies were able to respond to opportunities, including the openings afforded by the Black Baptist churches. By the time the slaves were emancipated in 1833, there were sixteen Wesleyan and fourteen Baptist stations scattered across the island, eight Moravian missions grouped, with the exception of one north coast station, in the southwest parishes on hills surrounding the Black River valley, and five Presbyterian stations strung along the north coast from Lucea in the west to Port Maria in the east. There were forty-four missionaries in all,[60] usually assisted by their wives, and mission membership totaled 27,000.

Licenses for mission work were first dispensed by a small minority of Jamaican whites with religious sympathies. Kingston became a center for both Baptists and Wesleyans under the influence of John Savage, a member of the Kingston Council. He won the support of James Laing, a fellow councilor who was in 1823 custos of Kingston and one of the most important attorneys in the island. After 1815, when a new Wesleyan missionary had to apply three times for a license to preach, no other missionary was refused a license. The Wesleyans established three chapels there and the Baptists founded two.[61] In St. Catherine the Baptists were particularly fortunate to find that the custos himself, Sir Francis Smith, attorney, clerk of the supreme court, and member of the Assembly, was a friend of the Reverend Joseph Fletcher, member of the B.M.S. committee. Smith's influence won the mission many influential friends, including the assemblyman and attorney M. B. Clare, M.D., who was knighted and made councilor in 1826.[62]

An English planter and barrister, Stephen Drew, an assemblyman who was converted to Methodism in Jamaica and acted as counsel for the defense in the 1802 case against Daniel Campbell, introduced the Wesleyans to St. Ann. Drew built a chapel on his own estate, Bellemont, and his friendship with Henry Cox, custos and assemblyman, ensured them licenses to preach, while his son-in-law John Fox, a proprietor and magistrate in St. Andrew, became a Wesleyan lay preacher.[63] Another English planter, Samuel Moulton Barrett, who returned to Jamaica determined to undertake good works, taught the slaves himself until a full-time Presbyterian missionary arrived at his expense on his Trelawney estates.[64] Samuel Vaughan, long-standing protector of the Black Baptist preacher Moses Baker, proved a firm friend to the Baptist missionaries on the north coast. It was planters of this type who promoted the Moravian mission in Westmoreland and St. Elizabeth. Hutchinson Muir Scott of Hopeton, Westmoreland, for example, invited visits to his estate in 1822, and later gave land and timber for a mission adjoining the estate called New Carmel; other Moravian missions benefited in the same way.[65]

In one parish, St. Thomas in the East, the Anglican clergy acted as intermediaries between the local planters and the missionaries. Both the Reverend John West and the Reverend John Trew worked with the slaves, and West was an advocate of Beilby Porteus's plan for teaching the slaves to read and write.[66] They introduced the Wesleyan missionaries to a network of sympathetic proprietors, including the proprietors of Golden Grove, the largest estate in the parish.[67] Sir Simon Taylor was replaced as custos of the parish by assemblyman Peter Robertson, who, as chief magistrate, gave the missionaries every assistance. Under these auspices the Wesleyan mission at Morant Bay was followed by another at Bath in the valley of the Plantain Garden River and at Manchioneal on the east coast.[68]

Scottish patrons, traditionally firm Presbyterians, gave their support to the S.M.S. From the earliest years of settlement Scotland supplied an important element in the Jamaican white population. "Jamaica," wrote Edward Long, "is greatly indebted to North Britain as very near one third of the inhabitants are either natives of that country, or descendants from those that were."[69] The connection continued as long as the slave system operated. Scotsmen established in Jamaica recruited their young relatives to train as sugar planters; penniless young men took ship from Glasgow and Whitehaven in the hope of finding a Gaelic-speaking patron on arrival. The Scots maintained their allegiance to the Presbyterian church and persistently petitioned the Assembly for funds to establish a Presbyterian kirk in Kingston until a grant was made in 1814. The Scottish Missionary Society, though the offspring of the United Secession church and not the Church of Scotland represented by the Kingston kirk, anticipated that men "reared in the doctrines and learning required for a preacher" in Scotland would not meet with the "aversion" roused by strangers.[70]

Two absentee Scottish plantation owners, William Stothert and Alexander Stirling, set an example by inviting the S.M.S. to send a missionary to their slaves in Trelawney. George Blyth, once established at Hampden estate, soon found that in Trelawney and St. Mary, "The greater part of the respectable people in the country are Scotsmen, who almost universally favour the Presbyterian form of religion."[71] Another S.M.S. missionary, set out to Hampstead estate in St. Mary, built a church in Port Maria and was so much in demand for estate work that a second man was sent to found the Carron Hall mission, twelve miles from Port Maria. When local Presbyterian loyalties were less strong, the S.M.S. had more difficulty in gaining access to the estates; the missionary at Lucea waited three years before being invited by one proprietor to instruct the slaves on four estates.[72]

The missionaries' patrons included, as already mentioned, planters who thought it politic to patronize them and believed they could do no harm. Richard Barrett was their most important single ally of this sort. His example encouraged others to have confidence in their own judgment of the missionaries. In Trelawney, for example, James Stewart, one of the few overseers recruited in Scotland ever to become an attorney, custos, and assemblyman, played host; he lent the Wesleyans the old police office as temporary premises in Falmouth in 1818, and a Baptist mission followed in 1826. Resident proprietors in Trelawney followed Stewart's lead and afforded the missionaries employment on the estates.[73]

The patrons, whatever their motive, did not lose sight of the need to guide, advise, and, above all, control the missionaries. To patrons who paid stipends, subsidized mission buildings, and had missionaries resident on their estates, they were employees. To patrons dispensing licenses, they were protégés. In either case their social behavior, their teaching, and their political sympathies were expected to conform to the standards for good behavior set by the patrons. Interest focused on three main points: that the missionaries' access to the slaves should be limited, that they should respect the church and the magistracy, and that they should not associate themselves in any way with the critics of slavery.

The missionaries had little enough time in which to teach the slaves. Estate visits were limited to the two-hour dinner break, called shell-blow; attendance at Sunday services, even in estate chapels, was drastically reduced during crop season. It was quite common for the magistrates to reduce the time available still further by making "candlelight" services illegal. Since darkness fell about 6 P.M., Sunday evening services were customarily transferred to the afternoon, but the prohibition deprived even slaves living near the chapel of the opportunity to attend week-night services and classes. This prohibition became one of the terms on which licenses were dispensed. Wesleyan licenses for Montego Bay, Spanish Town, and Kingston, three main population centers, were all limited in this way.[74] From time to time the missionaries tried to establish a customary right to hold services until about 8 P.M. The Wesleyan missionary at Stony Hill managed to achieve this, in spite of complaints to the magistrates, and by 1826, under the occasional supervision of a constable, some evening services were held in Montego Bay.[75] But candlelight services, no matter how early they ended, aroused suspicion, a fear that deeds could be plotted by night which did not bear discussion by day, a fear backed up by the strong objections of slave managers to their laborers dissipating their energy on night journeys.

The patrons' insistence on due respect was much less tangible than the controls, but just as real. They appealed, on the one hand, as white men to the color tie but, on the other hand, maintained the class barriers. Their courtesies and liberal gestures were intended to provoke gratitude and emulation, and eliminate any possibility of criticism. A good example of the manner in which the patrons flattered the missionaries' self-esteem was provided by Sir Francis Smith's gracious dispensation of a license to a new Wesleyan missionary in Spanish Town. He commented, "It is with pleasure the court allows you to take the oaths. The other gentlemen of your persuasion have conducted themselves in such a manner as to give satisfaction to the legislature and to do good to the community and we hope you will imitate their laudable example."[76] The license in question introduced restriction of candlelight services to Spanish Town for the first time. Marks of friendship shown to the missionaries personally, a greeting gift of fruit and provisions awaiting a new missionary at his station, a sick nurse sent to fever patients, a home given to the convalescent and the bereaved, a public collection made for a widow—these gave them a niche in Jamaican society and tended to stimulate an appetite for favors.

The plainest statement of what the ruling classes expected from the missionaries was made by the Reverend John Trew, who, not content with merely advising his missionary friends, wrote to the Wesleyan

Methodist Missionary Committee to suggest how their agents might best win the confidence of the authorities. The committee was advised to start them on the right foot by arming them with a letter of recommendation to the custos and magistrates. The committee should also "impress on their minds the necessity of paying honour where honour is due," and this meant treating with respect both the civil authorities and the Anglican church. Church privileges were to be respected and occasional attendance was advised. The missionaries were, in addition, required to show a meek deportment, a liberal spirit, and a willingness not to associate on intimate terms with free colored people in a manner contrary to the usage of the island.[77]

To a large extent the missionaries fulfilled these requirements. Whatever private doubts, reservations, or resentments they felt, few were impelled to express them. Retrospectively a Moravian missionary commented that the position of estate missionaries was that of "a spiritual police officer sent out to care for the interests of the proprietor";[78] mission policy, however, was directed to shoring up, by every possible means, the toleration afforded by planter patronage. When Moravian and Presbyterian missionaries worked with the cooperation of humanitarian planters, criticisms were uncalled for. But, in general, experience showed that the wishes of absentee proprietors, or of nonresident attorneys, were easily thwarted by uncooperative overseers who could easily prevent the slaves from attending shell-blow classes. Even so the missionaries were submissive for fear a complaint might be construed as criticism of the estate management or as an unwelcome assertion of their right to teach slaves.

The Baptist and Wesleyan missionaries were as unwilling as the Presbyterians and Moravians to attempt any improvement in their status, though the license system restricted their activities. The Wesleyans, at their quarterly district meeting, asked their missionary committee what their policy should be regarding the special limitations usually incorporated in their licenses. They were officially advised that restriction of weekday service was not a matter of conscience; the limitation must be accepted, not because the law was good but because due submission and exemplary conduct toward those in authority might encourage repeal. The most missionaries could attempt was to urge the whites in private conversation that the need for instruction was so great that these limitations meant a considerable interruption of the work.[79]

The Wesleyan missionaries settled down to working with the exist-

ing system and began to view it from a Jamaican point of view. They
argued that it was an advantage for each missionary to be placed directly
under the "protection" of the local magistrates, though the only protection they needed was against the hostile behavior of the magistrates, and
that the license differentiated accredited missionaries from people who
merely called themselves "parsons," a distinction that must have been
clear enough to any observer.[80] The Wesleyan mission, in fact, became
so concerned with meriting patronage that when a champion of the
Dissenters' rights, their patron Stephen Drew, proposed to agitate against
the imposition by the magistrates of restrictions on preaching hours and
argue his case in terms of the English Toleration Act of 1812, the district
meeting cooled his ardor. The missionaries felt privately that "it would
be very ungrateful and unbecoming . . . under present circumstances, to
make even the slightest attempt" to enlarge their privileges.[81] Officially,
in a series of resolutions, they respectfully requested him to allow matters
to "rest quietly" for fear that "anything that looks like a forcing of
greater privileges would only irritate and stir up old bad feelings."[82]
When Drew used his personal influence to persuade Henry Cox, custos
of St. Ann, to license the Wesleyan missionary at St. Ann's Bay according
to the requirements of the 1812 act, however, the mission was gratified;
broader implications they thought best to avoid. Drew contented himself
by advising the W.M.M.S. committee to circularize the 1812 act to the
custodes of every parish.[83]

The missionaries demonstrated their "liberal spirit" by conforming
as far as possible to the social conventions of the ruling class. They
adopted the standard of living customary for whites; a mission family in
Jamaica employed domestics, usually free colored servants or hired slaves,
on the same scale as respectable whites, and had a cook, a cleaner, and
probably a boy to look after the garden and the horse. They spent three
times as much on servant hire as their London colleagues, whose families,
however large, had only one servant. But the Wesleyan missionary committee's strictures on this point were ignored.[84] Respectability also demanded that missionaries, unlike their London counterparts, should ride
rather than walk. A "walk-foot buccra" (white man) was an object of
derision even to the slaves; it was the mark of a down-and-out, a white
man who had lost his place in society. In the flourishing Wesleyan and
Baptist missions, keeping a horse soon extended to keeping a chaise
needing two horses for country journeys. Again, the Wesleyan mission
was constantly criticized on this score by the London committee, but the

missionaries were more concerned to secure respect in Jamaica than avoid criticism from home.

Conformity with ruling-class conventions also influenced their relationship with free colored and black converts. The free colored and black populations were an increasingly important element in Jamaican society; by 1830 they outnumbered the whites, and decades before they had begun to achieve parity with the whites in the island militia. In Kingston, where the largest single militia unit was located, the whites were outnumbered by 1806 and in 1829 constituted little more than one-third of the entire force.[85] The free coloreds and blacks felt their strength and in 1813 began to petition the Assembly for the removal of repressive legislation. Many influences shaped their political development, including the antislavery movements and the Haitian exiles living in Kingston. The missions also made a significant contribution by affording free coloreds and blacks the status and experience to be derived from an active role in their churches. It is not surprising that Edward Jordon, who was the founder-editor of their first newspaper, *The Watchman and Jamaica Free Press*, and a leader in the fight for civil rights in the 1820s, was a leading member of the Kingston Wesleyan church.

Free blacks and coloreds played a vital part in mission work; they were lay preachers, deacons, and advisers to the missionary. When death or sickness interrupted regular services, they held the members together with prayer and class meetings. Missionaries "taking the word" to new districts found accommodation in their houses and very often were given a piece of land on which to build a chapel, while chapel building was subsidized by the interest-free credit they extended.[86] Their allegiance as a class was clearly demonstrated by the numbers who attended; in the Wesleyan mission they comprised as much as a quarter of the total membership, about two-thirds of the attendance in Kingston, and formed roughly a third of the Baptist congregations.[87]

The missionaries, however, did not accept free blacks or coloreds as ministers until they had been awarded full civic status in 1831. And as long as slavery lasted free black and colored women were not found acceptable as missionary wives. In the one instance where such a marriage occurred, the case was complicated by strictly moral considerations; the lady in question had formerly lived, Jamaica fashion, in "keeping," and the young missionary involved resigned from the ministry. It is evident that the "mental and religious" acquirements of many of the free black and colored women qualified them to become missionary wives, and the missionaries themselves recognized this to be the case. For young men dependent on the approval of the magistrates for licenses to preach, mixed marriages, however, were out of the question. Alliances of this sort could only serve, the missionaries thought, as "a weapon in the hands of our enemies to chastise us."[88]

In the pursuit of social standing the Presbyterian and Wesleyan missions had special assets; they were related to churches already accepted as part of the Jamaican establishment. The Presbyterian mission, though staffed by ministers of the United Secession church, tended to be identified with the Church of Scotland represented by the Kingston kirk, and, it will be recalled, in exploiting the "Scottish" loyalties of attorneys and proprietors the missionaries relied on this common tradition. However, the relation of the Wesleyan mission to the Anglican church was more complex than that of the Presbyterian mission to the Church of Scotland. The Wesleyan church was commonly regarded as an inferior brand of Anglicanism suitable for the lower classes. It is not surprising that the Wesleyan missionaries fought against this impression and tried to use their association with the Anglican church to bolster their position in Jamaican society. The society in London encouraged association with Anglican clergy,[89] and the missionaries welcomed opportunities to "stand in" at the parish church when the rector was sick, and to hold joint prayer and discussion meetings. To make the association between the two churches crystal clear, some missionaries took communion from time to time in the Anglican church and urged their members to do the same.[90] Their enthusiasm was curbed, however, when the Anglican Bishop Lipscomb proved hostile to mission work. Under his influence cooperation between the Anglicans and the Wesleyans dwindled.

The spirit of emulation left the Wesleyan mission with two interesting legacies. It became customary for Wesleyan missionaries to officiate in gowns and bands, an equivalent of the clergyman's cassock. The tradition was accepted without question until a district chairman from Antigua took charge of the mission; he had served twenty years as a missionary without ever wearing a gown and voiced an astonished protest to the society against this "silly custom." The W.M.M.S. ruled against the practice and gowns were abandoned.[91] A more enduring monument to the determination of the Wesleyan mission to rank with the Anglican church and achieve acceptance like the Church of Scotland was the second chapel built in Kingston, known as Wesley chapel. Opened in December, 1823, Wesley chapel was designed to outclass both the kirk and the parish church. It was a high square building, ornamented outside by a stone balustrade and decorated stone work, tall sashed windows, and a wide pedimented porchway to give dignity to the facade. Inside, its most striking feature was an enormously tall pulpit in carved mahogany supported by iron pillars, mounted from a spiral staircase of twenty treads that rocked like a boat. The pulpit alone was said to have cost £1,000, and the total cost of the building was admited to be £14,000 sterling.[92]

Wesley chapel was an extravagance; the initial outlay crippled the Kingston circuit with debt at a time when surplus funds from Kingston could have been used for vital repair work on chapels with less prosperous congregations.[93] The folly was never repeated. "With Wesley Chapel before our eyes every missionary should pray 'from vain imagination in chapel building, good Lord deliver me,' " commented one, and much appreciation was bestowed on the buildings that were "plain, neat, substantial and commodious."[94] The never-ending debt, the recurrent problem of how best to organize the Kingston finances, the embarrassing demands of free colored creditors, all made it abundantly clear that the chapel was a mistake. But the real price all the missions paid for the policy symbolized by Wesley chapel, of winning favors and achieving respectability, was political.

The missionaries developed a keen concern lest political activity in England on behalf of the slaves should upset their relationship with the slave owners. Experience showed that such agitation exposed the missions to suspicion, criticism, and abuse. This was demonstrated in 1815 when the African Institution, heir to the Society for the Abolition of the Slave Trade, launched its campaign to extend slave registration[95] to the colonies that had legislative assemblies.

The missionaries in Jamaica found themselves, consequently, under fire. The newspapers set themselves to rouse "every lurking prejudice" against them by "unfounded and invidious declamations."[96] The missions' patrons took the opportunity to impress the protégés that they must be above all suspicion of sympathy for, or connections with, the humanitarian party. James Stewart exemplified their attitude in an interview with a Baptist missionary. Was it part of the missionary's purpose, he asked, to examine the state of the island, or send to England accounts of its civil and political affairs? Did the missionary know anonymous letters accused him of holding nightly meetings on the estates? Or that his letters had been opened and found full of political information? Or that he was supposed to be in direct communication with Mr. Wilberforce? When the missionary denied these allegations, Stewart, having made sure the missionary was aware of all the charges against him, was prepared to say he considered them invidious and unfounded; at the same time, however, he advised him not to preach for a while.[97]

Patronage had its price. This experience, and the generally precarious tenure of the missions, led the Wesleyan district chairman the following year to specifically request the W.M.M.S. not to take part in any debates about the new Jamaican slave code for fear of provoking another "hot persecution" of the Jamaican mission.[98]

The circumstances in which the missionaries established a place for themselves in Jamaican society made them responsive to the influence of their patrons. The imperial government had asserted only the principle of religious toleration; it was the patrons who determined what measure of toleration should be practiced. The missionaries, therefore, as reformers of the slave system, found themselves allied with the planters who sought only to preserve it. Together they deplored humanitarian agitation. The missionaries had been co-opted by the planters, and only a powerful new influence operating on the missions' behalf could change this alignment.

The missions, however, had succeeded in establishing themselves despite strenuous, if sporadic, local opposition in a slave society at a time when the institution of slavery was already under attack in England. They owed their success partly to their own persistence, partly to the influence of the planters, both resident and absentee, but most significantly to the insistence of the imperial government that the Assembly had no right to make mission work illegal. The influence of the imperial government was to prove more than once an important factor in the protection and development of mission work. Given the survival of the missions, however, the crucial question is, what contribution did the missionaries make to the life of the slaves? What modifications, innovations, and improvements were they able to effect in the social life developed by the slaves within the structures created by the organization of plantation labor? The context for mission work established by the slaves' social, cultural, and religious life is the topic of the next chapter.

NOTES

1. Lowell J. Ragatz, *The Fall of the Planter Class in the British Caribbean, 1760–1833* (New York, 1928), p. 81.

2. The Assembly was founded in 1661. It had forty-three members in 1774: three each for Kingston, Port Royal, and Spanish Town and two for each parish.

3. Lewis B. Namier, *England in the Age of the American Revolution* (London and New York, 1966), p. 235.

4. Douglas Hall, *A Brief History of the West India Committee* (Barbados, 1971), p. 4.

5. Seymour Drescher's *Econocide* effectively destroys the statistical basis of the thesis established in Lowell J. Ragatz's *The Fall of the Planter Class,* published originally in 1928, which presents the commercial consequences of the American Revolution as the basis of West Indian economic decline. Drescher's contention that the decline was entirely the consequence of the abolition of the slave trade, however, is still open to question.

6. David B. Davis, *The Problem of Slavery in Western Culture* (Ithaca, N.Y., 1966), pp. 434, 435; George Lichtheim, *A Short History of Socialism* (London, 1970), p. 15.

7. Lichtheim, *Socialism,* p. 14.

8. Roger T. Anstey, *The Atlantic Slave Trade and British Abolition, 1760–1810* (London, 1975), p. 239.

9. Vessels were allowed to convey only five slaves per three tons of registered burden up to 210 tons and one for every ton above this. A trained surgeon was to be on board, and premiums of £100 or £50 were paid to all captains and doctors who made the Atlantic run with only 2 percent or less mortality rate, half these sums for 3 percent mortality rate. Ragatz, *Fall of the Planter Class,* p. 251.

10. Ibid., p. 267.

11. J. H. Buchner, *The Moravians in Jamaica* (London, 1854), p. 24.

12. William J. Townsend, Herbert B. Workman, and George Earys, eds., *A New History of Methodism* (London, 1909), 2 vols., 2:288.

13. Ragatz, *Fall of the Planter Class,* p. 281.

14. George G. Findlay and William W. Holdsworth, *The History of the Methodist Missionary Society* (London, 1921–24), 5 vols., 2:27–29. Stations were established in Antigua, Nevis, St. Christopher, St. Barthelemy, Tortola, Virgin Islands, St. Eustatius, Dominica, St. Vincent, Barbados, Grenada, Trinidad, Bahamas, Demerara, and Jamaica. *Wesleyan-Methodist Magazine,* Sept. 1815, p. 714.

15. The first Baptist mission, headed by Carey, went to India in 1794. Samuel Pearce Carey, *A Life of William Carey, Baptist Missionary* (London, 1936) p. 128.

16. Dugald Mackichan, *The Missionary Ideal in the Scottish Churches* (London, 1927), pp. 74–80.

17. The most important magazines were the Moravian *Periodical Accounts* and the Baptist *Annual Register* and the *Evangelical,* later the *Wesleyan-Methodist Magazine.* Eugene Stock, *The History of the Church Missionary Society* (London, 1899–1916) 3 vols., 1:60–64.

18. Richard R. Madden, *A Twelvemonths Residence in the West Indies* (London, 1835), 2 vols., 2:248–9.

19. Thomas Coke, *A History of the West Indies, containing the Natural, Civil and Ecclesiastical History of each Island* (Liverpool, 1808–11), 3 vols., 1:40–41.

20. Reginald Coupland, *Wilberforce* (Oxford, 1968), p. 378.

21. John Wesley, *Thoughts on Slavery* (London, 1774), pp. 55–56.

22. *Instructions for Members of Unitas Fratrum who minister in the Gospel among the Heathen*, pp. 44–45; S.M.S. "Instructions," par. 20, *Scottish Missionary and Philanthropic Register* (hereafter cited as *S.M.R.*) 13 (May, 1832):194–95; B.M.S., Letter of Instructions, p. 13; *A Statement of the Plan, Object and Effects of the Wesleyan Missions to the West Indies* (London, 1824), p. 8.

23. Edward Long, *The History of Jamaica* (London, 1774), 3 vols., 2:258.

24. The Anglican church did not prohibit the ownership of slaves. As late as 1826 seven of eighteen rectors owned properties worked by slaves or jobbing slaves, and all except two owned domestic slaves. Manchester to Bathurst, Nov. 13, 1826, C.O. 137/163.

25. See Chapter Four.

26. Henry T. de la Beche, *Notes on the Present Condition of the Negroes in Jamaica* (London, 1825), p. 27.

27. "Letters Showing the Rise and Progress of Early Negro Churches in Georgia and the West Indies," *Journal of Negro History* 1 (Jan. 1916):70–71, 75.

28. Ibid., pp. 72, 90–91; John Clarke, *Memorials of Baptist Missionaries in Jamaica* (London, 1869), p. 16.

29. "Letters Showing the Rise . . . of . . . Negro Churches," pp. 84, 89; William T. Whitley, *A History of British Baptists* (London, 1932), p. 255.

30. "Letters Showing the Rise . . . of . . . Negro Churches," pp. 72, 76.

31. Coke, *History*, 1:415–17; Peter Samuel, *The Wesleyan-Methodist Missions in Jamaica and Honduras* (London, 1850), p. 29.

32. Membership figures for Kingston in 1803 (the only station for which at this date there were regular returns) divide the congregation by color, sex, and status: whites, 14, browns, 98, blacks, 418; free, 246, enslaved, 284; men, 201, women, 329. Coke, *History*, 1:456; Edward Brathwaite, *The Development of Creole Society in Jamaica, 1770–1820* (Oxford, 1971), pp. 168–69.

33. Sheila Duncker, "The Free Coloured and Their Fight for Civil Rights in Jamaica, 1800–1830" (M.A. dissertation, University of London, 1960), pp. 76, 112, quoting Kingston Common Council Proceedings 1803–15, minutes of Aug. 23, 1813. Kingston became a corporate city in 1802. William J. Gardner, *History of Jamaica* (London, 1873), p. 260.

34. Ragatz, *Fall of the Planter Class*, pp. 219–20, 226.

35. John Clark, Walter Dendy, and James M. Phillippo, *The Voice of Jubilee* (London, 1865), pp. 32, 35.

36. Mary Turner, "The Bishop of Jamaica and Slave Instruction," *Journal of Ecclesiastical History* 26 (Oct., 1975):365.

37. It was financed partly by the Boyle Trust, dedicated to the education of Indian children by William and Mary College.

38. Brathwaite, *Creole Society*, p. 12. The commission was ineffective. The ecclesiastical court, established in 1799, met only five times in fifteen years and dealt with cases of absenteeism, discrimination against free colored parishioners, and a dispute between a clergyman and a planter over nonpayment of a puncheon of rum for a baptism ceremony. Turner, "Bishop of Jamaica," p. 365.

39. See Turner, "Bishop of Jamaica," p. 378.

40. Jamaica: *Journals of the Assembly,* 1802–7, Dec. 16–17, 1802, pp. 72–74, C.O. 140/91. The first reading of this bill was followed by consideration of a bill to make more effectual "An Act to prevent any intercourse or communication between the slaves of the island and foreign slaves of a certain description," passed originally in 1799, and a bill to establish regulations respecting persons of a certain description arriving in the island or resident therein. The Assembly completed three readings of these three bills in two days.

41. Mulgrave to Stanley, July 7, 1833, no. 9, enclosing judgment of Justice Bernard in Greenwood vs. Livingstone et al., Grand Court, June 20, 1833, C.O. 137/189; W.M.M.S. Correspondence, West Indies General (letters from missionaries in Jamaica to the W.M.M.S. committee in London), M.M.S. Archives (hereafter cited as W.M.M.S. Letters), Pennock, Kingston, Nov. 12, 1832, f. 116, Box 132.

42. Jamaica: *Journals of the Assembly,* 1802–7, Dec. 17, 1804, p. 287, C.O. 140/91.

43. Duncker, "The Free Coloured and . . . Civil Rights," pp. 123–24, quoting Kingston Common Council minutes, Dec. 14, 1807.

44. Coke, *History,* 2:19, 20–21.

45. Jamaica: *Journals of the Assembly, 1808–15,* Nov. 16, 1809, Additional Instruction, May 23, 1809, pp. 166–67, C.O. 140/96. The Wesleyan Methodist church exerted all its influence to obtain the disallowance of the 1807 act. The annual conference of the church sent a petition to the Privy Council in which they declared that they had spent £70,000 establishing the Jamaican mission, that they instructed 12,000–13,000 Negroes, and that the established clergy was insufficient for the needs of the island. They finally claimed that the law was "repugnant" to the spirit of religious toleration that "characterises our age and country." In another petition to the Lords Committee of the Privy Council for Trade and Plantations, they represented themselves as "a body incomparably out-numbering the white inhabitants of the British West Indies." Coke, *History,* 2:27–31.

46. David J. Murray, *The West Indies and the Development of Colonial Government 1801–1834* (Oxford, 1965), pp. 43–44.

47. Coke, *History,* 1:445–52.

48. The license provided by the quarter sessions took the following form: "Be it remembered that, in the General Quarter Sessions of the Peace holden at the town of (   ) in and for the said District, on (date) before (name), chairman and others, squires, justices of our sovereign Lord the King, assigned to keep the peace in the said district, came (name of applicant) of (place of origin) who professes to be a minister of the British Wesleyan Missionary connection. . . . When it appeared to the majority of the said justices that the said (name) was duly ordained as a Minister of the said British Wesleyan Missionary Connection.

      Signed   Chairman
                  Clerk of the Peace."

49. Peter Duncan, *A Narrative of the Wesleyan Mission to Jamaica* (London, 1849), p. 92.

50. Whitley, *British Baptists*, p. 255.

51. Clarke, *Memorials*, p. 16; Francis A. Cox, *A History of the Baptist Missionary Society 1792–1842* (London, 1842), 2 vols., 2:21.

52. The Black Baptist church at Old Harbour, St. Catherine (near Spanish Town), invited a B.M.S. missionary to take over in 1815. The B.M.S. also took over the church founded by George Gibb at Pembroke Hall, St. Mary, in 1834. After Gibb died in 1826, a free brown assistant, James Alexander Clarke, took over. The church was visited by the Baptist missionary James Phillippo, established in Spanish Town in 1824. Thomas Nicholas Swigle disappears from the records and George Leile's work as a public preacher seems to have come to an end in 1807; neither the Baptist missionaries in Kingston nor historians of the Baptist mission mention his church after that date. Leile spent some years in jail for debt; he visited England in 1822 and died shortly afterward. William Knibb attended the funeral. Leile may have continued to work as an itinerant preacher as Brathwaite suggests, but no evidence confirms this. He was a well-known public figure and would have needed the protection of the magistrates to work even informally. Brathwaite, *Creole Society*, p. 253; Cox, *History of the B.M.S.*, 2:23; Clarke, *Memorials*, pp. 16–18.

53. Bathurst to Manchester, Nov. 30, 1815, no. 22, pp. 220–21, C.O. 138/44.

54. Jamaica: *Journals of the Assembly, 1808–15*, Nov. 16, 1809, Petition to the Magistrates, p. 167, C.O. 140/96.

55. Ragatz, *Fall of the Planter Class*, p. 398.

56. Barry W. Higman, "The West India 'Interest' in Parliament 1807–33," *Historical Studies* 13 (Oct., 1967):3, 8.

57. Hope M. Waddell, *Twenty-nine Years in the West Indies and Central Africa 1829–1858* (London, 1863), p. 37.

58. John Owen, *The History of the Origin and First Ten Years of the British and Foreign Bible Society* (London, 1816), 2 vols., 2:289–92. It is interesting that the free colored population joined in this enterprise but formed their own separate organization; only the "more opulent" threw in with the whites.

59. Returns to Circular dispatch Apr. 7, 1817, enclosed, Manchester to Bathurst, Oct. 23, 1817, no. 152, C.O. 137/144. These charges were made in the parishes of St. Elizabeth and St. Thomas in the East.

60. The General Baptist Missionary Society made a short-lived attempt to found a mission in Jamaica in 1826. Three missionaries were sent out and stations were established at St. Ann's Bay and Lucea. These missions were handed over to the Particular Baptists in 1829 and 1831 respectively, following the death of one missionary and retirement of the other two. Cox, *History of the B.M.S.*, 2:33–34; Clark, Dendy, and Phillippo, *Voice of Jubilee*, pp. 51, 53.

   The Church Missionary Society sent two catechists to Jamaica in 1825 in response to a request from a slave owner, J. B. Wildman. The work did not expand under slavery because no agreement was reached between the society and the bishop of Jamaica as to the terms under which their representatives could serve in his diocese. C.M.S. Committee, *Confidential Address on operations in the West Indies*, pp. 5–10.

   The number of missionaries serving the island in 1834 was forty-four, compared with thirty-three magistrates appointed to administer the apprenticeship scheme, though this figure was later increased to sixty-three. William L. Burn, *Emancipation and Apprenticeship in the British West Indies* (London, 1937), p. 197.

61. W.M.M.S. Letters, Johnston, Kingston, Nov. 20, 1819, f. 33, Box 114; Samuel, *Wesleyan-Methodist Missions*, pp. 47, 48, 55; Edward Bean Underhill, *The West Indies: Their Social and Religious Condition* (London, 1862), p. 207.

62. James M. Phillippo, "Rough Sketch of Facts connected with the Personal History of the Writer, of his Life and Correspondence from the years 1798–1824, and thence onward," p. 175 ms. vol., Box W.I./2, B.M.S. Archives (hereafter cited as Phillippo, "Personal History"); Cox, *History of the B.M.S.*, 2:23; W.M.M.S. Letters, Shipman, Aug. 16, 1817, f. 33, Box 113.

63. Samuel, *Wesleyan-Methodist Missions*, p. 195; W.M.M.S. Letters, Murray, Spanish Town, July 9, 1827, f. 165, Box 124.

64. Samuel Moulton Barrett was living on the receivership of his estate to which he was appointed by Chancery. He was an old acquaintance of the Earl of Mulgrave, governor in 1832–34. His financial difficulties made it impossible for Mulgrave to appoint him to the Legislative Council. Mulgrave to Howick, Aug. 6, 1832, Private, C.O. 137/183; *S.M.R.* 9 (July, 1828):291, Blyth, Apr. 10.

65. Buchner, *Moravians in Jamaica*, pp. 72–73. Matthew Farquharson of Spring Vale estate, ten miles from Hopeton, clerk of the peace to the St. Elizabeth vestry, held religious meetings among his slaves, invited missionary visits, and helped the foundation of the New Fulnec mission. The Cokes at Paynestown and the Coopers at Cruse estates also held services, ran small schools, and gave the missionaries every assistance. On the north coast the Seniors at Mosquito Cove (Mrs. Scott was a Senior),

visited by the Moravian missionary from Irwin Hill, were similarly inspired. *Periodical Accounts* (hereafter cited as *P.A.*) 9 (1823):322; 10 (1826):126; 11 (1829):458, 351.

66. Manchester to Bathurst, Oct. 23, 1817, no. 152, enclosing Rev. J. West, June 4, 1817, C.O. 137/144.

67. W.M.M.S. Letters, Horne, Morant Bay, June 28, 1819, f. 68, Box 114.

68. Samuel, *Wesleyan-Methodist Missions*, pp. 244–45, 257, 258.

69. Long, *History*, 2:206–7.

70. *S.M.R.* 4 (July, 1823):290–92.

71. *S.M.R.* 6 (Dec., 1825):485, Blyth, Sept. 14; 13 (June, 1832):242, Cowan, Mar. 16.

72. *S.M.R.* 12 (Jan., 1831):6, Watson, Lucea, Aug. 2, 1830.

73. W.M.M.S. Letters, Shipman, Falmouth, Feb. 19, 1818, f. 18, Box 113.

74. W.M.M.S. Letters, Shipman, Bath, Dec. 15, 1822, f. 168, Box 118.

75. W.M.M.S. Letters, Young, Stony Hill, Feb. 8, 1825, f. 33, Box 122; Crofts, Montego Bay, Nov. 7, 1826, f. 255, Box 123.

76. W.M.M.S. Letters, Crofts, Grateful Hill, June 25, 1822, f. 72, Box 118.

77. W.M.M.S. Letters, Trew, London, July 13, 1820, f. 13, Box 115.

78. Buchner, *Moravians in Jamaica,* p. 18.

79. W.M.M.S. Committee to the District Chairman, Jamaica, Sept. 8, 1821, Box 24, M.M.S. Archives.

80. W.M.M.S. Letters, Shipman, Spanish Town, July 18, 1817, f. 26, Box 113.

81. W.M.M.S. Letters, Binning, Spanish Town, Jan. 20, 1823, f. 184, Box 118.

82. Minutes of the District Meeting, Jamaica, Jan. 11, 1823, Box 148, M.M.S. Archives.

83. Samuel, *Wesleyan-Methodist Missions,* p. 195; W.M.M.S. Letters, Drew, Mar. 5, 1823, f. 208, Box 118.

84. W.M.M.S. Committee to the District Chairman, Jamaica, Dec. 6, 1825, Box 24, M.M.S. Archives. The cost of servant hire in Jamaica was £60 p.a. compared to £20 p.a. in London.

85. Duncker, "The Free Coloured and . . . Civil Rights," p. 12.

86. Land was given by free colored or black converts for the Baptist chapel in St. Thomas in the Vale and the Wesleyan chapels at Grateful Hill and at Hope Bay. Phillippo, "Personal History," inset, p. 109; Samuel, *Wesleyan-Methodist Missions,* p. 150; W.M.M.S. Letters, Morgan, Kingston, Dec. 19, 1824, f. 163, Box 128. Interest-free credit subsidized the Wesleyan mission built at Ocho Rios; when the premises were destroyed in 1832, Miss Catherine Jarvis, the creditor, was still unpaid. After the rebellion, when the missionaries seemed in danger of being driven from the island, the relatives of a Kingston creditor with £1,350 sunk in Wesley chapel sued for £350. W.M.M.S. Letters, Whitehouse, Bellemont, Jan. 5, 1829, f. 112, Box 127; Kingston, Aug. 24, 1832, f. 53, Box 132; Kingston, Mar. 5, f. 49, Apr. 29, 1833, f. 78, Box 133.

87. W.M.M.S. Letters, Duncan, Kingston, Sept. 3, 1825, f. 181, Box 122.

88. W.M.M.S. Letters, Shipman, Bellemont, Sept. 3, 1823, f. 143, Box 119.

89. W.M.M.S. Committee to the District Chairman, Jamaica, Dec. 16, 1824, Box 24, M.M.S. Archives.

90. W.M.M.S. Letters, Binning, Spanish Town, Oct. 22, 1819, f. 21, Box 114; Aug. 13, 1821, f. 27, Box 117; Duncan, Bath, May 1, 1823, f. 49, Box 119.

91. W.M.M.S. Letters, Morgan, Kingston, Mar. 16, 1829, f. 159, Box 127; Wilcox, Kingston, July 24, 1834, f. 30, Box 135.

92. W.M.M.S. Letters, Atkins, Stony Hill, July 21, 1834, f. 22, Box 135. *Wesleyan-Methodist Magazine,* Sept., 1825, p. 627, replied to charges in the *New Baptist Magazine* that it cost £30,000 and was better fitted for a theater. In Jamaican currency £1 (i.e., 20 shillings) was worth approximately 14 shillings sterling. All sums are given in sterling unless otherwise specified.

93. W.M.M.S. Letters, Jenkins, Morant Bay, July 14, 1826, f. 173; Murray, Spanish Town, Oct. 14, 1826, f. 239, Box 123.

94. W.M.M.S. Letters, Corlett, Port Royal, Aug. 16, 1831, f. 179; Murray, Montego Bay, Feb. 8, 1831, f. 28, Box 130.

95. Slave registration was imposed on the crown colonies in 1812. Jamaica finally passed its own Registration Act in 1818. See Ragatz, *Fall of the Planter Class,* pp. 386–99.

96. Clark, Dendy, and Phillippo, *Voice of Jubilee,* p. 142, quoting letter from Rowe, May 1, 1816.

97. Ibid., pp. 142–43. Stewart's claim about the opened letters was clearly a bluff. Rowe was not in communication with Wilberforce. His letters, however, were occasionally passed on to Wilberforce by the secretary of the B.M.S. William Wilberforce to Dr. John Ryland, May 22, 1815, "Letters from Wilberforce to Dr. Ryland," ms. vol., Baptist College Library, Bristol.

98. W.M.M.S. Letters, Shipman, Spanish Town, May 16, 1817, f. 33, Box 113.

CHAPTER TWO

The Jamaican Slaves

THE PROPAGANDA OF the antislavery campaigns established a slave stereotype whose life was made up of work and punishment, a creature symbolized by the chained, suppliant figure on the Wedgewood medallion, whipped into subjection, shackled by the demands of estate labor, his outstretched hands craving the white man's charity. The stereotype reflected a large measure of truth. The daily round of plantation labor and plantation discipline defined the parameters of life allotted to the slaves. Chattel slavery was, by definition, a system that claimed to control every aspect of the laborers' lives.

The plantation system, therefore, organized primarily as a method of production, had also to serve the slaves' social needs. The context in which these needs were met was dictated by the demands of estate work, but the content was created by the continuous interaction between the slaves and their conditions of work. The slaves were chattels who had been ripped from their homelands, packed into slave ships, thrust into forced labor gangs. But every slave, on arrival in the colony, incorporated a body of knowledge and experience he used, like a voluntary immigrant, in the struggle for survival. As a result, the first generation of slaves created among themselves new languages, new religious and social forms, in short, distinctive cultures particularized in each island and territory. The missionaries found, consequently, that obstruction from the magistrates was only the beginning of their problems; teaching the slaves Christianity involved combatting religious ideas, social forms, and cultural values developed within the plantation system.

The content of the slaves' culture is particularly difficult to establish, first, because the written evidence about the Jamaican population is less plentiful and less reliable than the source material usually available to labor historians, or even to historians of U.S. slavery, and, second, because our knowledge of African history is still relatively limited. Historical investigation of religion in Africa, for example, a subject which could lend important insights into the slaves' cultural development, has only just begun.[1] As a result, the slaves' original cultural baggage in this area, as in others, cannot be defined, and the dynamics of developments that took place within the plantation system are an area for speculation only. Within these limitations this chapter attempts to outline the main features of the Jamaican slave society the missionaries tried to influence, and to indicate the chief areas of conflict between mission teaching and the slaves' traditional culture.

The missionaries' teaching challenged the slaves' established religious beliefs, denigrated their culture, and attempted to impose new social mores. It offered the slaves a new, coherent world view in which all men, whites as well as blacks, were in the hands of a universally powerful god who called them, equally, to judgment. The conflict between the missionaries' message and traditional practices created a ferment among the slaves, reflected in part by the creation of the mission churches and also by the development of new religious practices and new leaders among the slaves themselves.

The missionaries were dealing with a predominantly creole slave population; African-born slaves comprised only 25 percent of the population emancipated in 1834,[2] and national differences among them, easily observable a generation before, had largely disappeared. The slaves in Jamaica, drawn originally from all the slave trading areas of Africa, had become essentially one nation.[3]

Almost all the slaves were plantation workers; barely 8 percent worked in the towns. Most of the slaves were concentrated along the rim of the north coast, from Lucea to St. Ann's Bay: in a broad belt across the island, in the valleys between the Blue Mountains and the western ranges, and in the sugar plains and coffee mountains of the eastern parishes. Only the Blue Mountains, parts of the hill country, and the arid plains of the south were uninhabited.[4]

Of the plantation slaves 75 percent worked in comparatively large-scale units of more than fifty workers and some in units of 600. Small-scale slave holding, characteristic of the United States, where most of the slaves were in units of less than fifty, had no significant place in the Jamaican economy. Almost half the slaves, 150,000, were engaged in sugar manufacture, 45,000 were used in coffee production, and 40,000 worked on cattle pens.[5] The rest of the rural slaves were engaged in a variety of occupations; some produced pimento, which was a specialty in St. Ann, and others logwood, ebony, and fustic. Slaves also worked as fishermen, salt rakers, and charcoal and lime burners and manned the wharves, the wagons, and the droggers which plied between the island's ports. Groups of "jobbers," hired workers, were kept to assist with the heavy work or with skilled work on the estates.[6]

When the missionaries arrived in Jamaica, they were invariably impressed, initially, with the slaves' resilience and vitality. One of them wrote: "I expected to find at my arrival an ignorant, depressed, and miserable set of people, whose knowledge was as little as their condition was destitute. It is not saying enough to assert I was disappointed; I was astonishingly disappointed."[7] But the system was infinitely more repressive than these superficial first impressions indicated. Slavery in Jamaica killed. The slaves were carried off by fevers and debilities. The most commonly named diseases were dropsy, dysentery, leprosy, pleurisy, and liver conditions, and in the low-lying wet areas tetanus and rheumatism were common.[8] Medical treatment was perfunctory; and "hot houses," the plantation hospitals, were in the charge of old women who might, at best, know some herbal remedies and traditional cures.

The high rate of natural decrease was not matched by natural increase, and the slave population as a whole, in the period 1817–32, had a natural decrease rate of between −0.7 to −4.8 per thousand. By occupation, the highest rate of natural decrease was on the sugar estates. There were more women sugar workers than men, but the unhealthy location of the estates, the intensity of the labor demanded, and the marginal level of subsistence were crucial factors in preventing natural increase. Even in the jobbing gangs, where there were fewer women than men, the rate of natural decrease was lower than on the sugar estates. Only plantations that combined coffee cultivation with livestock rearing, or coffee with pimento, or livestock with pimento, had more than a five per thousand natural increase, and these employed only a small proportion of the slaves.[9]

The missionaries learned by experience the conditions in which the slaves lived and the limited opportunities they had for absorbing Christianity. The demands of estate labor were heaviest on the sugar estates. Throughout the crop, or harvest, season, which ran from December to June on the south side of the island and variously from February through November on the north side, the slaves did shift work, resting for only five- or six-hour spells so as to feed the sugar mill continuously with freshly cut cane. Crop season overlapped with the season for planting cane, and this, too, was an arduous process for which jobbing slaves were often employed. Many of the missionaries, in St. Thomas in the East, St. James, Hanover, Trelawney, and St. Elizabeth, served primarily the sugar estate workers, and some, the Moravians at Irwin and Mesopotamia and the Presbyterians at Hampden and Cornwall, were actually situated on sugar estates.

Coffee cultivation, typical of Manchester and the mountain regions of Port Royal, St. Mary, and St. George, was less demanding; it involved chiefly weeding, pruning, and picking and roasting the beans, work usually allocated on a task basis, so the slaves were sometimes able to finish by the late afternoon. Missions in the mountain districts of St. Mary, St. Andrew, and St. Elizabeth benefited from the slaves' comparative freedom. These missions also served the free colored settlers in these areas. The livestock pens, situated in the back lands of the sugar-growing plains, also put less pressure on the slaves.

Most missionaries built up knowledge of the slaves' routine by making rounds of weekday visits to the estates to stimulate attendance on Sundays. The visits revealed the extent to which the slaves were at the mercy of the work routine and the "temper and character" of the management.[10] On one estate the slaves declared "that the living they live is too bad, that their heart is broken with work and punishment," but on another property the people were "very comfortable in their worldly circumstances, and when an opportunity of hearing the gospel is offered they feel themselves quite at liberty to embrace it."[11] But, in general, the slaves had only a marginal level of material existence.

The organization of production on the plantations generated a hierarchy among the slaves, a series of divisions that assisted in the maintenance of plantation discipline. Over the generations occupational status became intrinsically connected to skin shade as white fathers tended to do what they could, conveniently, for their colored offspring. Wealthy planters and attorneys manumitted, educated, and endowed at least some of them, but most colored progeny remained slaves. Since the whites were convinced that their offspring were a superior species to the black, they automatically monopolized all the most privileged positions on the plantations. The connection between color and occupational status was so strong that colored women slaves on some plantations lived together in household groups to avoid connection with any other than white mates, and so secure whatever little advantage the system had to offer for themselves and their children.[12]

The most privileged group of slaves took no part in production; they administered to the comfort of their masters. Domestic slaves were better dressed and, above all, better fed than their contemporaries in the field. The difference in diet was demonstrated when sickly children from the slave village were sent to live at the great house for a few weeks; they "very soon evince in their countenances the change in their mode of living, they become fat, sleek and shining. . . ."[13] Domestic work was largely a colored preserve and was the only occupation with any status open to women.

The most privileged individual slave was the headman in charge of the overall organization of plantation work. He worked closely with the white management and was assisted by the drivers, who turned out the work gangs at daybreak and supervised them in the fields. These slaves were associated with the skilled workers, the smiths, wheelwrights, coopers, harness makers, and the highly specialized boiler men in charge of sugar manufacture. On the sugar estates this privileged group comprised as much as 12–15 percent of the slave population.[14]

These slaves enjoyed a standard of living comparable to that of the domestics; headmen, drivers, and tradespeople always had special allowances of pork, herring, flour, sugar, and rum, and headmen were customarily given large provision grounds. Other perquisites could include a comfortable two- or three-room house with proper furniture, free supplies of rum and sugar, the right to keep unlimited numbers of stock, poultry, pigs, a mule, and even another slave as servant.[15]

At the bottom of the hierarchy were the field slaves; on the sugar plantations they were divided into a prestigious first, followed by a second and third, gang. Demotion to field work was calamitous. When a visiting proprietor punished one headman in this way, the man's whole family came to plead for his reinstatement. When the proprietor proved obdurate, the new headman, in the name of all the workers, begged that the offender be allowed to return to being a wagoner, "for that all the negroes said, it would be *too sad a thing* for them to see a man who had held the highest place among them, degraded quite to be a common field negro."[16] Under this pressure the owner relented and the ex-headman became a wagoner.

Slaves at every level of the hierarchy could be not only demoted but flogged. The use of the whip was regarded as necessary to secure production as well as maintain discipline. It was used by the slave drivers in charge of every plantation gang and by their supervisors, the bookkeepers, to keep the slaves working the fields and to punish all forms of misbehavior: work badly done, damage to estate property, or fighting and stealing among themselves. Legally there were limits to the punishments which could be meted out on the estate. According to the 1816 slave code, no slave was to be given more than thirty-nine lashes at any one time, and any punishment of more than ten lashes was to be given in the presence of the overseer, who supervised all work gangs, or the attorney, the owner's representative. In the case of improper punishment the slave had a right of appeal to the magistrates and vestry, sitting as a council of protection, which could prosecute the offender. A few cases of this sort, brought eventually to the attention of the Colonial Office, demonstrated both how ineffectual this mechanism was and that the legal limits of floggings were not observed. Indiscriminant corporal punishment was used, as one missionary remarked, to deprive every slave of character and make him, however intelligent, a man of degraded condition.[17]

The status hierarchy generated by plantation production contrasted sharply with mission church organization. The slaves' status on the plantation was dictated by the accident of birth and the will of the manager. The mission churches made both church membership and promotion within the church a reward of merit. They gave the slaves an opportunity to earn status, to exercise some control over it, and to associate with a white man without a whip at his command.

Plantation production imposed a social structure on the slave population; within this structure, however, the plantations also allowed the slaves roles as individual producers, growing crops for internal consumption and for sale in the island market. The comparative abundance of land in Jamaica made it convenient for the slave owners, from the earliest days of slavery, to allocate the slaves not only house plots and adjacent gardens but provision grounds, usually located on the back lands of the plantation.[18] The size of the provision grounds varied. Some managers allowed the slaves to cultivate as much as they could manage, but had difficulty themselves in estimating just how much this meant.[19] A survey of the slaves' provision lands on an estate belonging to Lord Seaford (the absentee proprietor Charles Ellis) in 1825 showed that the smallest landholding was about ten yards square and the largest thirteen acres.[20] On average, each slave worked between three-quarters and one and one-third acres of land and owned two or three chickens, a hog, and a half or a third share in a goat or a cow.[21]

The provision grounds, first mentioned in an act of 1678, were intended originally simply to supply the slaves with all their food except the rations of salt meat and fish supplied by the estate management: their "ground provisions," cocos, yams, cassavas, as well as plantains and corn.[22] The grounds, however, vitally influenced the slaves' family organization and their relation to the slave system itself.

It was customary for the slaves to cultivate their grounds in household groups, and the households usually represented families. This did not mean that Jamaican slave managers encouraged the development of family life among the slaves. The 1816 slave code promised rewards for reproduction, including exemption from field work for mothers of six children. But, in practice, pregnant laborers were abused by bookkeepers and overseers; on two estates belonging to one proprietor bookkeepers kicked pregnant women, in one case crippling the woman and in the other killing the child. It is not surprising that in these circumstances the missionaries found it necessary to teach that abortion was a sin and warn their congregations, "Never do anything to injure your children born or unborn. . . . It is *murder* and they who do it will surely perish."[23]

Of the children born, many were victims of tetanus, or died when thrust prematurely onto a diet of corn meal and sugar, or were carelessly allowed to eat whatever they laid their hands on when their mothers returned to field work.[24] The plantation system did not make the production of children a function that justified the development of families. Marriage, therefore, was not encouraged. There was a widespread opinion in Jamaica, elevated into law by the 1826 slave code, that the slaves could marry only with their masters' permission. Marriage was a privilege, one most slave managers were prepared to withhold. Marriage for the slaves, like civil rights for the free colored and black population, implied a humanity the whites were unwilling to concede as a right and preferred to retain as a privilege to confer.

In these circumstances many contemporary observers concluded, "Every estate . . . every negro hut was a common brothel; every female a prostitute, and every man a libertine." More observant writers, like Edward Long, remarked, however, that the slaves all had "so much decency as to call their sexual attachments by a conjugal name" and claimed, "They are all married, (in their way), to a husband, or wife, pro tempore, or have other family connections, in almost every parish throughout the island."[25]

The slaves, in fact, succeeded in establishing families that their owners, while reluctant to concede legal recognition, acknowledged. The focus for family life was the provision grounds, which the families worked in common. It is possible that, as an analysis of a small group of estate returns suggests, most of the slaves lived in some form of family group. Some families consisted of mothers living with their children and their nieces and nephews, or of grandmothers, mothers, and children. The majority of the families in the sample, however, consisted of a man and woman of marriageable age living with the woman's children. One of the privileges of slaves at the top of the hierarchy on these plantations was two "wives," an established connection with two different family groups. Other households consisted of men and women living together, brothers and sisters living together, and single-person households. The greater part of the population, however, lived in standard or matriarchal family groups.[26]

The provision grounds that the households cultivated in common became, by custom, slave property; children were carefully instructed as to the boundaries of their grounds, and estate managers allowed them to be "inherited." The household—more particularly, the family households with their common property interest in their grounds and houses— enabled the slaves to establish a nucleus of family solidarities to sustain them in the vicissitudes of life.

From the missionaries' point of view, the slaves' established relationship patterns, and the sexual mores that accompanied them, presented difficult problems. The slaves' acknowledgment of family ties gave them something to build on, but the diversity of relationship patterns meant that, quite apart from the legal problems surrounding marriage, the missionaries had to instruct the slaves in the very concept of Christian marriage. Even the households appearing to approximate the Christian ideal were not necessarily either stable or monogamous. And although only a few slaves practiced polygamy, sequential partnerships were, as the missionaries discovered, common. The legal problems surrounding the implementation of marriage proved secondary to the difficulty of persuading the slaves to embrace it.

The provision grounds had a further significance beyond their role in family relationships; they established the slaves as independent producers and traders within the slave system. From the earliest years of settlement regular markets were held at Spanish Town and Port Royal, attended by slaves with goods to sell.[27] The weekly Sunday markets supplied the towns with fruit and vegetables, poultry and eggs, redistributing corn and yams from areas specializing in them, and the slaves' provision grounds became essential to the internal economy of the island. The slaves' right to trade was legally established by 1711, and by 1735 they were licensed to sell provisions, fresh fruit, milk, poultry, and small stock as well as artifacts, baskets, and earthenware pots. The slaves, in fact, were also exporters; they sold gums, arrowroot, oilnuts, cowhorns, and goatskins to small merchants who sold them hardware and clothing for exchange.[28] It is not surprising that, at the end of the eighteenth century, Edward Long estimated that at least one-fifth of the small currency in the island was in the hands of the slaves.

The slaves' right to trade created an area within the slave system in which they enjoyed some of the functions and rights of a free peasantry. The early slave codes, to reduce the danger of rebellion and minimize opportunities for selling stolen goods, made it illegal for slaves to travel without a ticket signed by their owners. By the end of the eighteenth century, however, tickets were never required in practice; the slaves' role in the island's internal economy had become too important to be restrained by pass laws.[29] As a result, they were free to travel to market, sometimes carrying headloads fifteen or twenty miles to reach a busy center.

The market also put a little money in their pockets and gave them a choice as to how to spend it. How much the slaves benefited economically from marketing depended on how much land they had, how much time they were allowed to work it, how industrious and skillful in bargaining they were, and whether their plantation was near an important commercial center like Kingston or Spanish Town, or tucked away in the interior parishes with access only to a country crossroads market. One of Jamaica's apologists for slavery, Alexander Barclay, recounted how the slaves on Holland estate in St. Thomas in the East were able to run a coasting vessel to take their produce to the Kingston market and bring back muslins, crockery, and extra supplies of saltfish. Their earnings were variously estimated, proslavery writers claiming it was as much as one shilling a week.[30] After abolition the ex-slaves in Jamaica were expected to do a week's work for less than two shillings plus the use of their house and grounds, so the slaves' earning power should not be exaggerated.

The process by which the slaves made their earnings was, perhaps, more important than the money itself. The market connected the slaves with the world outside their plantation; it created contacts with neighboring plantations, established linkages between the coast and interior, and spread news, not only of family and plantation disputes but of political events within the island and even in England. Travelers were astonished to find that news brought by the mail packet from England could be circulating at inland markets only three days later.[31]

The slaves' functions as free peasants promoted the survival and development of precisely those intellectual capacities which the slave system was intended to destroy: curiosity about the world and determination to exert control over life. The slaves' dual role—as estate laborers subjected to all the repressive mechanisms of the slave system, and as individual producers enjoying the functions of free peasants—created a tension within the slave system. It concretized the contradiction on which plantation slavery was based, between, on the one hand, the slaves as chattels and, on the other, their intrinsic human capacities.

The mission churches exacerbated this tension: they developed the slaves' functions as free peasants. To their established right to leave the plantation and trade at the Sunday market was added the opportunity to attend the mission churches; to their ability to earn money and buy goods was added the opportunity to contribute to their church and achieve status within it. The missionaries, moreover, addressed themselves to the slaves as people with souls to be saved, capable of intellectual and moral judgments, and the activities they encouraged were presented in a philosophical framework that posited the spiritual equality of all men.

The slaves' rights as producers and traders encouraged them to develop a sense of their rights as laborers on the estates. This development was encouraged by the fact that their immediate white managers were poorly paid and frequently proved to be short-term appointments, whose status allowed the more privileged domestic slaves to perceive themselves as superior. One old house slave asked a young white store keeper, "Me have fe me [my] *house,* for me *ground,* for me *nigger* where for you house, you ground, you nigger?"[32] The strongest demonstration of the slaves' sense of corporate rights was made when "their" plantation went out of production and they were sent to work elsewhere. On these occasions the bulk of the slaves had to be evicted, literally driven from the property, intimidated by floggings and workhouse sentences.[33] Even in the normal working day the slaves vigilantly defended their established work routines; as the slave owners themselves remarked, they knew "very well what duty they have to do and are very impatient of any interference." New overseers and bookkeepers were carefully watched both to protect existing routines and, where possible, to secure improvements.[34]

The slaves were equally vigilant in defense of their privileges; they considered they were entitled not simply to allowances of salt provisions but their *customary* salt provisions. The substitution of salt pork for salt herring, or of oatmeal for flour, could lead to complaints to the magistrates. The magistrates, on the whole, tolerated this exercise; the substitutions were usually forced on the estate managers by shipping problems. There were occasions, however, when the slaves protested against the hours they were expected to work on the estate to the detriment of their provision grounds. Such claims brought into the open the fundamental conflict of interest between the slaves and the estate managers and alarmed the authorities. The slaves were challenging their owners' inalienable rights. Such manifestations were severely repressed; the slaves from two estates who protested to the Montego Bay magistrates on this account were all flogged, publicly, in the marketplace.[35] The slaves, however, to defend their existing rights within the plantation system were evidently developing new forms of opposition to it. Where their forefathers had rebelled to escape from slavery and establish a new life for themselves in the hills, in the last decades before emancipation the slaves were staking their claim to rights within the system that threatened to destroy it.

The incidence of slave rebellions, in fact, diminished once the slave trade ended and an increasing number of slaves identified primarily with the plantation. Slaves were sent to trial occasionally for conspiracies, but in the decade before 1831 there was only one small-scale attempt, in 1824 by the slaves of three estates in Hanover, at rebellion. Slave managers as individuals were rarely attacked, and even cases of arson were unusual.[36] Individual slaves, however, still attempted to escape the system; between 2,500 and 3,000 runaways were reported every year in the last decade of slavery.

The runaways had some hope of success. The mulattos and quadroons especially commanded the knowledge and the nerve to establish themselves as free within Jamaica, or to escape from the island altogether. If they could get to a town and find some means of supporting themselves as "higglers" (small traders) or tradesmen, their owners might advertise in vain for years. At the ports they might find work on local trading vessels or, better still, a captain short of crew willing to ship them for foreign parts. Success required good luck, good sense, audacity, and the connivance of friends or relatives. A random selection of advertisements for runaways gives the following descriptions: "a mulatto boy, a very plausible character, may endeavour to pass for free"; "a young creole wench of yellow complexion, very dressy"; "an African, passes for creole."[37] News of successful escapes sometimes reached home; one ex-slave settled in England, became a bandsman in the Coldstream Guards, married a white wife, and had two sons. The guardsman's letter, dated 1822, described his uniform, a red jacket with gold lace, and his wages, fourteen shillings a week. He took care to describe the shade of his children for his West Indian friends and family as "the colar of Sarah litel boy James."[38] But with no overland connection with a free society it was impossible for any equivalent of the American underground railroad to develop in Jamaica.

In contrast to the United States, where the majority of runaways were robust fellows under thirty-five years old,[39] in Jamaica they were characteristically middle-aged field hands, many of them Africans without family ties, who had nothing in front of them but a steady demotion to the third gang and an old age as night watchman.[40] Usually hunger drove them back to the plantation, and it was common practice for a repentant runaway to ask a neighboring white man to intercede for him and give him a "begging paper." A few managed to acquire guns, establish themselves in the bush, and claim supernatural powers. They were like bandits, symbols of resistance to the system oppressing their fellows on the estates, and they sometimes became the focus of small rebellious conspiracies, as in Trelawney in 1825 and St. Catherine in 1821.

The most usual form of protest against the system consisted of devices that have been defined as "pre-political": the slaves malingered, they worked slowly, they misunderstood orders, they took advantage wherever they could. "It is a difficult thing to get a negro to understand anything which he does not wish to hear," wrote one observer; "the more you try to explain a matter that is disagreeable to him, the more incapable he appears of comprehension."[41] The slaves' "laziness" and irresponsibility, the tricks they resorted to, the pains they invented, were a final guarantee to the whites of their inferiority.

The power of the whites forced the slaves to cringe, to evade, to lie, in order to win advantage. Alternatively, they flattered by praise and faithful service; their children, even, were tribute to the masters. "Look Massa, look here! him nice lilly neger for Massa!" cried one woman holding up her baby to a visiting proprietor. Even when there was an immediate prospect of manumission, the habit of reassuring the master, of playing the faithful servant, remained. A mulatto carpenter who was claiming freedom explained: "It is not that I wish to go away, sir; it is only for the name and honour of being free; but I would always stay here and be your servant; and I had rather be an underworkman on Cornwall, than a head carpenter anywhere else."[42]

The slaves themselves recognized their position perfectly; it was embodied in their folk hero, Anansi the Spider-man, a version of Ananse, the folk hero of the Akan. Anansi expressed the ideology of survival within the slave system. He was small, powerless, easily crushed under foot, but had a supreme cunning that always enabled him to outwit his more powerful enemies. The victories of Anansi put in heroic proportions the small, successful evasions of responsibility, the momentary advantage gained by some lying tale, the slaves' own desperate maneuvers. The victories of the folk hero Anansi were themselves the last desperate maneuver of a people driven to idealize intelligent cunning. The slaves had a special noun for a really cunning rogue: he was a "ginal." The ginal and the ideology of deception epitomized the consciousness the slave system created among the slaves, the consciousness mission teaching challenged. But as long as the slaves had no other ideal, the slave managers were safe.

The comparative stability of the slave system was, as the experience of the first preachers to the slaves demonstrated, essential to the expansion of mission work; it also encouraged the slave owners to allow the slaves to develop, within their villages, a cultural life that included their own religion. Slave culture incorporated many "African" elements. Ever since the publication of Melville J. Herskovits's *The Myth of the Negro Past* in 1941,[43] the extent and nature of these elements have been an area of both dispute and investigation. Recent anthropological researches have demonstrated that, while many apparently African cultural survivals are in fact innovations, instances can be found where, for example, complex religious rituals have been transmitted with perfect accuracy for at least three centuries.[44] It is clear that removal from their homelands stripped the slaves of their indigenous culture in the sense that it cut them off from the institutions embodying it, but each slave was a depository of what Sidney Mintz and Richard Price have defined as "cultural materials." These cultural materials included both specialist knowledge and "cognitive orientations," basic assumptions about social relations, the way in which the world functions phenomenologically, and attitudes toward change, which informed the development of plantation society.[45]

In the first decade of slavery the Jamaican slaves imported cultural materials that facilitated amalgamation. The majority of them were drawn from a West African provenance, more particularly from the Gold Coast, the Bights of Benin and Biafra, and Sierra Leone.[46] These peoples do not share a common religious tradition or a common language, but their languages and their religions are closely related, and this comparative cohesiveness may have stamped Jamaican slave culture with explicitly West African words, music, and religious forms.

The development of creole languages combining African and European elements was a necessity for both slaves and masters, and some evidence suggests that these languages were created in the first decades of slavery. The slaves first established on the plantations were able to acculturate newcomers so that successive waves of slave labor learned the language their predecessors had made. This was the case in Surinam, established initially by English planters, where a creole incorporating English elements developed during the twenty years the territory was in English hands. This remained the slaves' language even when Surinam was transferred to Dutch ownership.[47] In Jamaica evidence suggests that the African base of the creole language was definitively stamped by Twi, language of the Akans from the Gold Coast, the planters' favourite "Coromantees," who dominated the labor force in the early decades of settlement. Studies of Jamaican creole in the twentieth century have revealed that the African words surviving in the vocabulary are predominantly Twi.[48] This creole language, the slave's first creation, constituted the missionaries' first teaching problem.

The slaves, once established on the plantations, made versions of their musical instruments, which were known in Jamaica at this period as "goombah" drums, caramantee flutes (made from the trumpet tree), kittie-katties (boards beaten by sticks), shakie-shakies (calabashes with pebbles in them), and a type of African musical bow made with a bent stick and dried grass. They continued to use these as well as learning to play the violin and flute common to the whites. Their particular African dances survived while the slave trade continued but were gradually adapted and amalgamated out of recognition, though the style and vigor remained.

The slaves were encouraged by the whites to amuse themselves with music and dance. The managers recognized that their workers needed circuses as well as bread; as the American slave Frederick Douglass observed, "To enslave men successfully and safely it is necessary to keep their minds occupied with thoughts and aspirations short of the liberty of which they are deprived."[49] The yearly festivals, particularly Christmas, became seasonal circuses in which the slaves provided the whites with exotic entertainment. On these occasions the field slaves, dressed in whatever finery they could lay hands on, invaded the great house and the adjacent yard to dance. For the domestic slaves, committed to the mincing dances and scraping fiddles of their betters, it was a testing time, for the drum rhythms evoked a response the gavottes and minuets could not stimulate, and they were remarked to cast "many a wistful look" at the goombah dancers.[50] It was a tradition the missionaries found difficult to combat, more particularly since drumming and dancing were intertwined with the religious practices they were determined to root out.

Before the Black Baptist preachers and the missionaries started work, no attempts had been made by the planters to influence directly the slaves' ideas about life and the universe. The slaves, however, stripped of country and family, had to exercise some form of control over their environment. They adapted the techniques developed in their homelands to serve their new needs. Deprived of priests and organization, theological distinctions became blurred and a common pattern of religious practice emerged. Amalgamations may have been facilitated by the fact that, judging by studies made in the twentieth century, there were strong elements of uniformity among the religions of West Africa, where 80 percent of the slaves originated.

The religions of West Africa are polytheistic. They posit a belief in a supreme being, in nature spirits, in the spirits of the ancestors, and in magic, the use of supernatural powers to achieve good or bad ends. Ancestor worship and witchcraft, in fact, are common throughout Africa south of the Sahara. In each West African society priests train in religious practices to preside over public ceremonies and over the personal rites that attend illness, birth, puberty, marriage, and death. The idea of the supreme being is thought by some authorities to be indigenous and to pre-date missionary activity. In any case, the role assigned to the supreme being in these religions is quite different from that assigned to the Christian God. God in West Africa is the great creator but not the great law giver; among the Yoruba and the Ibo he is not worshipped, and is given less attention than the nature gods or the ancestors.

These spirits have a powerful day-to-day influence on the good or bad fortune of every individual, and the religious specialists—priests, mediums, diviners, and doctors—are all engaged, one way or another, in mediating between the individual and the spirit world. Every event, every illness, is assumed to have a cause, a spiritual root, a religious significance, and the specialists are there to rationalize, ritualize, or cure it. Mediums communicate directly between god and man; they are possessed and speak in tongues. Diviners are trained to conduct elaborate rituals to interpret the past or the future, and doctors provide good medicine, herbs and magic, often in the form of amulets or figures to put on the house and grounds, to keep away bad fortune. Doctors also have the power of bad medicine, black magic to cause harm, illness, and death. Death itself is always regarded as being caused by bad magic or a revengeful spirit, and burial ceremonies incorporate rituals intended to reveal who has wished death on the corpse. But death itself is not seen as a great divide; the spirits of the dead remain related to the living as one of the spiritual powers in their lives. Life after death is envisaged as a form of family reunion where life continues like life on earth.[51]

To what extent these findings represent the religions the slaves knew cannot be precisely ascertained, but it is clear that there were similar beliefs and practices among the Jamaican slaves. Stripped of the social structures that maintained these world views, the slaves were driven to rely not only on the established experts in their midst but on their common knowledge to create, as circumstances demanded, new experts among themselves. Birth and death had to be ritualized, the control of the spirit world had to continue. New rituals based on old memories were invented, experts created by emergencies developed a new expertise. It is clear from accounts by two contemporary observers of the slaves, one first published in 1793 and one written in 1820, that although memories of particular African spirit hierarchies persisted among the Jamaican slaves as long as the slave trade continued, religious practices derived chiefly from the slaves' common knowledge of ancestor worship and witchcraft.

Bryan Edwards's account includes a description of the spirit hierarchy of the Coromantee, the Akan slaves. Their supreme god was Accompong, a being of infinite goodness who was worshipped by prayer and thanksgiving, not by sacrifices. Their nature spirits included the god of the earth, served by libations and first fruits, and the god of the sea, for whom a hog was sacrificed when a ship returned home. The Coromantee also acknowledged Obboney, a malicious deity who pervaded earth, air, and sea. Edwards gives some prominence to ancestor worship; he attributes to each family a "tutelary saint," the original founder of the house, whose death is celebrated annually by the heads of every household belonging to the clan. The other important element in the slaves' religion was magic, called obeah, and the new experts were called obeah men and women and myal men.[52]

John Shipman, a Wesleyan Methodist missionary, by 1820 had already worked six years in Jamaica and wrote from Montego Bay, parish capital of one of the most densely populated parishes. His informants included free black and colored church members as well as whites, and they provided a comparatively well-informed, current assessment of slave practices. Shipman's account[53] prefaces a longer discussion of the necessity of teaching Christianity and the best methods of doing so. He makes no mention of African gods; so far as his knowledge extended, the slaves' traditional religion was by that time composed of two elements: their ideas about their ancestors and the practice of obeah. His account of both elements is more detailed than Edwards's but in no way contradicts it.

Shipman defines obeah as witchcraft, a phenomenon with which all the missionaries with some experience of rural England were familiar. Obeah was used to make charms to protect both individuals and property; this was considered harmless. It was also used to "discover secrets," that is, as a means of divination, and his examples related to identifying thieves and plotting vengeance. All this magic was in the hands of obeah men. Shipman also briefly mentions the myal men, who reportedly would work themselves into a "perfect phrensy and utter prophesy."[54] It is clear from Shipman's account that the slaves, like present-day Africans uprooted from their distinctive cultures, stripped of a regularly trained priesthood, and subjected to the confusion and degradation of labor migration, work camps, and urbanization, relied on the witchcraft elements in their religion and on ancestor worship.[55] The existence of the myal men, however—and they remained an active phenomenon long after slavery was abolished—suggests that the slaves also retained some organized cult worship of nature spirits. This will be discussed below.

The ancestral spirits were the slaves' best protection, but, as Shipman observed, the dead were easily offended and punished the living with the worst misfortunes, sickness and death. Sickly children were given new names in the hope of placating offended spirits. Death was always attributed either to offended ancestors or to the machinations of an enemy. Funerals were, therefore, important occasions on which to demonstrate respect for the ancestors as well as celebrate the departure of a new spirit. The ceremonies were prolonged and noisy events and involved much feasting and conviviality. The mourners beat drums and sounded their "wild, discordant musical instruments . . . dancing and throwing themselves into the wildest attitudes, singing at the same time in a vociferous manner their senseless, heathenish songs."[56] The coffin bearers staggered with their load, apparently pushed in diverse directions by the corpse, sometimes stopping at the house of an enemy or a debtor. At the graveside a feast was held and the corpse was offered food and drink and included in the conversation. The funeral ceremonies did not end with a feast at the burial; there were Christmas visits to the graves and feasts on the ninth and fortieth nights after the funeral, a custom which still survives in rural Jamaica and can be paralleled, in form, in contemporary African communities among the Fanti and the Umbundu.[57] The ancestors' spiritual significance made the slaves particularly attached to their burial grounds, reinforcing the ties with the estate established by the "possession" of house and grounds.[58]

The priesthood that controlled the spirit world had been reduced to a well-known, multipurpose figure, the obeah man or woman, and to the less clearly defined myal man. To what extent these experts were trained, in the sense of learning their lore from an established figure, is not clear. One obeah man sent for trial in 1824 claimed to be one of a fraternity 150 strong; certainly the slaves on every plantation had access to one.[59] Evidence suggests that they were usually African rather than creole. The Popo people from Dahomey had a particular reputation as obeahs, and it is interesting that in the twentieth century the Fon in Dahomey have one of the most highly organized religions in West Africa. Their priests and mediums are accepted as experts among neighboring people and the Fon have proved highly resistant to Christianity and Mohammedanism.[60] It would not be surprising if their enslaved ancestors had become the backbone of Jamaica's traditional religion.

The obeahs, who often combined positions as spiritual leaders with authority as headmen and drivers, united the attributes of diviners and medicine men; they were conversant with good and bad magic and with herbs.[61] For a population dogged by sickness in a notoriously unhealthy climate, all forms of remedies, both spiritual and medicinal, were eagerly sought. Slaves went to the obeahs for personal consultation, explained their problem, and bought an individual solution, very often a charm for warding off evil spirits. The obeahs supplied amulets made up of magic ingredients, a few feathers, a cat's tooth, and grave dirt, ingredients that were always looked for when an obeah man's hut was raided. They provided bottles filled with rainwater with a few quills stuck in the top to hang around the houses and provision grounds to scare away thieves.[62] These charms are similar in form to those used in rural communities in the West Indies in the twentieth century and by Fanti priests in Ghana, where a bottle with quills serves as a sign of sickness.[63]

Obeah men also advised clients on how to interpret their dreams. Dreams were an important channel of communication with the spirit world, and the traditional Africa methods of fasting, night watching, and sleeping in the bush were used to evoke dream signs.[64] At the same time the slaves consulted the obeah on how to wreak vengeance on their enemies. Vengeance was necessarily a clandestine affair; open quarreling and fisticuffs were a breach of plantation discipline, and slaves driven to actual fighting or attempted murder were sent to the workhouse or the slave court. Vengeance was best taken by proxy, through influence over the spirit world exercised by the obeah, for a price. The obeah induced sickness, or death, by rituals that tied up the victim's spirit with string, or stabbed it through the heart as it appeared reflected in a bowl of water, or caught his "shadow" and put it in a miniature coffin. When rituals failed to induce results, ground glass and arsenic were resorted to.[65]

The obeah interpreted the spirit world; the myal men were in direct communication with it in the manner of mediums in West Africa. The myal men were usually categorized by white observers as obeahs with higher powers, but it is possible that the myal men were cult leaders and represent a Jamaican version of African forms of organized worship. Certainly the myal men did not operate alone; they were always presented as group leaders. Their rituals, when observed, took place around trees, often silk cotton trees (trees commonly serve as shrines in West Africa), and consisted of drumming and dancing during which the myal man was taken by the spirit and possession spread to his followers. The ritual may have been used to propitiate the spirit world in general, and to counteract the evil influence of the "duppies," spirits of the dead.[66] There is a striking resemblance in form between the practices of the myal men and of Fanti priests (belonging to the Akan people) observed in the twentieth century. Fanti priests, after being called to the service of a particular deity, can evoke the deity by means of dancing and act as a medium. During the ritual the "spirit" spreads from the priest to his followers and their reactions seem epileptic. It is interesting that another

Akan people, the Ashanti, recruit their priests by training those who become possessed during a ceremony; this is interpreted as a divine call and is obviously a method easily transferred to plantation use.[67] Myal cults continued in operation long after slavery was abolished and, as Philip D. Curtin suggests, "more theology may have survived with it than the record shows."[68]

The slaves' traditional religion was, in effect, licensed by the whites. Legally, obeah was a felony to be punished by execution. In the eighteenth century, however, it was considered a joke until it was discovered that slaves in the 1760 rebellion had bound themselves by obeah oaths.[69] Then it was taken seriously for a time, but as rebellion became less frequent and obeah was being used primarily to regulate relationships among the slaves, the whites relaxed into the sort of uneasy tolerance they extended to the missionaries. The continued existence of obeah, however, demonstrated that the whites had no absolute control over the ideas influencing the slave population. The slaves' thought was not free, but it was open to new ideas.

Christianity challenged the slaves to adopt new ideas about the spirit world, the nature of God, and the destiny of man. Their response was reflected not only in the growth of the Black Baptist and mission churches but in the development of an attendant proliferation of syncretic sects, variously referred to as "Native Baptist," "Native Methodist," or "Spirit Christian." The sects appear to have originated with the work of the Black Baptists and were further stimulated by the mission churches. By 1820 John Shipman, in his analysis of the religious condition of the Jamaican slaves, found it necessary to devote one whole section to a discussion of "the moral condition of the Negroes when placed under the tuition of uninformed, and self-created Instructors." These preachers were not only numerous but, in some cases, well established. There were reputedly two or three illegal "chapels" in Kingston by 1830, as well as on some of the estates.[70]

The Native Baptist leaders were recruited from the free colored and black as well as the slave population. "Every man," wrote John Shipman, "who is able to use a form of prayer, however imperfectly, immediately thinks he has a right to set up as a *Teacher*, or *Preacher* and endeavours to turn it to worldly advantage."[71] Characteristically, they emphasized all the ecstatic and experiential elements in religion: the Spirit and not the Word. There were sects which mortified the flesh and sects where the spirit spoke in tongues. Some repudiated the Bible on the strength of the text "the letter killeth, but the Spirit giveth Life." Followers were expected to be possessed of "the spirit" before they were admitted to baptism, and the spirit was sought by penances, fasting, and sleeping in the bush. The baptism ceremony itself took on a new significance; it was no longer a symbol of grace but an extension of grace itself. Conversion, therefore, meant not embracing a strict code of Christian morality but being above morality. It followed that, in the rubric of these Baptists, John replaced Christ as the savior figure.[72]

The linkages between some of the sects and the orthodox churches were, however, very close. There were instances where membership of the two overlapped; the Presbyterian missionary Waddell, for example, met members of the Baptist mission church in Montego Bay who claimed to be Native Baptists and called the mission church John the Baptist's church.[73] At the same time there were leaders of independent sects that the missionaries themselves recognized as Christian. One such case was that of George Lewis, an African christianized in Virginia, who had been a member of Leile's Kingston church. He traveled about in St. Elizabeth and Manchester and produced "a general enquiry after the truth" that was followed up by the Moravian missionaries. The slaves called Lewis's meetings "the Negroes home religion," and Lewis evidently encouraged practices typical of the sects but repudiated by the mission churches; slaves fasted for three days when he visited a plantation, and at his meetings many were taken by the spirit or, as the slaves expressed it, were taken by "convince." The Moravian missionary John Lang, however, recognized him as an orthodox Christian and gave him assistance.[74]

"Native Baptist" was clearly a generic term for a proliferation of sects in which the slaves developed religious forms, more or less Christian in content, that reflected their needs more closely than the orthodox churches, black or white. The missionaries regarded the Native Baptists as both ideological enemies and a political threat to the good reputation of their own churches, and the planters regarded them as amusement fit for chattels. Both tended to record only the most outrageous and spectacular stories about them. There were stories of leaders who gave signed tickets to their members in imitation of the missionaries and of one enterprising fellow who, following the appointment of an Anglican bishop to Jamaica, signed himself as the "First Baptist Bishop of Jamaica." There was a sect in Spanish Town, where the Jews had a synagogue, which was said to eat no pig and kept Sabbath on a Saturday.[75] But developments paralleling the proliferation of Native Baptists can be found wherever Christianity spread.[76]

To the missionaries, the slaves' traditional religion and the Native Baptists appeared to be part and parcel of the same problem. The Native Baptist leaders were defined, accurately enough, as "Christianised obeahs," whose sects simply compounded error with error. The missionaries considered that "the only way to destroy error is to diffuse Truth." The slaves had to be taught to "*think* and *act* rationally." They identified their problem in Jamaica as the problem that faced preachers in England. "There is an immense Mass of Superstition, and always will be, in the ignorant Mind," commented the Baptist missionary Knibb to a parliamentary committee; "it is the same in this Country."[77]

The sects, however, represented a significant new development among the slaves; they demonstrated the extent to which the slaves were capable of using and absorbing new ideas. They demonstrated that some of the slaves were reaching for new satisfactions, new rationalizations, new compensations in life. At the same time the slaves were looking for leadership to their fellows and to free blacks in groups that operated outside the supervision of the whites. The proliferation of the Native Baptist sects was, therefore, a development full of political implications. The sects demonstrated that the slaves adapted the missionaries' religious teaching for their own ends.

The assumption on which the missions were founded, tolerated by influential planters, promoted by the antislavery movement, and encouraged by the imperial government was that Christianity would civilize the slaves and prepare them for the gift of freedom rather than politicize them and encourage them to demand it. But the existence of the sects was a constant reminder that the results of missionary teaching could not be determined by the missionaries or the magistrates; the results could only be determined by the slaves themselves.

NOTES

1. See Terence O. Ranger and Isaria N. Kikambo, *The Historical Study of African Religion* (London, 1972).
2. Barry W. Higman, *Slave Population and Economy in Jamaica 1807–1834* (Cambridge, 1976), p. 76.
3. Philip D. Curtin, *The Atlantic Slave Trade: A Census* (Madison, Wis.,

1969), p. 160, Table 46; Great Britain, Parliamentary Papers (Commons), "Report from the Select Committee on the Extinction of Slavery Throughout the British Dominions: with the Minutes of Evidence; Appendix and Index" (no. 721), 1831–32, 20:503, evidence of Vice-Admiral Sir Charles Rowley (hereafter cited as P.P. (Commons) (no. 721), 1831–32, 20).

4. Higman, *Slave Population*, p. 53, Table 6. There was an average concentration of 247.4 slaves to the cultivated square mile. The data derive from an analysis of 960 properties, which accounted for 58 percent of the rural slave population in the period 1829–32.

5. Ibid., p. 275, Table A3.15; p. 16, Table 2, gives the following figures: 49.5 percent of the slaves in sugar, 14.4 percent in coffee, and 12.8 percent on pens.

6. Ibid., pp. 24, 36–42.

7. George Jackson, *A Memoir of the Rev. John. Jenkins, late a Wesleyan Missionary in the Island of Jamaica* (London, 1832), p. 87, quoting letter from John Jenkins, Aug. 21, 1824.

8. Higman, *Slave Population*, pp. 113–15.

9. Ibid., p. 102, Table 15; p. 123, Table 24.

10. John Stewart, *A View of the Past and Present State of the Island of Jamaica* (Edinburgh, 1823), p. 222.

11. S.M.R. 15 (Apr., 1834):131, Waddell, Feb. 4; 13 (Oct., 1832):413, Cowan, July 4.

12. Barry W. Higman, "Household Structure and Fertility on Jamaican Slave Plantations: A Nineteenth Century Example," *Population Studies* 27 (Nov., 1973):537.

13. [B. M. Senior], *Jamaica as it was, as it is, and as it may be* (London, 1835), p. 29.

14. Michael Craton, *Searching for the Invisible Man* (Cambridge, Mass., 1978), p. 141, establishes that on Worthy Park estate, 1787–1838, the upper élite of headmen and drivers comprised 2.9 percent of the slave population and the lower élite of domestics, factory craftsmen, and others comprised 10.3 percent, making 13.2 percent over the period. This corroborates the findings of Orlando Patterson, *The Sociology of Slavery* (London, 1967), pp. 60–61.

15. Great Britain, Parliamentary Papers (Lords), *Minutes of Evidence taken before the Select Committee of the House of Lords appointed to inquire into The Laws and Usages of the several West India Colonies in relation to the Slave Population* (no. 127), 1831–32, 306:52, evidence of John Baillie (hereafter cited as P.P. (Lords) (no. 127), 1831–32, 306 or 307).

16. Matthew G. Lewis, *Journal of a West Indian Proprietor* (London, 1834), p. 373.

17. The investigations are discussed below, Chapter Five; Burn, *Emancipation and Apprenticeship*, pp. 55–56; P.P. (Lords) (no. 127), 1831–32, 306:430, evidence of Rev. J. Barry.

18. Patterson, *Sociology of Slavery*, p. 217.

19. P.P. (Commons) (no. 721), 1831–32, 20:384–85, evidence of J. Simpson.

20. P.P. (Lords) (no. 127), 1831–32, 307: Appendix F.3, 1392–3, nos. 1, 2, 3, pp. 1376–93, "Reports of the State and Condition of Old Montepelier, New Montpelier and Shettlewood; Negro Houses and Provision Grounds, and the number of stock possessed by each family . . . taken August 1, 1825."

21. In Ireland 45 percent of family holdings in 1841 were only one to five acres. Thomas W. Freeman, *Pre-Famine Ireland* (Manchester, 1957), p. 54.

22. Patterson, *Sociology of Slavery*, p. 217. The parish of Vere was exceptional. Here the slaves had no provision grounds and were supplied instead with corn, saltfish, or pork. Some of the corn was used to rear poultry for sale at the market.

23. Lewis, *Journal*, pp. 388–89; P.P. (Lords) (no. 127), 1831–32, 306:274–75, evidence of Sir. M. B. Clare, M.D.; "A series of Tracts for Slaves in the West Indies," 2 ms. vols., pts. 1–4, pt. 4: Address after Marriage, Box 588, M.M.S. Archives (hereafter cited as "A series of Tracts").

24. Joseph Sturge and Thomas Harvey, *The West Indies in 1837* (London, 1838), pp. 122–23. One proprietor, H. M. Scott, set up an infant school on his estate to supervise the young children and had only seven children between the ages of two and fifteen die in nine years.

25. James M. Phillippo, *Jamaica: Its Past and Present State* (London, 1843), p. 218; Patterson, *Sociology of Slavery*, p. 163, quoting Long, *History*, 2:414.

26. Higman, "Household Structure," pp. 534–39.

27. Sidney W. Mintz and Douglas Hall, "The Origins of the Jamaican Internal Marketing System," in Sidney W. Mintz, comp., *Papers in Caribbean Anthropology* (New Haven, Conn., 1960), pp. 13–14.

28. Ibid., pp. 15, 17.

29. Ibid., p. 14.

30. Alexander Barclay, *A Practical View of the Present State of Slavery in the West Indies* (London, 1826), p. 265; Patterson, *Sociology of Slavery*, p. 228.

31. P.P. (Commons) (no. 721), 1831–32, 20:199, evidence of Vice-Admiral Sir Charles Fleming.

32. Barclay, *Practical View*, pp. 265–66, footnote.

33. P.P. (Commons) (no. 721), 1831–32, 20:25, evidence of W. Taylor; 513, evidence of J. B. Wildman.

34. P.P. (Commons) (no. 721), 1831–32, 20:352, evidence of Robert Scott.

35. P.P. (Lords) (no. 127), 1831–32, 306:646, evidence of Rev. P. Duncan.

36. Some crimes against property were defined as capital offenses by the 1816 slave code. These included arson, house breaking, stock stealing, and mutilating a fellow slave. Such crimes were tried by special slave courts consisting of three magistrates and a twelve-man jury. The slave court returns for 1820–25 establish that, in the parishes with the largest slave populations (20,000, or more), only thirty to thirty-eight slaves were

convicted by slave courts of capital crimes in the whole five-year period. Jamaica: *Votes of the Assembly,* 1825, Appendix 59, pp. 373–402, C.O. 114/112.

37. *Royal Gazette,* Mar. 29, 1823, p. 8, C.O. 141/20.
38. *West India Sketch Book* (London 1826), 2 vols, 2:226.
39. John W. Blassingame, *The Slave Community: Plantation Life in the Antebellum South* (New York, 1972), p. 113.
40. Higman, *Slave Population,* pp. 178–79, Table 40.
41. Madden, *Twelvemonths Residence,* 2:155–56.
42. Lewis, *Journal,* p. 76.
43. Melville J. Herskovits, *The Myth of the Negro Past* (New York, 1941).
44. Sidney W. Mintz and Richard Price, *An Anthropological Approach to the Afro-American Past: A Caribbean Perspective* (Philadelphia, 1976), pp. 27, 28. The authors cite examples of marriage patterns among the Saramaka that derive from twentieth-century conditions rather than African tradition, and wood carvings by Bush Negroes, traditionally regarded as pro-typical African art in the Americas, now shown to be largely a nineteenth-century creation. On the other hand, the "ordeal" used as the highest court in Saramaka involves pushing a medicated feather through the tongue of the accused to determine guilt or innocence, a practice which can be traced directly to the eighteenth-century kingdom of Benin.
45. Ibid., p. 5.
46. Curtin, *Atlantic Slave Trade,* p. 144, fig. 12.
47. Mintz and Price, *Anthropological Approach,* p. 25.
48. The language question is fully discussed in Robert B. Le Page's *Jamaican Creole* (London, 1960).
49. Frederick Douglass, *My Bondage and My Freedom* (New York, 1969), p. 253.
50. Cynric R. Williams, *A Tour through the Island of Jamaica . . . in the Year 1823* (London, 1827), p. 27.
51. Geoffrey Parrinder, *West African Religion* (London, 1961), pp. 11–24.
52. Bryan Edwards, *The History, Civil and Commercial of the British Colonies in the West Indies* (London, 1801), 3 vols., 2:85–86.
53. John Shipman, "Thoughts on the present state of Religion among the Negroes in Jamaica. A plan for their moral and religious improvement suggested by which a knowledge of the Christian religion may be communicated to them with but (comparatively) little clerical assistance: and without teaching them to Read. And the propriety and necessity of their Instruction considered in a variety of Arguments," 1820, 2 ms. vols., Box 558, M.M.S. Archives (hereafter cited as Shipman, "Thoughts on Religion among the Negroes").
54. Ibid., pp. 9–11.
55. Max Gluckman, "The Magic of Despair," in *Order and Rebellion in Tribal Africa* (London, 1971), pp. 141–43.
56. Stewart, *View of the Past and Present,* pp. 274–75; Barclay, *Practical*

View, pp. 135–36; Madden, *Twelvemonths Residence,* 1:189; Shipman, "Thoughts on Religion among the Negroes," p. 5.

57. James B. Christiansen, "The Adaptive Function of the Fanti Priesthood," in William R. Bascom and Melville J. Herskovits, eds., *Continuity and Change in African Culture* (Chicago, 1959), p. 275; Gladwyn M. Childs, *Umbundu Kinship and Character* (London, 1949), p. 57; Patterson, *Sociology of Slavery,* pp. 198–202. It is not clear whether the elaborate burials were part of ritual ancestor worship.

58. Philip D. Curtin, *Two Jamaicas: The Role of Ideas in a Tropical Colony, 1830–65* (Cambridge, Mass., 1958), p. 31.

59. Phillippo, *Jamaica,* p. 249; Patterson, *Sociology of Slavery,* p. 190.

60. Patterson, *Sociology of Slavery,* p. 189; Parrinder, *West African Religion,* p. 3.

61. Barclay, *Practical View,* p. 185; Patterson, *Sociology of Slavery,* p. 191.

62. Patterson, *Sociology of Slavery,* p. 190; Phillippo, *Jamaica,* p. 247; Stewart, *View of the Past and Present,* p. 277.

63. Melville J. and Frances Herskovits, *Trinidad Village* (New York, 1947), p. 247; Christiansen, "Adaptive Function of the Fanti Priesthood," p. 263.

64. *Missionary Herald,* Apr., 1822, p. 174, letter from Coultart, Dec. 10, 1821.

65. Patterson, *Sociology of Slavery,* pp. 186–87, 189; Stewart, *View of the Past and Present,* p. 277; Shipman, "Thoughts on Religion among the Negroes," p. 12.

66. Curtin, *Two Jamaicas,* p. 130; Waddell, *Twenty-nine Years in the West Indies,* p. 137; Phillippo, *Jamaica,* p. 248.

67. Christiansen, "Adaptive Function of the Fanti Priesthood," pp. 257–58; Parrinder, *West African Religion,* pp. 78–79.

68. Curtin, *Two Jamaicas,* p. 30.

69. Edwards, *History,* 2:95.

70. P.P. (Lords) (no. 127), 1831–32, 307:807, evidence of Rev. W. Knibb.

71. Shipman, "Thoughts on Religion among the Negroes," p. 41.

72. Curtin, *Two Jamaicas,* pp. 33–34.

73. Waddell, *Twenty-nine Years in the West Indies,* pp. 35–36.

74. Buchner, *Moravians in Jamaica,* pp. 47–52.

75. Shipman, "Thoughts on Religion among the Negroes," pp. 42–49; P.P. (Lords) (no. 127), 1831–32, 306:623, evidence of W. Taylor.

76. The religious forms developed among the twentieth-century Zulus provide one example. Two clear tendencies emerged among the Zulus: Ethiopian-type churches formed in imitation of the white mission churches but under black leadership, and a Zionist element defined theologically as a "sycretistic Bantu movement, with healing, speaking in tongues, purification rites, and taboos as the main expressions of faith." The Zionist sects were led by prophets who claimed to have been called to the work through supernatural revelation in dreams. They began as eccentric visionaries with no fixed place to live who went about preaching an apoca-

lyptic message and gathering followers. Their worship was characterized by sacred dances, watchnight services, and animal sacrifices. They, too, relied on the Spirit rather than the Bible for guidance, although some were ready with particular quotations to defend specific theological points, just as some of the Baptists Waddell spoke to could quote chapter and verse without being able to read. The savior of these sects was also John the Baptist. Although the Zionist churches had no central organization, and each prophet, like the Daddies in Jamaica, followed their own visions and fancies, they nevertheless displayed an amazing uniformity. As Sundkler comments, they reflected "the fundamental needs and aspirations of the broad masses." Bengt G. M. Sundkler, *Bantu Prophets in South Africa* (London, 1948), pp. 53–55, 276.

77. Shipman, "Thoughts on Religion among the Negroes," p. 49; P.P. (Lords) (no. 127), 307:807, 810, evidence of Rev. W. Knibb.

CHAPTER THREE

The Missionaries
and the Slaves

THE MISSIONARIES WENT to Jamaica to improve life for the slaves within
the parameters defined by the slave system, and on these terms they won
the cooperation of a small liberal element among the slave owners. For
the missionaries, as for their patrons, religious instruction for the slaves
was entirely directed to the rescue of their souls from sin and preparation
for life eternal. To achieve this end, however, the missionaries had to
attack the slaves' established culture, to root out their religious ideas, to
divorce them from the social traditions and moral assumptions of plantation life, to replace Anansi, the supreme ginal, with Christian the Pilgrim, who fought his was through life. In doing so they appealed to the
intellectual and moral capacities that the slave system, in principle, denied its chattels and introduced them, in the mission churches, to new
activities and organizational forms based on the assumption that all men
were equal before God. Mission work among the slaves, in short, was an
innovation with a disruptive potential.

Its political significance, moreover, was underlined by the planters,
who remained throughout the period divided on the issue of mission
work. Mission patrons gave priority to meeting the imperial government's requirements on religious toleration; their opponents were more
concerned with the missionaries' connections with the antislavery movement. Missions enjoyed, at best, an uneasy tolerance that made attendance at the mission churches an activity which exposed the slaves to
punishment.

In the last resort the missionaries' neutral stance on the slavery issue
was no more than a declaration of intent: they did not intend their
message to souls in bondage to be translated into a message to people in
bondage; they undertook to point the path to salvation, not the road to
liberation. But their work created reverberations among the slaves over

which they had no control. This chapter outlines what the missionaries taught and the goals they aimed to achieve. It also analyzes those elements in mission teaching and activity that sharpened tensions between the slaves and the slave system and opened the way for the slaves to use Christianity as a politicizing force to fuel the conviction that "better must come" in this life as well as the next.

The impact of mission teaching was vitally influenced by the attitudes that informed it. The missionaries, it will be recalled, dependent on the planters for licenses, tended to respond to the "aristocratic embrace" and identify their interests with the interests of the patrons. Their class origins, to a degree, encouraged this tendency. They were recruited from the sons of small traders, skilled workers, and farmers who made up the bulk of their parent churches; though most came from chapel-going families, few had relatives who were ministers. To become a missionary represented, for most of them, a distinctly upward social step. Of the Baptists sent to Jamaica, for example, at least seven had trained initially as artisans, and only one, Thomas Burchell, son of a west country clothier, was distinctly middle class.[1]

The missionaries themselves were aware of what they termed the "worldly" aspect of their aspirations, the conflict between ambition and service to others. "I have endeavoured to examine the motives which have induced me to make this choice," wrote one, "and though I have too often discovered them to be unworthy of so noble an undertaking, yet I do trust that they arise from a desire to be useful to the cause of Christ. I trust that I do not deceive myself."[2] This definition, however, provided only a rough rule of thumb to guide decisions in the complexities of the political situation they confronted in Jamaica, particularly since the neutral policy was itself no real guide. It is not surprising to find that there were times when actions the missionaries could justify as service to the cause of Christ, in fact, reflected their ambition to achieve respectability in the eyes of the whites.

The missionaries, however, could never become, like the Anglican clergy, a mere adjunct of the planter class. Their occupation as instructors to the slaves declassed them, and their supposed antislavery connection made them suspect. Every courtesy extended by their patrons was counterbalanced by innumerable incivilities; time and again they were made aware that "no Englishman, except a missionary, would be treated with so much contempt."[3] The tensions stirred by mission work relegated them firmly to a social no-man's-land, beyond the pale of white society, to which they were admitted only as an occasional privilege. Their position as outsiders was underlined by an income significantly below that of Anglican curates; the W.M.M.S., for example, paid £130–250 for married men compared to the curates' £500. The missionaries consequently formed a professional group that socialized chiefly with one another, reinforcing the principles and convictions on which their work was based.

Relationships among the mission groups were publicly cordial. The Moravians, product of an international church, had a sharp sense of Jamaica as part of a global mission field, and their north coast station at Irwin became a regular meeting place for all the missionaries in the area. Where the Baptists and Wesleyans had town stations in common, they met for prayers, attended each others' special services, and shared the pleasure of welcoming new arrivals. Bi-monthly and quarterly meetings also brought together Moravians and Wesleyans to conduct their missions' business, which allowed them to spend the occasional comfortable evening "taking a view of the extent and importance of our missionary work and looking forward to a place of eternal recompense."[4] Outside the town stations, however, most of the missionaries most of the time were completely dependent on their family circles for social support, a circumstance that prompted some missionary wives, like Mary Knibb, to seize the opportunity to work as partners with their husbands. They awarded themselves informally the authority enjoyed officially by mission "sisters" only in the Moravian church.[5]

Many of the Wesleyan missionaries in their first years of service were denied even domestic comfort. Sent out to complete their training under the supervision of an experienced missionary, they qualified for marriage, and a marriage allowance, only when their training was completed. No less than a third of the Wesleyan missionaries in the island at any one time were in this position, and some were no more than twenty years of age. W.M.M.S. policy was strongly criticized by senior men in the field,[6] and the sexual and moral stresses to which these young men were subjected, in a society where "the sacred halo" of a missionary living alone with a man servant was no guarantee against scandal, were reflected in their letters home to the W.M.M.S. They pleaded for fiancées to be sent out, or for permission to return to England to find wives, or even, in the case of one young man stationed forty miles from a mission family and "very tried," for permission to "look out for a wife."[7] It is remarkable that only one of them left mission service to marry a free colored woman.

The missionaries' dependence on one another, and their comparative isolation in the daily round of mission work helped preserve the assumptions they carried to Jamaica about their role as pastors and the slaves' role as converts, assumptions that cut across the established social conventions of slave society and fundamentally contradicted the posture they adopted as planter protégés. The missionaries trained as popular preachers. Their models were the eighteenth-century successors to the Apostles, Wesley and Whitfield, Coke and Carey, preachers to the masses and innovators of mission work. Their theology, the Presbyterians of the United Secession church excepted, was the theology of the religious revival and stressed the experiential nature of Christianity, its universality, the qualities which restored it to the poor, the ignorant, and the oppressed.

For Baptist and Wesleyan recruits the tenor of their theology was reinforced by practical experience. Trainees were sent to preach not only to established congregations of the comfortably converted but to the home heathen of the slums and marketplaces. Recruits with no natural eloquence had to hammer out from carefully written drafts a forceful, passionate preaching style to catch the attention of crowds on street corners, and to hold their own against the heckling of "free thinkers, infidels and Papists," who put up more vociferous opposition than was ever recorded from the slaves.[8] The missionaries, themselves the product of the popular preachers of the revival, were trained to repeat this process. As teachers their approach was democratic, not authoritarian, and their easy familiarity with their converts was remarked on by contemporary Anglican clergy. "His minister converses with him [the slave] freely; and thus he sees no mark by which he is reminded of Slavery. . . . He possesses the temporary Elements of Liberty and Independence and during the hours of labour he looks forward to joining his Chapel, as a source of Joy and Gladness."[9] To accost a slave as "friend" identified a white man as a missionary, not a "buckra."[10]

Education and experience also prepared them for opposition from the authorities. Their formal studies included the history and constitution of their churches. Compacted into these studies, particular to each church in terms of theology and internal development, were the political experiences common to them all. Each church had its origins in debates, divisions, and controversies that attempted to determine the true path to salvation at the expense, where necessary, of conflict with both the government and the Anglican church. And political action in the pursuit of religious principles remained a live tradition in Britain, since the fundamental issue, the individual's right to religious freedom, was not entirely resolved. Measures of this freedom, it will be recalled, had been portioned out during the eighteenth century by the Toleration Acts, but full freedom for Dissenters was not accorded until 1812, within the memory of most of the missionaries and all their mentors, after a sharp political struggle. Full political rights for all denominations were granted only in 1828. Some of the missionaries, therefore, submitted reluctantly to the compromises dictated by the pursuit of planter patronage; they remained convinced that "it will not do to be too tame under our difficulties and trials. It is true that by opposing injurious and unjust impositions we may subject ourselves to further contumely and fiercer persecution, but better to endure this than be deemed by our successors a hindrance and a curse. . . . What would the dissenters in England be now, but for the firmness of the puritans and nonconformists in defence of their rights."[11]

The missionaries' key assumption, however, the assumption that struck most deeply and most subtly at the authority of the planters, was simply that the slaves were capable of choosing salvation and participating, like free citizens, in the mission churches. The missionaries were convinced that, of all the categories of foreign heathen, the slaves, victims of British cupidity, were among the most deserving and had already demonstrated, by the formation of the Black Baptist churches, outstanding capacities as Christians. The B.M.S., it will be recalled, had planned its mission to Jamaica in terms of assistance to George Leile, and Leile's contact with Dr. John Ryland, principal of the Bristol Baptist Academy, made it a regular recruiting ground for missionaries to Jamaica; no less than eight trained there.[12]

To the belief that the slaves were part of the brotherhood of man, and shared the common need for salvation, the missionaries literally gave their lives. The young volunteers no doubt envisaged themselves entering their last reward from the mission field, old and full of labors. But few lived long enough to be worn out with zeal, like the Wesleyan George Johnston, who was fifty-six when he died.[13] Most did not survive even ten years' service; Jamaica was a grave for Europeans, and no insurance company would insure a life there. Every exertion, to visit an estate, to attend an outstation, threatened fever, and death struck often enough to keep the survivors in mind of mortality. They watched over the death beds of wives and children; "I came to Jamaica by your direction," a Wesleyan missionary wrote, "and brought with me a lovely family. Within the space of two years I have lost . . . three children, an affectionate wife, and my own health." The survivors were plagued with fevers, debilities, convalescence, and enormous doctors' bills; the expenses of a few weeks' sickness quickly mounted to £50, a third of the year's salary for single men.[14]

The missionaries' conditions of work, training, and professional commitment all militated against the influence of their patrons. As professionals, moreover, the missionaries in Jamaica remained ultimately responsive to ideological developments in Britain. They were employed by societies whose missionary committees,[15] four or five men meeting at most once a month, left responsibility for routine business very largely in their hands. Even the W.M.M.S., which attempted more detailed regulation of mission finances, sick leaves, rotation of stations, as well as their employees' marital status, depended on the district chairman to act as its representative. The committees, however, kept the missionaries supplied with church publications, encouraged them to write detailed accounts of their work, and generally supervised their development. As one young Wesleyan was told when he ventured to complain that he had had no reply to twenty-two letters, "Your letters are always read; and you thus move under the Committee's eye."[16]

The missionary committees, however, were also responsible for relating mission policy to the policies adopted by their parent churches. The Baptist and Wesleyan missionaries were vitally affected by the fact that in 1823 their parent churches came out in full support of the campaign for the abolition of slavery. As later chapters will demonstrate, it was this development, in conjunction with the imperial government's program for the reform of slavery, that provided the political leverage to emancipate these missionaries, in the last years of slavery, from dependence on their patrons.

The conflicting influences to which most of the missionaries during most of the period were subjected, pressured by circumstance to identify with planter patrons and dedicated professionally to the service of the slaves, produced a wide range of individual responses among them. At one extreme was the Wesleyan James Horne, who once shocked and shamed his colleagues by whipping his elderly slave manservant;[17] at the other was the Baptist William Knibb, whose wholehearted commitment to the slaves made him one of Jamaica's most outstanding missionaries and a leading propagandist for the antislavery cause in Britain. But any missionary who addressed himself seriously to his work—and cases of indiscipline were rare—was bending his energies to assist the slaves to develop the capacities the system in principle denied.

Building the mission churches was an arduous and complex process. The missionary's first problem was communication. They learned by experience the distinctive rhythms and pronunciation of Jamaican creole and acquired a stock of idioms to convey their ideas. Their first sermons, however, were often too literary and argumentative. The Presbyterians, in particular, inexperienced in teaching illiterate heathen, quickly discovered that sermons suitable for congregations at home made no sense whatever to the slaves. "Began a series of discourses on the character of God," a Presbyterian missionary wrote soon after his arrival in Jamaica. "Although I though this as plain a discourse as I had ever preached . . . I found during the examination afterwards that I had never delivered one to them which they had understood less."[18] Evangelical preaching stirred consciences most effectively, since it was easier, as an experienced missionary commented, to impress the slaves' minds with "feeling application" than with argument;[19] in other words, the emotional tone of the sermon might be effective though the congregation had understood only one word in ten.

But what appeared initially as simply a language problem proved to be a battle with the slaves' traditional religion; they were trying to implant entirely new ideas about the nature of the spirit world and the nature of God. Nothing in the slaves' theology prepared them for the idea of God the law giver. The slaves also proved resistant to the basic Christian concept of sin; it tended, when first confronted, to intensify their feelings of inferiority induced by the slave system. Though the "wages of sin" was the text of innumerable sermons to newly founded groups, the missionaries found it was generally "a long time before a Negro would admit himself to be a sinful creature,"[20] and welcomed storms and earth tremors as means of rousing from "the sleep of sin those who would not be wakened by gentler methods."[21] The slaves admitted to sin only when they had grasped that to acknowledge their sinfulness was to acknowledge, as Christians, their individual spiritual value. The supreme importance the missionaries attached to the convert's soul, the strenuous measures they recommended to secure its salvation, ultimately enhanced their converts' sense of their own worth and laid the foundation for changes in their conduct.

Once congregation members confessed to a sense of sin, they attended classes to deepen awareness and learn the essentials of the Christian faith. The missionaries found that the most effective teaching materials were children's catechisms designed for rote learning, and the Wesleyan district chairman, John Shipman, devised a special version for the slaves of Wesley's *Instructions for Children*. Shipman's catechism[22] shows the content of this teaching and its emphases: seven lessons dealt with religious knowledge and no less than five with its social consequences, the practice of Christian morality.

The catechism hammered home the lessons already outlined on the nature of God and of sin and detailed methods of earning redemption. Redemption was won by faith, by grace, and by correct morality. Faith in God, created in each individual by the workings of the Holy Ghost, was the beginning of redemption. But the grace of God was continually necessary to save the convert from falling into sinful words and sinful works; the chief means of grace were the sacraments, prayer night and morning, both publicly and privately, daily searching of the scripture, and meditation on it at all times. These practices were to be sustained throughout the convert's life.

The slaves were familiar with versions of these forms of religious worship; spiritual visitations were evoked by the myal men and the Native Baptists as well as by the missionaries. Prayer and fasting were practiced by the missions' rivals to the point that experienced missionaries de-emphasized some Christian practices, such as fasting before communion, that sanctioned these "superstitions."

The main thrust of mission teaching, however, directly conflicted with both the slaves' religious ideas and their established social mores. The salvation of the individual's soul, and the achievement of rewards in heaven, demanded that converts adhere to the pattern of social and moral conduct that mission teaching dictated. Religious practices, the missionaries emphasized, could not in themselves secure salvation; an internal or spiritual revolution was not enough. Christian conviction had to have social consequences. Here the missionaries were breaking completely new ground. This key Christian concept, that there was a vital connection between conduct in this world and fate in the world to come, was completely novel to the slaves. In the slaves' traditional religion nothing that happened on earth affected their prospect of feasting with the ancestors in the afterlife. The spirits had no power to trick or punish beyond the grave. The Native Baptists, characteristically, emphasized the purely spiritual means of salvation.

The missionaries invited the slaves who had accepted the idea that all men were equally sinners, to be judged by an Almighty God, to implement changes in their daily lives: to practice, in the sight of their families, their work mates, and their masters, the principles they learned in chapel. The capacity to implement radical changes in their way of life on the plantation was a measure of individual worth and of their hope of salvation.

The missionaries' morality cut across all the social practices of plantation life, including the slaves' sexual mores; no less than two whole sections of the catechism were devoted to the importance of Christian marriage. Confronted by what were, in their eyes, irregular and haphazard relationships among the slaves, the missionaries preached monogamy;[23] as Shipman's catechism demonstrated, they had to begin by explaining both the reason for marriage, "fulfillment of God's command," and exactly what it was, the uniting of one man with one woman with God as witness. Many questions had to be dealt with: should they marry before they cohabit? May not a man or woman take another man or woman? What is living together without marriage called? The punishments for adultery, whoredom, and fornication had to be underlined: condemnation to the lake of fire and brimstone, "which is the second death."[24]

The only alternative to monogamy countenanced by the missionaries was chastity. In the Presbyterian mission even slaves who were still "hearers," and not full-fledged church members, had to declare they would live in faithful concubinage and apply for marriage as soon as possible. The Wesleyan district decided that members must either marry or be chaste, and even if a marriage was broken because a wife or husband was sold, they advised submission to God's will. The Moravian church, which instituted its own form of marriage valid among church members, took a more liberal view. If church members married and promised fidelity, a broken vow meant exclusion from the church. If a man already had more than one wife, however, he could only become monogamous with their consent; failing this, he was allowed to join the church but not to hold office in it. In cases where a marriage was broken up by the sale of one of the partners, they allowed for re-marriage, especially where small children were involved, but would not advise or encourage it.[25]

The missionaries' teaching encountered strong opposition from the slaves. The slaves' arguments were fully and frankly stated in an anonymous pamphlet written by a Wesleyan missionary who had served many years in the West Indies.[26] The pamphlet, which was never published by the W.M.M.S., takes the form of conversations among the missionary, Quaco, the head driver on an estate, and Quasheba, the woman he is living with. When the missionary argued that fornication was a sin and threatened the sinner with the lake of fire and brimstone, Quaco pointed to the example of his betters: "Buccra can read book [the Bible], but have plenty women." The missionary stressed that God was no respecter of persons and drove Quaco to his second argument, the fact that he might be separated from his wife. The missionary urged him to face his immediate duty and confront that poblem when it arose. Quaco then stated his underlying fear, that marriage would make Quasheba "think too much of himself [*sic*]" and not give him much satisfaction. This confession prompted a spirited attack on his "unmanly and unchristian" attitude; slave men, the missionary declared, like to keep their women in a kind of brutal subjection and view them as slaves, not companions. Quasheba, in fact, showed no signs of subjection and demonstrated great pride in her economic independence. "Me raise plenty stock and take 'em to market . . . me make cassava bread . . . me work sometime till second cock crow." She saw no reason to believe that marriage could change a man's habits. "He no mean to mend. . . . You no know him Massa. He got women everywhere . . . he run about too much, too much, . . . he caree for me, nor for the pickanees not so much as so (showing the end of her finger)." This couple is eventually led to the altar by Quaco's fear of punishment, allied with Quasheba's hope of a God-guided reform.

The pamphlet writer took a straightforward example where the man "have woman everywhere" but only one established family group. The Presbyterian missionary Waddell, who lived on an estate in the midst of his congregation, found such cases the simplest to deal with, since the established couple had only to be persuaded to marry. But very often a man had abandoned one wife and family for a new, younger wife and already had new family ties. Others, contemplating a sanctioned union, wanted to abandon all their old connections and start with a new choice.

"As a general rule," Waddell wrote, "vagaries of fancy were discouraged"; the men were persuaded, where possible, to return to their first wife and family and, "generally speaking, good sense and right feeling, guided by the divine word, prevailed, and difficulties were satisfactorily arranged."[27] The example set by married missionaries was an important element in persuading converts that marriage and church membership were intertwined. But those really concerned for salvation had to be prepared, in the last resort, to live chastely. As one woman said, abandoning a partner she had lived with for many years who refused to marry her, "Me must give account of myself to God and him of himself. My soul very valuable, me have no time to wait for him."[28]

The morality demanded by the road to salvation also included a total ban on drumming and dancing. The slaves' musical creativity, as such, found a place in the mission churches, where the missionaries were pleased to find that the slaves gave old hymns new tunes infused with their own rhythms and harmonies. But dancing and drumming and the drinking that accompanied them were condemned as heathen practices. European as well as African dancing was indicted, though the latter was instinctively recognized as the greater enemy; it was connected with the slaves' traditional religion, and the alien drum rhythms suggested pits of sexual iniquity more fearful than scraping fiddles could evoke. The three-day Christmas holiday was a testing time even for settled congregations. While rowdy heathenish processions, with "revolting attitudes in their dances," filled the slave villages and the streets outside the chapels, the missionaries tried to encourage their congregations by contrasting their clean, dignified appearance with the "half-mad, half-naked" goombah dancers. Occasionally the overseers cooperated and rewarded orderly conduct by killing cattle for a feast. Even so, the festivities usually took their toll of converts; at best, Christian and African celebrations were juxtaposed and if the drums were silent on one estate, they were busy nearby. The missionary was fortunate if, drummed to sleep on Christmas Eve, he was roused by carol singing on Christmas morning.[29]

The missionaries made no easy converts. "Very few turn to God," one missionary concluded. This painful conviction "often hangs like a dead weight on all my exertions and, after a week of incessant toil, causes me to sit down and mourn over the unproductiveness of all my labours."[30] But their attack on social customs introduced new ideas among the slaves, opened up new choices for them, and, most important, encouraged them to claim new rights and privileges on the plantation.

Applications for permission to marry, which forced the masters to acknowledge formally that slaves had family obligations, multiplied. To curb this development the planters attempted, in the 1826 slave code, to make their consent a legal rather than a customary requirement, a move frustrated by the disallowance of the code.

The missionaries attempted to counter any disruption their teaching might provoke by tightly hedging the path to salvation by duty and obedience. Converts were required to be obedient to their masters. The missionaries, on the instruction of their parent societies, enforced "the same exhortations which the Apostles of our Lord administered to the slaves of ancient nations, when by their ministry they embraced Christianity,"[31] in order to promote the "due discharge of the duties of the lower Classes and the total destruction of every principle of discontent and insubordination."[32] They were to repeat, in Jamaica, the achievement of the religious revival in England and uplift the moral consciousness of the laboring classes, without disturbing the existing power structure.

Shipman's catechism indicated how this was to be done. Of five lessons on Christian morality, three were devoted to the duties of servants. Masters were required simply to be "just, humane and charitable." The instructions to servants were more detailed. The blatant sins of lying and stealing were condemned, and the pitfalls of being a mere "eye servant" were carefully explained. The slaves were reminded that God willed men to earn their bread by the sweat of their brows; so converts must labor diligently and not trifle their masters' time. With the industrious hand went the respectful attitude; they must not answer their master back but "show by their respectful silence, due submission" and should not indulge in evil speaking in private.

The missionaries applied this advice; when drought threatened standing cane, the slaves were urged to work harder, and when labor relations were strained, they advised submission.[33] Stealing was condemned, particularly in relation to the master's property. Shipman's catechism queried,

> Is it right for servants to steal from their masters?
> No, because God has commanded us "Thou shalt not steal."
>
> Even if they are not observed?
> But God sees and will punish them.
>
> How are thieves punished in this world?
> By being whipped, confined, banished and sometimes hanged.

> But is this all the punishment they are subject to?
> No, if they repent not God will punish them in hellfire for ever.

Even the sugar allowance, which was commonly regarded by estate managers as a perquisite of office for the sugar boiler, was condemned as stealing by the Presbyterians.[34]

The Bible was rich in examples of faithful servants, and the pattern of virtue held up to the slaves was Onesimus. Here was an example of a runaway slave who went to Rome, heard St. Paul preaching, and was so moved by the sermon he went to Paul afterward and explained how he had left his master. Paul sent him home again with a letter in which he asked the master to forgive him. The Onesimus story was hammered home in sermons and classes; a Wesleyan missionary asked a class of boys,

> Was [Onesimus] a good and dutiful slave?
> No, he was a very bad one, for he was a thief and runaway.
>
> And how did the slave behave himself after his repentance and
>   conversion to Jesus Christ?
> He behaved himself well and was profitable to his master.
>
> Does religion produce the same effect now on slaves that have
>   it?
> Yes, they neither rob nor run away, but are good servants.[35]

The missionaries' conscious political message, applied on their own terms, simply added a new twist to the slaves' established pattern of adaptability, Anansi style, to the demands of the system. For some of the slaves the missionaries were able to report that the practice of these principles brought distinct advantages. The virtues of thrift and sobriety produced as striking effects in the slave villages as in the English mining towns. "The hovel became a house . . . instead of the rum bottle some neat article of clothing, or useful appendage to the family came from town . . . a most harmonious and interesting association of refinement and religion soon displayed itself, alike in their persons, their habits and morals. . . ." Reverence for the master, soft answers, and silence were said to save converts from "many a cut and slash."[36] In all essentials, however, the missionaries emphasized primarily that the rewards of a Christian life would be reached beyond the grave.

The prospects for saved and sinner in the life hereafter were described in the final lessons of the catechism as the climax of mission teaching.

What sort of place is hell?
A dark, bottomless pit full of brimstone.

Will both their souls and bodies be tormented?
Yes, every part of them at once.

Who will be their tormentors?
Their own conscience, the devils and one another.

How long will their torments last?
Forever.

This description was easily translated into the slaves' own experiences. One described hell as a place where "twenty thousand driba [drivers] . . . poke you wid fire stick." By comparison the joys of heaven, though also lasting forever, seemed nebulous:

What sort of place is Heaven?
Full of Light and Glory.

How will good men live there?
In Joy and happiness greater than they can now desire or think.

Wherein will happiness lie?
In enjoyment of God.

How will they spend their time?
Singing praise to God.

Converts in their death-bed speeches sometimes demonstrated their sense of heaven as a place of comfort and glory: "So the world 'tan wid me now, it ready to trow me off, but den O me hope, me hope though me no sure, me will den fall into de arms of Jesus."[37]

Shipman's catechism displayed the contradiction at the heart of mission teaching: on the one hand a conscious appeal for conformity to the system, on the other a characteristic Protestant emphasis on each individual's responsibility to seek salvation. Once accepted, this responsibility dictated that converts must repudiate their existing religious ideas, established mores, customary pleasures, and even family connections and, further, claim new rights for themselves on the plantation. Logically, converts set on this road had every intellectual incentive to question the social practices of not only the plantation but the society of which it was part, and were justified in doing so by the missionaries' basic message that all men were equally sinners in the eyes of God.

The missionaries' intellectual challenge appealed to the slaves as embodiments of the moral and intellectual capacities the slave system simultaneously exploited and denied. The impact of this appeal was heightened by the fact that this basic contradiction was already expressed in the organization of plantation production: the slaves played a dual role, as chattel laborers and as small producers and traders who enjoyed some of the functions of free peasants. On this basis the slaves had already defined, within estate organization, certain customary rights, and were accustomed to defending them. The invitation to join the mission churches encouraged them to extend their existing rights, and diminish the rights their owners exercised.

The missionaries, as religious teachers, also revived, strengthened, and developed the religious element in the slaves' indigenous culture, which had always served to regulate and rationalize their relationship with the universe and society. The slaves' religion was traditionally associated with rebellion; obeah oaths had bound the rebels of 1760, obeah was still a felony, and the slave owners occasionally hanged or transported its practitioners.

The factor that brought all these elements into play in the regular round of mission work, and threw into relief every nuance of mission teaching connecting its critique of plantation culture with condemnation of the social structure of which it was part, was the opposition it excited among the slave owners. Their sensitivity to the security of the slave system, whether threatened by external or internal violence, internal or external political developments, first marked by their attack on the Wesleyan chapel and the imprisonment of the Black Baptist preachers Leile and Baker, was repeatedly reactivated. They identified the missionaries not simply as "outsiders," as socially not quite white, but as a disruptive element and, ultimately, enemies of the system.

The slaves observed when the missionaries' estate visits were bedeviled by overseers who kept the gangs working at a distance, or cut down the dinner break so there was no time to attend a meeting. They took note when Sunday services in the town chapels were interrupted by young rowdies or by interfering constables checking that services were ending before sunset. They picked up at market rumors of trouble with the magistrates. From time to time there were spectacular, dramatic incidents which trumpeted white antagonism loud and clear. Following chapters discuss, for example, an attack on the Wesleyan mission and the imprisonment of missionaries at St. Ann's Bay.

While the missionaries risked prison, the slaves risked flogging. Routine harassments were directed against the missionaries; at times of political tension, however, efforts were also made to keep the slaves from chapel. Their free time was cut down and sometimes alternative instruction by an Anglican curate was provided; more often, direct orders were given and punishment inflicted.[38] Onesimus, in short, could not make his master play Philemon. Slaves who took their Christianity seriously cut themselves off from the customary compensations of plantation life; they stayed sober, avoided dances, perhaps even married, and certainly thought their own thoughts. They necessarily exuded a certain independence the managers feared would undermine their authority.

James Williams, an apprenticed laborer whose verbatim account of his experiences made an influential pamphlet in the anti-apprenticeship campaign,[39] exemplifies this conflict. Williams happened to see other apprentices on the estate put in the dungeons for refusing to go to breakfast when ordered to do so, and his master, who was standing nearby, chose to try and provoke him. "He ask me what I got to say about it; I say, Sir, I have nothing to do with it, I don't interfere; he say, You do interfere; I tell him no—he raise up his stick three times to lick me down." At this, Williams protested and was locked up with the rest, but he had the final word: "While they was putting me in, I said 'It wasn't a man made this world and man can't command it: the one that made the world shall come again, to receive it, and that is Jesus Christ!' "[40] James Williams was driven to verbal defiance, but he was punished for his silent appraisal of the scene before him.

It was, however, the slave activists, exerting themselves to serve the mission cause, who excited peculiar animosity. A Wesleyan slave leader at St. Ann's Bay, who refused to take the slaves from his plantation to the Anglican church instead, was imprisoned in irons and flogged almost to death. A Baptist slave deacon was taken to court on a false charge, imprisoned, and publicly flogged. As the missionaries knew, such cases, detailed in Chapter Five, were only the tip of the iceberg; in the last resort the slave system, true to its own logic, denied the slaves the right to seek salvation.

Christianity, therefore, while affording the slaves many of the spiritual satisfactions they associated with religion, also elaborated the social bases for conflict, sharpened tensions, and stimulated new forms of resistance to slavery. The mission churches, moreover, by transferring to slave society organizations created in the struggle for freedom of conscience in Britain, provided the slaves with opportunities to establish new claims to status, acquire new skills, and undertake responsibilities that indicated directly the equality of slave and free, black and white.

The missionaries, in recruiting church members, gave absolute priority to combatting the slaves' rival religious traditions, which in fact facilitated their own success. Their battle proved endless. Established congregations had to be reminded from the pulpit that they must have nothing to do with obeah, but watchmen remained around their houses and "jumbies" (the spirits of the dead) provided an endless stock-in-trade of stories for their children. Estate visits revealed preparations for "superstitious rites" to quiet restless spirits. Even the funeral services the missionaries themselves conducted were inbued with the slaves' traditional sense that death was a festive occasion, and the most earnest sermons failed to induce a properly Christian response. The slaves continued to think of heaven as a place where they feasted with the ancestors; the missionaries found this a "prejudice very natural to their circumstances," but it required "no ordinary degree of moral force to make them forgo the hope for the hope of a country in heaven."[41]

Native Baptist influence was even more insidious; it was difficult to detect and was, in effect, encouraged by the work of the missionaries themselves. It is not surprising that from time to time the missionaries had to admit defeat in the struggle with these rival traditions; their converts fell back into "debasing and disgusting practises" and prompted weary exclamations: "Oh, my dear brother, the prejudice, the obstinate headstrong prejudices of ignorance, who can describe them?"[42]

The missionaries understood that to combat this ignorance they had to provide, above all, regular instruction, "line upon line and precept upon precept," taught in the simplest language possible to establish a new framework of thought. Yet the missions were always short-staffed, and the missionaries' grueling weekly rounds of visits, involving as many as a hundred miles of traveling in a week, were easily disrupted by bad weather or a sick horse. Death and sickness complicated matters still further; even established stations were sometimes left with one missionary to provide services for two churches, and to have assistance on country circuits from literate free colored and white members as lay preachers was the exception, not the rule.[43]

The slaves' opportunities for learning were also limited. The most eager converts had to divide their Sundays between the provision grounds, the market, and the chapel, while the demands of crop season (the sugar harvest) made attendance at church or at meetings on the estate virtually impossible. Some missionaries stopped estate visits altogether with a final prayer that their exhortations might be remembered, but they acknowledged that "by the time the sugar harvest is over everything is forgotten . . . and it is necessary to begin the work of instruction all over again." And when drought affected the provision grounds, as in 1825, the people were left short of food and money and were too depressed to show any enthusiasm for church going. More trivial circumstances reduced congregations; a missionary might conscientiously struggle through rain and mud to fulfill his commitments, only to find that the people had stayed at home.

In these circumstances the average attendance, even of accredited members, was low. The Wesleyan missionaries at Bath, St. Ann's Bay, and Montego Bay found that estate slaves attended sometimes once every six to twelve weeks, at most once a month. As one missionary queried, "How much of the Gospel may be learnt by hearing it two hours a month?"[44]

The standards the missionaries established were, in their own minds, a compromise between the requirements set out in the catechism and the realities they confronted. For the slaves the status of church membership represented a real achievement. Each candidate for admission was examined personally by his minister in the main tenets of Christianity. The missionaries attempted to distinguish, in the examination, between mere verbal facility and sincerity, between the "ginals" and the genuine converts. Enthusiasm and eloquence often went hand in hand with novelty; praying could be in fashion among the slaves. Converts whose fluent testimonies to a change of heart were lyrical with biblical phrases could not necessarily be trusted, for "though conversant with the language of Zion, and apt in the use of religious phrases, [they] have not yet fully seen into the heinous nature of sin."[45]

Presbyterian and Moravian candidates were also tested for their will and ability to "live Christian"; "I have found it my duty," one missionary wrote, "to exert a rigid faithfulness approaching, all things considered, a severity . . . caution and watchfulness ought ever to be inseperable from the ministerial office."[46] The Baptists and Wesleyans, cut off from the estates, were in no position to make this test. More important, these missionaries, once convinced of the candidate's sense of sin, put a greater reliance on the infinite power of grace; given faith and good intentions in the convert, prayer and the working of God's mercy might do the rest.[47] Members, however, were periodically re-examined and communicant status was reserved, except in the Baptist church, for tried members. Between a third and a half of Wesleyan church members achieved communicant status, and most Presbyterians and Moravians.[48] In the last resort, church discipline was maintained by the expulsion of backsliders. Members were expelled for nonattendance, fornication, "the prevailing sin of the country," adultery, drunkenness, and occasionally "obeahism." From time to time the bejeweled free colored women were disciplined for their love of ornament.[49]

The Wesleyan expulsion rate could be as high as 10 percent of the total membership. This was partly because their itinerant system regularly exposed the class lists to the scrutiny of a newly appointed missionary who frequently concluded that it would be necessary to "pull down" before "building up."[50] In the Presbyterian and Moravian churches only 3 to 4 percent of church members were expelled yearly.[51] Presbyterian members, however, lost privileges not only for their own sins but for condoning sin in their family. This applied to mothers who maintained contact with daughters living as concubines; no less than three members at Hampden were excluded on this account in one year.[52] Baptist backsliders, in contrast, were rarely disciplined. By 1834, however, when mission membership totaled 27,000, Wesleyans, Moravians, and Baptists all had stations where one missionary had charge of more than 800 converts,[53] a scale which made effective supervision impossible. All the denominations had to rely primarily upon the slaves' profession of faith.

These procedures, however unsatisfactory by the missionaries' standards, appealed to and fostered the slaves' sense of individual merit and potential for achievement. And the testimonies the missionaries found acceptable demonstrated that the slaves did acquire a grasp of Christian principles. Baptist members, for example, testified as follows:

> What is sin?
> All that don't fitten.
> All the badness me do foretime.
>
> What has Jesus Christ done for our salvation?
> Him 'tand fe we.
> Him get himself wound fe we.
>
> Why do you love the Saviour?
> For Him come down and be crucified an' Him 'till pray.
>
> Do you think Jesus will hear you when you pray and never say
> No to you when you ask a favour of Him?

Massa, Him have mercy upon we and Him deal wid we as we
deal wid Him.[54]

Not all candidates testified in such idiomatic language; the Moravian converts used more formal terms. "When I think about this great
feast and how I shall appear before my Lord and Saviour . . . I feel myself
very unworthy of this grace, but my lord is everytime very gracious to
me and I feel him near my heart"; "I am not worthy, but my Saviour is
too good. He was treated too cruelful when he suffered on the Cross for
my sins." But the slaves lent the old phrases fresh validity. It was with
"a pathos altogether indescribable, but which was felt like electricity
through all the household," that an old man exclaimed, "but above all
the Gospel has brought God into my heart and made me wise unto
salvation."[55]

The splendid ceremony in which Baptist candidates were admitted
to membership encapsulated all the comforts the mission churches afforded the slaves. The candidates and their friends assembled in the
chapel the night before the baptism. No service could be held, but it was
understood that this was a time for solemn meditation. In the very early
hours of the morning the missionary joined them for prayer; then, before
sunrise, the company moved to the nearest river or seashore. The candidates, all robed in white, were assembled by their class leaders while the
missionary waded waist-deep into the water and the ceremony began.
Each one was led by his class leader to the missionary, who, emphasizing
once more that baptism must mark a change of heart, immersed him. On
the bank the waiting crowd sang hymns while some made fires and boiled
coffee. Spectators arrived by horse and chaise to survey the scene. The
orderly crowds, the white-robed candidates, the sacrificial fires, and the
holy music under the luminous blue dome of the sky before sunrise
created a memorable occasion.[56]

Ritual, religious fervor, the missionary's personal attention, contact
with friends, time spent away from the plantation, clean and neatly
dressed, to contemplate a better life and pray for strength in this one—
these were the comforts recaptured, in little, by every Sunday service.
Church membership, however, did more than comfort the slaves for the
hardships of life; by making status the reward of merit, the mission
churches undermined the values on which the authority structure of the
plantation and the society it represented were based. On the plantation,
status derived from the accident of skin shade and the will of the managers. The status of church membership, by contrast, was available to all

who chose to aspire to it; in addition, continued good conduct secured their good standing and won promotion. On the plantations no slave, however privileged, enjoyed security of tenure, and most slaves were condemned by age to downward mobility. The meritocracy of the mission churches, therefore, afforded particular comforts to the field slaves at the bottom of the plantation hierarchy and to all women who could not aspire to white mates.

More important, however, it underlined the arbitrary nature of the divisions between slaves and masters. The missionaries themselves, anxious to enhance the status of church membership, emphasized that Christians, black and white, slave and free, were equal. Membership in the mission churches meant membership in the church universal. The connection between slave converts and members of the missions' parent churches was symbolized by the membership tickets. The Wesleyans and the Baptists had their tickets printed in England; they were thus not a mark of a merely local association but linked them directly with the friends in England who supported mission work.[57] The slaves, in response, were always eager to have their tickets renewed and their anxious importuning, "me no able to come often, massa" made it difficult for the missionaries to refuse them.[58]

Slave converts, like their free counterparts, contributed money to their churches. Moravian and Presbyterian members did so occasionally and for a specific purpose: for chapel repairs or new furnishings. Baptist and Wesleyan members did so regularly, paying class money and quarterly subscriptions of ten pence and one shilling and eight pence a quarter respectively. Baptist "inquirers" also paid class money, and new groups contributed to the missionaries' traveling expenses. Members of these churches also formed auxiliary mission societies, which held special meetings to hear letters from missionaries in other fields and collect money, in their turn, for mission work. The slaves felt a special sympathy for Africa and called their collections "throwing up for Guinea country."[59] The missionaries intended these activities to cement the slaves' connection, symbolized by the membership tickets, with "all the sympathies hopes and joys which arise from communion with the General Church."[60] In doing so they encouraged the slaves to feel that as Christians they enjoyed advantages denied benighted heathen, but the inference that as Christians they merited free status was equally clear.

All the slaves' contributions were, of course, voluntary; only about one-half of the Baptist members paid their subscriptions, making the average contribution about a half-penny a week. The chapels were invariably burdened by debt and owed as much to capital invested by free colored members and to contributions from England as to slave offerings.[61] The slaves' subscriptions nevertheless meant that mission development was partly their own creation; they could identify the chapel they attended as their own and see neighboring chapels as the work of other slaves. The missionaries, who kept their converts well informed about money problems, made it clear that the chapels were monuments to their collective effort, an expression of their organized opinion.

This lesson was underlined by the planters themselves, who correctly perceived the increasing number of mission churches as a threat to their authority and attempted, by the 1826 slave code, to make slave contributions to the missions illegal. They advertised their anxiety to every congregation in the island when the code was disallowed, by calling the missionaries to Spanish Town for an investigation of mission finances before a special sectarian committee.[62] The Assembly's efforts to intimidate the missionaries and their converts were, however, unsuccessful and, in the years that followed, the mission churches expanded more rapidly than ever before.

The slaves' activities within the mission churches invested their spiritual equality with elements of social practice. Mission schools carried this process a step further by demonstrating their intellectual equality with the whites. The missionary societies recognized that the slaves had been reduced by avarice and neglect to a state of intellectual torpor that afforded the slave owners a "pretext for the favourite notion of their natural inferiority." The B.M.S. took the initiative to combat this state of affairs and sent out a salaried schoolmaster, Thomas Knibb, to Kingston in 1822.[63]

The planters, on their side, were convinced that education schemes would "revolutionize the country,"[64] and initially most of the missionaries in the field acquiesced in this judgment. John Shipman's catechism, for example, was specifically designed to "promote the Christian religion without teaching the slaves to read." The lead given by the B.M.S. and developments in imperial government policy, however, prompted the Wesleyans and the Moravians to reconsider their position.

In 1823 the imperial government gave priority in its program for the reform of slavery to religious instruction for the slaves.[65] The W.M.M.S. seized the opportunity to prompt the establishment of a regular system of Sunday schools and, where possible, day schools. The following year the Moravians followed suit. The Presbyterian missionaries, who arrived in the wake of the reform program, undertook schools and classes as a matter of course.[66]

Schools made fresh demands on limited resources. The home societies gave little financial assistance, and money for schools had to be scraped together from English charities, fee-paying pupils, and sympathetic slave owners.[67] The burden of teaching fell chiefly on the missionaries and their wives,[68] and even books were scarce. The missionaries were left begging for tracts and alphabets while they dreamed of presenting each literate pupil with a copy of the Bible and *The Pilgrim's Progress*.[69]

In these circumstances the Presbyterians and the Moravians, who worked with the full support of the slave owners, ran the most successful day schools for slave children. The patrons either provided or subsidized a schoolhouse, contributed to the teacher's salary, and arranged for the estate children to attend regularly.[70] The Moravians had seven schools with sixty to a hundred pupils each; two Presbyterian schools were on a similar scale, and smaller groups were served at other stations. These missionaries also ran a number of schools for free colored children in Port Maria and Lucea and among the small cultivators.[71]

The most successful independent school was the Baptist school in Kingston. It was largely the creation of William Knibb, who took it over in 1825 after the death of its founder, his elder brother Thomas. He found a leaking schoolhouse set beside a gully used alternately as a rubbish dump and a drain during the rains, the slates all broken and the pencils lost. Knibb revived public interest by holding successful public examinations, and in 1826 he built a new schoolhouse for 224 scholars including sixty-five slaves. The three Rs were taught to all pupils and history and grammar to the more advanced.[72] Free colored parents, however, had strong prejudices against their children associating with slaves; it needed a schoolmaster with personality to make mixed classes attractive, and when Knibb left the Kingston school it declined. A Baptist school in Spanish Town and a Wesleyan school in Kingston, each serving about a hundred scholars, had difficulty in keeping open; the Wesleyan school had only forty fee payers of the 150 it needed.[73] The mission day schools, however, in 1834 served in all some 1,300 children, of whom about 900 were slaves.[74]

All the missions, with the exception of some Baptist stations, ran Sunday schools where reading was taught to adults and children. These schools fluctuated widely in efficiency and popularity from year to year, but the overall attendance figures were high: the Moravians had 700–800 pupils and the Wesleyans about 500. The turnover, however, was rapid, as pupils rarely attended more than three months at a stretch.[75]

Most adults were reached by morning and evening classes. The Presbyterians were particularly keen on this work; the missionary in Lucea had 6 A.M. Sunday morning meetings in progress for domestic slaves within a few weeks of his arrival, and other classes were held for two hours every evening. At Cornwall estate the missionary's house was crowded night after night. Even in crop time, when the sugar harvest made heavy demands on every estate worker,

> One class with books sat round the table, another faced a lesson-board on the wall. The rest were sound asleep on the floor. . . . When their turn came, however, the sleepers jumped up, rubbing their eyes. . . . Out of crop their craving for lessons was insatiable. They would not be done. "One word more, minister, only one." "Missis, wharra dis be," was the incessant cry. Those who had learnt to read began to write, and one missionary commented: "It is an interesting sight to see some of them as soon as they drop the hoe in the evening, run and take up the quill and wield it so well."[76]

The schools and classes fed an appetite among the people that amazed their teachers. The slaves showed a "strong desire" for learning that, given the minimum opportunity, made progress possible beyond all reasonable expectation. One missionary marveled: "They have no stated person to teach them and are without books suited to their capacity, but they will beg a lesson from this and the other individual, and in some instances have learnt to read with considerable fluency." The number of children attending the mission schools is, therefore, little guide to the number of slaves affected by mission education. In the vicinity of the mission stations any ambitious adult could find means of instruction; schoolchildren in Kingston earned between three and ten pence a week teaching adults.[77]

The slaves sometimes used their new-found knowledge to seek exclusively spiritual guidance; one slave on Hampden estate returned a book to the little mission library because, "After we 'pell out two or three pages we no see nothin' for we soul."[78] Slaves who could read the Bible, however, had thrust into their hands the sanction and inspiration of English protest movements from Wycliffe to the Levellers, and some found lessons there the missionaries did not teach. Bible readers read newspapers and picked up more information about what was happening in the world than market or dining-room gossip revealed. Literacy opened new avenues of thought and encouraged the emergence of new leaders among the slaves. Although schools and classes were never a major feature of mission work before emancipation, they were one of the most important; they demonstrated the intellectual capacities the system attempted to deny and contributed to the complex developments that made the 1831 rebellion possible.

The mission churches made one further contribution to the slaves' political development: they awarded trusted converts responsible positions in the church hierarchy. Members took part in every level of administration. Chapel servants maintained the buildings and prepared for services; deacons and stewards made collections, took up membership dues, visited the sick, and occasionally distributed charity. And at the top of the hierarchy were assistants recruited to help the missionaries conduct and supervise membership classes.

The slaves' role in church organization reinforced all the positive values of church membership; it underlined the slaves' intellectual and moral worth, their equality as Christians with their counterparts in England, and opened new avenues for achievement. At the same time, however, their role revealed the extent to which the function of Christian converts within the mission churches was determined, ultimately, by their slave status. This comprehension, shared to some degree by all church members, was experienced most fully by the handful of slaves who acted as assistants to the missionaries.

The role of these "leaders," as developed in the mission churches, was an adaptation of the practice of the missions' parent churches where laymen customarily not only taught classes but preached. In the Baptist and Wesleyan churches these laymen were appointed by the minister, whereas Moravian and Presbyterian congregations elected respectively their "helpers" and "elders"; in the Presbyterian church the elders were then ordained by the minister.

The right of slave converts to preach and teach was specifically denied by the 1816 slave code. This legal restriction was reinforced by the missionaries' anxiety to maintain, as far as possible, the distinction between church members and the independent preachers of the Native Baptist and Native Methodist sects. They were also initially reluctant to appoint illiterates to positions of authority.[79] But as their churches grew and their confidence in the slaves developed, converts were appointed to act as class supervisors. The extent to which slave leaders were used varied among the different churches. The Presbyterians and Moravians, working under the direct protection of planter patrons and untroubled by legal niceties or questions of reputation, appointed as many as the size of their congregations required.[80] The Baptists had no uniform policy; Knibb at Falmouth had fifty leaders in a church of 600 members, while Burchell at Montego Bay had only fifteen in a church the same size because he did not appoint estate slaves as leaders. The Wesleyans initially refrained from appointing slave leaders, but were encouraged in the practice by the W.M.M.S.; the society took its lead from the imperial government's disallowance of the 1826 slave code partly on account of its restrictions on mutual instruction by the slaves. Thereafter the Wesleyans increasingly followed the pattern established by the Moravians and Presbyterians.[81]

The leaders were instructed to hold no private meetings and undertook no formal teaching role; they were, however, responsible for the moral supervision of classes of both established and prospective members. The contribution these class leaders made to mission development was acknowledged by the missionaries to be unique. They were able to communicate their faith in a manner that was impossible for the missionary himself. Twelve months' attendance in a class with "holy, zealous Christians" of their own condition could have more impact on potential converts than three years of mission teaching. As one missionary commented, "If a missionary preaches and prays like an angel the negroes are not soon affected or moved. They think he has learnt his trade better than some of the church ministers. But when met in class by an able and pious class leader and hearing other blacks spread the love of God with so much life, and pray with so much liberty and power, they are overcome at once and ignorance and disbelief soon give way."[82]

The leaders were also able to extend the influence of the mission churches beyond the circle reached by Sunday sermons and outstation visits; they introduced new candidates for membership and simultaneously built up their own following among the slaves, inspiring imitators who might themselves have no official position in the mission churches. One such woman brought a "family" of one hundred converts to the Baptist missionary Burchell, on a visit to Falmouth. She was well versed in the Bible and traveled from place to place "picking up sinners"; she declared her intention "by de help of Massa Christ to hale all she can to de Gospel."[83]

The distinction between moral supervision and teaching, between prayer and preaching, was practically impossible for the missionaries to establish and maintain; the leaders worked to a large extent independently and enjoyed great authority over church members. Their relationship with the missionaries, consequently, was not always easy. They resented any interference in the size of their classes, any querying of their reports on members' conduct, and criticism could make them quarrelsome and aggressive.[84] Within the narrow compass of their meetings with the missionary, however, the slave leaders could speak up like free citizens in a manner that on the estates would have exposed them to punishment.

The privileges enjoyed by these slaves sharpened the contrast between the status the mission churches afforded their converts and their status on the plantations, but the limitations of these privileges also demonstrated that the forms of equality the mission churches could afford the slaves were themselves determined by the slave system. Slave leaders within the church continued to be burdened by their slave status in terms of the functions they could perform and the authority they enjoyed.

Their position was overshadowed by free black and colored members, who enjoyed greater responsibilities as lay preachers and circuit stewards. The missionaries found it necessary, from time to time, to prevent these free assistants from taking charge of leaders' meetings. The appointment of new slave leaders, moreover, could rouse resentment among free colored leaders.[85] In general, however, it was the slave leaders' relationship with the missionaries themselves that underlined their inferior status. Though the leaders could dispute the missionary's judgment, they could not overrule him or achieve an equivalent authority. Leaders in the churches, like headmen on the plantations, were doomed to subordination.

Both slave and free leaders evidently attempted to resolve this contradiction, in part, as their disputes with the missionaries made clear, by establishing themselves as undisputed authorities over their classes within the church. But their frustrations also found other outlets; the round of mission work tended to generate, in the vicinity of the mission stations, satellites of religious groups led by free coloreds and blacks as well as slaves, some more and some less connected with the mission churches. Such groups were established around Halse Hall estate, for example, where a Wesleyan missionary preached every two weeks with the permission of the absentee proprietor, and around Grateful Hill, a Wesleyan station in the mountains outside Kingston.[86] There were ample opportunity and incentive for mission church leaders and their imitators to set themselves up as sect leaders in the Native Baptist tradition.

Such leaders introduced into the sects skills and experiences that revived, to a degree, the standards first set for black pastors by the American Black Baptists; they were comparatively expert in theology and some were literate. Their expertise enhanced their authority and, as literacy spread among the slave population, became increasingly important to secure credibility. As one young slave expressed it, "Before time them leader hold book and talk, and we believe their word came from book. Now it not so, we find them out; they hold book upside down, and no saby read one word. Ah, minister, plenty false prophets live for neger-house."[87] At the same time, the connection with the mission churches provided an established framework for the activities of the groups that was potentially islandwide.

The missionaries, though conscious of a need to differentiate mission members from sect members, seemed blind to the possibility that their most trusted converts might make independent use of the knowledge and skills they had acquired. They assumed that these pillars of their churches accepted Christianity as they taught it. Since Christianity challenged the slaves' fundamental religious ideas and social practices, the opposite inference was equally valid: slaves who were capable of accepting Christianity could prove capable of developing their own version of it. And this version might prove less conformable to the slave system than the missionaries'.

Their failure to perceive this danger, or at least to record it, may reflect their attitude to the Native Baptists. Working with the positive support of only a small section of the ruling class, the missionaries were too concerned for the continuance of mission work and their own reputation to view them as anything other than ignorants trading on ignorance. Contemporaries working in Sierra Leone with free Africans had to regard equivalent developments with more respect. They considered the independent teachers "wild Africans," but they sent home sober accounts of their success that acknowledged the emergence of a "system of independency."[88]

The planters, however, whose hostility to the missions and mistrust of the slaves were never far below the surface, suspected the missions of active collusion with the sects and sensed in it some indefinable threat to the slave system. Police interviews with Baptist and Wesleyan missionaries always probed for these connections, and the Assembly's official committee of investigation in 1827 paid particular attention to the problem.[89] No connection was proved; indeed, no connection of the sort the planters suspected existed. Nevertheless, their suspicions were not unfounded; unknown to the missionaries, their own leaders were capable of playing a dual role and developing their own version of the Christian message and its political implications.

As members of the mission churches, however, the slaves demonstrated a clear understanding of the social equality mission membership inferred. On Hampden estates, for example, the official opening of their chapel attracted a large congregation that included many of the overseers and bookkeepers from the surrounding estates, who were chiefly Scotsmen. Many of these visitors were unable to find seats; the slaves, however, made no voluntary attempt to give up their places to their superiors. Some of the Hampden slaves, when requested to do so, vacated their special benches, but in the gallery slaves were occupying pews while their masters stood jammed in the aisles a few feet away.[90] The slaves, sitting comfortably during the sermon while their masters, customarily elevated on horseback and armed with whips, stood sweatily a few yards away, clearly had some inkling that in God's house all men were equal.

They were also unwilling to attend services at all in their master's great house or in premises associated with their work as slaves. To do so made them "boiling-house Christians." One missionary commented, "Their masters' houses appear to them improper places for God's worship . . . and to my certain knowledge many of them would rather walk nine miles to chapel to hear me than as many paces to hear me in Buccra house."[91] Only the chapel independent of the estate was a satisfactory symbol of the values it taught.

The slaves' political consciousness, though fed and watered by the mission churches, came to fruition outside them, in the religious groups they developed under the tuition of leaders recruited among themselves. It was in these groups that their political ideas took their most radical form.

This process has been observed in Africa, both among industrial workers in South Africa subjected to the political restrictions of apartheid and in the Congo under the Belgians. Throughout these areas separatist Christian sects have proliferated under the leadership of Africans, which combine religious functions, such as cleansing from sin and protection from witchcraft, with political aims and look forward to the end of white domination.[92] Even in early nineteenth-century England, where church members could carry their concern for equality and social justice into a range of political associations, brotherhoods, and unions, churches became political clubs. In Huddersfield the New Connection Methodists were known as the Tom Paine Methodists, since they discussed Tom Paine at chapel meetings together with the works of their founder, Alexander Kilham. In Halifax a group of Methodists purchased their own accommodation and ran it as a Jacobin chapel. The Primitive Methodist sect identified their church so closely with the trade union movement as to make it practically a labor religion, and the church supplied almost all the trade union leaders for the agricultural laborers and the Durham and Northumberland miners throughout the century.[93]

In Jamaica the leadership group in the 1831 rebellion suggests that a particularly important part was played in this development by mission-based Native Baptist preachers, some of whom, like Sam Sharpe himself, were mission church leaders.

Political consciousness among the Native Baptist sects developed initially on racist lines; from rejecting the use of the Bible and relying on dreams to reveal the will of God, as some claimed to do, it was a short step to refusing to associate with members of the mission churches as followers of the white man.[94] The slaves' overwhelming political concern, however, was not to differentiate themselves from their white masters but to claim equality with them in the form of free status.

Mission teaching, with its dual emphasis on the spiritual equality of all men and the connection between conduct in this world and fate in the world to come, opened the way for the slaves to question, as generations before them had done elsewhere, why Christian values were not practiced in the society they knew. Why were black and white equal after death but slave and master in life? Mission activities and organization provided, within the confines of church membership, small concrete examples of the equality of slave and free in Christian fellowship, developed new leadership elements among the slaves, and stimulated the network of religious meetings that proved capable of providing the organizational groundwork of the 1831 rebellion. And the missionaries themselves provided the slaves with a new model of authority, authority based not on the whip but on example and persuasion, authority used not to degrade and dehumanize but to establish the equality of all men as sinners capable of salvation and prepared, eventually, to challenge the masters who denied the slaves this fundamental human right. In their daily round of duty they set up countercurrents to the main thrust of authority in the society, making eddies that imperceptibly eroded its very base, eddies sensed even by slaves who never lifted their eyes from the hoe as the missionary went by.

The slaves transformed the missionaries' implicit message into action in the political circumstances created by the decade-long campaign for the abolition of slavery launched in 1823. It is to the effects of this campaign, which were felt by every class in Jamaican society and vitally influenced the political stance of the missionaries themselves, that we must now turn.

NOTES

1. William F. Burchell, *Memoir of Thomas Burchell* (London, 1849), p. 2; Edward Bean Underhill, *Life of J. M. Phillippo, Missionary in Jamaica* (London, 1881), p. 2; John H. Hinton, *Memoir of William Knibb, Missionary in Jamaica* (London, 1847), pp. 1–2. Moravian missionaries were recruited from settlements in England, Germany, and Pennsylvania. Some of the English missionaries sent to Jamaica were recruited from the settlements of Ockbrook, Fulnec, and Fairfield in the north country and Gracehill in Ireland. Recruits from the German communities had to spend some time on arrival in Jamaica with a mission family in order to learn the language.

2. Hinton, *Memoir of William Knibb*, p. 19, quoting letter to Thomas Knibb, Apr. 2, 1823.

3. Burchell, *Memoir of Thomas Burchell*, pp. 68–69.

4. *P.A.* 7 (1818):22, Light, Irwin Hill, Apr. 12, 1818; W.M.M.S. Letters, Box, Savanna-la-Mar, Oct. 10, 1829, f. 113, Box 128; Crofts journal, Spanish Town, May 28, 1824, f. 29, Box 121.

5. The Moravian Mission Board sent out single women as mission sisters. They usually married on arrival in Jamaica.

6. W.M.M.S. Letters, Shipman, Morant Bay, Feb. 28, 1822, f. 17, Box 118.

7. W.M.M.S. Letters, Greenwood, Port Antonio, Mar. 2, 1831, f. 40, Box 130.

8. Underhill, *Life of J. M. Phillippo*, pp. 19, 22.

9. Bp. Lipscomb to Bathurst, Oct. 17, 1825, f. 59, enclosure 4, Rev. H. Beams to Archdeacon Pope, July, 1825, C.O. 137/267.

10. Burchell, *Memoir of Thomas Burchell*, p. 84.

11. Ibid., p. 74.

12. Baptist missionaries sent to Jamaica in the period 1814–34 and trained at Broadmead Baptist College, Bristol: T. Burchell, S. Nicholls, Lee Com-

pere, Eb. Phillips, J. Coultart, J. Rowe, J. Kingdom, J. Shoveller. Bristol Baptist College, *Annual Report*, 1953–54, pp. 24–32.

13. Samuel, *Wesleyan-Methodist Missions*, p. 136.

14. W.M.M.S. Letters, Murray, Kingston, Oct. 11, 1828, f. 60, Box 127; Crofts, Stony Hill, Aug. 5, 1825, f. 157, Box 122.

15. The W.M.M.S. was organized after Coke's death at the instigation of Jabez Bunting, subsequently secretary of the society and president of the Wesleyan-Methodist Conference. The society was allotted a regular share of church funds; between 1819 and 1834, as the church increased its membership, W.M.M.S. income doubled from £25,000 to £50,000 a year.

    The Moravian Mission Board was appointed by the General Synod of the church in Germany and supervised the work undertaken by the provincial synods. The British provincial synod's missionary branch, the Society for the Furtherance of the Gospel, was established in 1741. The Moravians, who always provided proportionately a greater number of missionaries than any other church, relied heavily on interdenominational support. Their most important single source of income during the period of mission expansion in Jamaica was the London Association, formed in 1817. Their income was never more than £8,000 a year.

    The Baptist and Scottish missionary societies had committees elected at the annual meeting of the societies' subscribers. They relied on voluntary denominational support from auxiliary societies, Sunday school collections, church collections, and donations. The S.M.S. had an income of £6,000–8,000 a year; the B.M.S. increased its income from £8,000 to £17,000 a year between 1819 and 1834.

16. Thomas P. Jackson, *Memoir of the Life and Writings of the Rev. Richard Watson* (London, 1834–37), 12 vols., 1:413, Watson to Young, Oct. 10, 1825.

17. Minutes of the District Meeting, Jamaica, Feb. 14, 1826, Box 148, M.M.S. Archives.

18. *S.M.R.* 14 (Aug. 1833):299, Cowan journal, Carron Hall, July 22, 1832.

19. W.M.M.S. Letters, Ratcliffe, Kingston, Oct. 20, 1817, f. 12, Box 113.

20. *P.A.* 12 (1831):314, diary of Mesopotamia.

21. W.M.M.S Letters, Duncan, Bath, May 28, 1824, journal, Apr. 14, f. 20, Box 121.

22. Shipman, "Thoughts on Religion among the Negroes."

23. Missionaries in Africa, confronted by organized polygamy, were more cautious, and the precept "thou shalt not commit adultery" was preached initially without reference to how many wives were involved. Waddell, *Twenty-nine Years in the West Indies*, p. 276.

24. Shipman, "Thoughts on Religion among the Negroes," pp. 12–13, 21.

25. *S.M.R.* 8 (May, 1827):212, Blyth, Endeavour, Jan. 1; minutes of the District Meeting, Jamaica, Feb. 16, 1819, f. 35, Box 114, M.M.S. Archives; Buchner, *Moravians in Jamaica*, pp. 44–45.

26. "A series of Tracts," pts. 1–4. Extracts have been published in Brathwaite, *Creole Society*, Appendix V, pp. 331–36.

27. Waddell, *Twenty-nine Years in the West Indies*, p. 40.

28. S.M.R. 4 (Apr., 1825):160, Blyth, Nov. 6, 1824.

29. Phillippo, "Personal History," p. 78; W.M.M.S. Letters, Burrows, Kingston, Jan. 7, 1833, f. 12, Box 133; *S.M.R.* 6 (Sept., 1825):385, Blyth journal, Jan. 3; *P.A.* 13 (1834):19, diary of New Fulnec, Christmas, 1832.

30. S.M.R. 11 (June, 1830):340, Chamberlain, June 13.

31. *Statement of the Plan . . . of the Wesleyan Missions*, p. 8.

32. W.M.M.S. Letters, Ratcliffe, Kingston, Apr. 9, 1818, f. 44, Box 113.

33. Shipman, "Thoughts on Religion among the Negroes," lessons 6, 7, and 8; *S.M.R.* 6 (Sept., 1825):287, Blyth, Mar. 29; 7 (Sept., 1826):386, Blyth, July 5, 1825.

34. Shipman, "Thoughts on Religion among the Negroes," lesson 6; *S.M.R.* 9 (Apr., 1828):148–49, Blyth, Hampden, Jan. 7.

35. W.M.M.S. Letters, Young, Kingston, Mar. 6, 1823, f. 210, Box 118.

36. *Statement of the Plan . . . of the Wesleyan Missions*, p. 34; W.M.M.S. Letters, Kerr, Morant Bay, Dec. 14, 1829, journal, July 12, f. 157, Box 128.

37. Williams, *Tour through the Island of Jamaica*, p. 108; B.M.S., *Annual Report*, 1823, p. 26, T. Knibb, Port Royal.

38. Burchell, *Memoir of Thomas Burchell*, pp. 78–79, quoting letter from Burchell to Dyer, Jan. 18, 1825.

39. James Williams, *A Narrative of Events since the First of August, 1834* (London, 1837).

40. Ibid., pp. 10–11.

41. "A series of Tracts," pt. 4: Address after Marriage; *P.A.* 12 (1831):363, diary of New Fulnec, July 28; W.M.M.S. Letters, Crofts, Spanish Town, June 25, 1822, f. 72, Box 118; May 28, 1824, f. 29, Box 121; *S.M.R.* 15 (July, 1834):252, Cowan journal, May 13, 1833.

42. Burchell, *Memoir of Thomas Burchell*, p. 87.

43. Wesleyan lay preachers worked in the following parishes: St. Ann, Mr. Watkis, Mr. Martin; St. James, a person unnamed at Ramble, nr. Montego Bay; St. Thomas in the East, Mr. Langslowe, previously Wesleyan missionary at Morant Bay; St. Andrew, Mr. Lee and Mr. Harris, free coloured, John Fox, white planter. W.M.M.S. Letters, Wood, Stony Hill, July 3, 1829, f. 40, Box 128.

44. *P.A.* 9 (1823):347–48, diary of Irwin Hill; W.M.M.S. Letters, Crofts, Spanish Town, Mar. 14, 1825, f. 40; Duncan, Bath, Oct. 5, 1824, f. 8, Box 122; Whitehouse, Bath, July 16, 1827, f. 131, Box 125; Murray, Montego Bay, Apr. 5, 1831, f. 68, Box 130; Samuel, Bath, Dec. 18, 1832, f. 140, Box 132.

45. S.M.R. 13 (Oct., 1832):412, Cowan, Carron Hall, July 4; 14 (May, 1833):172, Waddell, Cornwall, Jan. 18; *P.A.* 13 (1834):67, diary of Fairfield, Aug. 22, 1833.

46. S.M.R. 12 (July, 1831):290, Chamberlain, Hampstead, Jan. 16. The Mo-

ravian and Presbyterian missions grew at the rate of about seventy a year, e.g., Hampden, 1828–29, 146–220 members; Fairfield, 1825–31, 424–814 members. *S.M.R.* 11 (May, 1830):196; *P.A.* 9 (1823):485; 12 (1831):127.

47. The Baptist mission in Spanish Town admitted 400 new members one year and the Wesleyan mission at Morant Bay admitted an average of 370 new members for four years. *Missionary Herald,* Sept. 1829, p. 397; W.M.M.S., *Annual Reports,* 1819–22, pp. xvii, xviii, xv, xviii.

48. Wesleyan missions: Bath, 1,302 members, 442 communicants; Manchioneal, 736 members, 345 communicants; Presbyterian mission: Hampden, 220 members, 220 communicants; Moravian mission: Fairfield, 691 members, 584 communicants. W.M.M.S. Letters, Whitehouse, July 16, 1827, f. 171, Box 125; *S.M.R.* 11 (May, 1830):196, Blyth, Hampden, Feb. 1; *P.A.* 11 (1829):84, 245, Ellis, Fairfield, Jan. 2, Nov. 4.

49. W.M.M.S. Letters, Whitehouse, Bath, Nov. 20, 1827, f. 21, Box 126.

50. Each quarterly examination also took its toll; at Bath there were nineteen expulsions one quarter, fifty-two the next; at Morant Bay as many as 200 were expelled one year. The expulsion rate was criticized by the committee in London, which advised a longer training period for candidates and more careful selection of members. W.M.M.S. Letters, Orton, Falmouth, Sept. 1, 1826, f. 122, Box 123; Whitehouse, July 16, 1827, f. 171, Box 125; Nov. 20, 1827, f. 21, Box 126; Kerr, Kingston, Oct. 10, 1829, f. 114, Box 128; W.M.M.S. Committee to the District Chairman, Jamaica, Dec. 10, 1826, Box 24, M.M.S. Archives.

51. *P.A.* 11 (1829):84, Ellis, Fairfield, Jan. 2, 1829, records twenty-nine exclusions in a church of 691 full members. *S.M.R.* 15 (June, 1834):212, Blyth, Hampden, Jan. 16, records twelve exclusions in a church of 376 full members.

52. *S.M.R.* 12 (June, 1831):244, Blyth, Hampden, Jan. 3.

53. Missions with 800-plus members: *Wesleyan*—Kingston, Montego Bay, Spanish Town, Falmouth, Morant Bay, St. Ann's Bay; *Baptist*—Kingston, Falmouth, Spanish Town, Crooked Spring, Montego Bay, Salter's Hill; *Moravian*—Fairfield. Total membership in 1834: Wesleyan, 12,000; Baptist, 11,000; Moravian, 2,500; Presbyterian, 650.

54. *Missionary Herald,* Jan., 1832, p. 42; Feb., 1832, pp. 85–86.

55. *P.A.* 12 (1831):20, diary of Fairfield, Aug. 8, 1830: 9 (1823):318, Ellis, Fairfield, Mar. 9, 1825; W.M.M.S. Letters, Kerr, Morant Bay, Dec. 14, 1829, f. 157, Box 128.

56. *Missionary Herald,* Feb., 1832, p. 86; Nov., 1830, p. 494; letter from T. Knibb, Kingston, Feb. 11, 1823, Box W.I./3, B.M.S. Archives.

57. Jamaica: *Votes of the Assembly,* 1828, App. 60, pp. 415, 444, C.O. 140/116.

58. W.M.M.S. Letters, Crofts, Spanish Town, May 28, 1824, f. 29, Box 121.

59. Jamaica: *Votes of the Assembly,* 1828, App. 60, p. 432, C.O. 140/116.

60. W.M.M.S. Committee to the District Chairman, Jamaica, Sept. 8, 1821, Box 24, M.M.S. Archives.

61. *P.A.* 13 (1834):82, Zorn, Spring Vale, 1831; *S.M.R.* 14 (Nov., 1833):422, Cowan, Carron Hall, July 4; *Missionary Herald*, May, 1823, p. 262, letter from T. Knibb; Jamaica: *Votes of the Assembly*, 1828, App. 60, pp. 403–4, 407–8, 427, 440, C.O. 140/116; P.P. (Lords) (no. 127), 1831–32, 307:768, evidence of Rev. W. Knibb.

62. Jamaica: *Votes of the Assembly*, 1828, App. 60, p. 402. The Sectarian Committee was appointed "to inquire and report the names of all sectarians or dissenters . . . resident within this island, also to . . . report what offerings or monies are, or have been received or taken by such sectarians or dissenters from any slaves or other persons attending the places of worship . . . and what offerings or monies . . . taken or received by unlicensed persons . . . class-leaders, or otherwise, . . . and in what manner . . . disposed of, and also to ascertain and report whether any and what regulations are necessary relative to the receiving of offerings. . . ." C.O. 140/116.

63. *Baptist Magazine*, Sept., 1832, p. 401; Hinton, *Memoir of William Knibb*, p. 11.

64. Phillippo, "Personal History," p. 94.

65. Circular dispatch, May 28, 1823, enclosing Resolutions, May 15, 1823, f. 134, C.O. 854/1.

66. Minutes of the District Meeting, Jamaica, Jan. 5, 1825, Box 148, M.M.S. Archives; Duncan, *Narrative of the Wesleyan Mission to Jamaica*, p. 167; Buchner, *Moravians in Jamaica*, pp. 80–81.

67. The S.M.S. contributed £50 toward the schoolhouse at Cinnamon Hill and £20 p.a. toward the teacher's salary, financed a school in Lucea for one year, and contributed £20 to the schoolhouse at Hampden estate. The B.M.S. paid £20 to buy out a soldier to serve as a teacher in Spanish Town. The Ladies Society for Negro Education made several small grants; Quaker funds subsidized a Baptist school in Spanish Town.

68. The Moravians made an attempt to train their own teachers. This idea, first considered in 1828, led to the foundation in 1833 of a normal school at the Fairfield mission with four girls, two brown and two white, whose fees were paid by patrons wishing to save them from concubinage; the establishment was called, appropriately, "Refuge." *P.A.* 11 (1829):36, Scholefield to Sec. of Ladies Society, Oct. 6, 1828; 13 (1834):315, Ellis, Fairfield, Nov. 7, 1833. When funds were available, free colored people were employed as teachers, e.g., by the Moravians for small schools among the free cultivators and by the Presbyterians.

69. The S.M.S. and the Moravian Mission Board supplied alphabets and spelling cards printed by the British and Foreign Bible Society. *P.A.* 10 (1826):349; *S.M.R.* 12 (Sept., 1831):391. Wesleyan and Baptist missionaries constantly begged for gifts from England; contributions were made by the Religious Tract Society, the Sunday School Union, and the Society of Friends. A touch dear to Knibb, scholars in the Baptist Sunday school of his home town, Kettering, sent their reward books. *Missionary Herald*, June, 1827, p. 295; Mar., 1829, p. 130.

70. The Presbyterian patrons William Stothert and Alexander Stirling gave £100 toward the schoolhouse at Hampden and paid a salary for a teacher. Samuel Moulton Barrett subsidized the schoolhouse at Cinnamon Hill.

71. *P.A.* 13 (1834):71–72, "Report of the Schools in Jamaica," March; *S.M.R.* 14 (Nov., 1833):421; 12 (July, 1831):292.

72. The East Queen St. Baptist School was modeled on the Borough Road School, London. Hinton, *Memoir of William Knibb,* pp. 50–53; letter from W. Knibb, Feb. 7, 1826, Box W.I./3, B.M.S. Archives.

73. Minutes of the District Meeting, Jamaica, Jan. 10, 1833, Box 149, M.M.S. Archives.

74. Approximately 1,300 children were attending mission day schools by 1834. Assuming that as many as 50 percent of the children at Baptist schools were free coloreds and blacks, about 1,100 were slave children. The detailed breakdown is as follows: *Moravian schools*—Irwin Hill, 30 (slaves); New Bethlehem, 60 (slaves); New Fulnec, 50 (slaves); New Eden, c. 50 (slaves); Fairfield, 16–20 (slaves); Hopeton, 100 (slaves); Cruse, 60 (slaves); Woodlands, 20 (free); Somerset, 50–80 (free); Springfield, 12–20 (free). *Wesleyan schools*—Kingston, 48 (slaves); 46 (free). *Baptist schools*—Kingston, 272 (slaves and free); Spanish Town, 120 (slaves and free). *Presbyterian schools*—Lucea, 26 (slaves), 48 (free); Hampden, 127 (slaves); Cinnamon Hill, c. 100 (slaves); Carron Hall, 12 (slaves), 14 (free); Port Maria, 30 (free). *P.A.* 13 (1834):71–72; minutes of the District Meeting, Jamaica, Jan. 10, 1833, Box 149, M.M.S. Archives; B.M.S., *Annual Report,* 1834, p. 20; *Baptist Magazine,* Sept., 1832, p. 399; *S.M.R.* 12 (June, July, 1831):245, 292; 14 (July, Nov., 1833):267, 421.

75. *P.A.* 13 (1834):70, "Report of the Schools in Jamaica"; 11 (1829):35, Scholefield, New Carmel, Oct. 3, 1828; W.M.M.S., *Annual Report,* 1832–33, p. 82.

76. *S.M.R.* 8 (Nov., 1827):489, Watson, Lucea, Sept. 2; 14 (Aug., 1833):298, Waddell, Apr. 4; Waddell, *Twenty-nine Years in the West Indies,* pp. 34–35.

77. *S.M.R.* 8 (May, 1827):212, Blyth, Endeavour, Jan. 1; 14 (Aug., 1833):298, Cowan journal, Carron Hall, May 1; Hinton, *Memoir of William Knibb,* p. 52.

78. *S.M.R.* 12 (June, 1831):245, Blyth, Hampden, Jan. 2.

79. Shipman, "Thoughts on Religion among the Negroes," p. 49; W.M.M.S. Letters, Whitehouse, Bath, July 16, 1827, f. 161, Box 125.

80. Waddell, *Twenty-nine Years in the West Indies,* p. 111; Buchner, *Moravians in Jamaica,* p. 79.

81. P.P. (Commons) (no. 721), 1831–32, 20:282, evidence of Rev. W. Knibb; Jamaica: *Votes of the Assembly,* 1828, App. 60, p. 441, C.O. 140/116. W.M.M.S. Letters, Whitehouse, St. Ann's Bay, July 1, 1829, f. 21, Box 128.

82. W.M.M.S. Letters, Wiggins, Morant Bay, Aug. 20, 1817, f. 25, Box 113; Duncan, Montego Bay, June 1, 1829, f. 14, Box 128.

83. *Missionary Herald,* Aug., 1827, p. 387, letter from Burchell, Montego Bay, Apr. 10.

84. W.M.M.S. Letters, Duncan, Bath, Sept. 3, 1824, f. 104, Box 121; Waddell, *Twenty-nine Years in the West Indies,* pp. 111–13.

85. W.M.M.S. Letters, Whitehouse, St. Ann's Bay, July 1, 1829, f. 21, Box 128; Murray, Kingston, Mar. 14, 1828, f. 112, Box 126.

86. Bp. Lipscomb to Bathurst, Sept. 17, 1825, f. 49, enclosure 1, Rev. G. Burton to Lipscomb, Aug. 18, 1825, f. 51; Bp. Lipscomb to Bathurst, Nov. 28, 1825, f. 69, enclosure 1, Rev. C. R. Fearon to Lipscomb, Oct. 26, 1825, f. 72, C.O. 137/267.

87. Waddell, *Twenty-nine Years in the West Indies,* p. 35.

88. Emmanuel A. Ayendele, *Holy Johnson, Pioneer of African Nationalism* (London, 1970), p. 21.

89. W.M.M.S. Letters, Horne, Feb. 12, 1822, journal, Feb. 8, f. 11, Box 118.

90. *S.M.R.* 9 (Oct., 1828):434, Blyth, July 7.

91. W.M.M.S. Letters, Crofts, Stony Hill, Aug. 5, 1825, f. 157; Young, Stony Hill, Aug. 5, 1825, f. 156, Box 122.

92. Basil Davidson, *The African Awakening* (London, 1955), pp. 156–61; Gluckman, *Order and Rebellion,* pp. 143–44.

93. Edward P. Thompson, *The Making of the English Working Class* (London, 1963), pp. 44–45; Eric J. Hobsbawm, "Methodism and the Threat of Revolution in Britain," *History Today* 7 (Feb., 1957):118, and *Primitive Rebels* (Manchester, 1959), p. 138.

94. P.P. (Lords) (no. 127), 1831–32, 307:744, 767, evidence of Rev. W. Knibb.

CHAPTER FOUR

The Humanitarian Challenge

T HE ATTACK LAUNCHED in 1823 by the antislavery movement on the institution of slavery produced complex effects on both sides of the Atlantic and altered the political framework in which the missionaries operated. The imperial government, to pre-empt the abolitionists' initial demand for reform of the slave system, produced the amelioration program, which gave priority to the provision of religious instruction for the slaves. The missionaries became unofficial agents of imperial policy with a claim to imperial protection. At the same time, however, the campaign and the reform program generated strong reactions throughout the West Indies. In Jamaica the planters entrenched themselves to defend every vestige of their power as slave holders; the free colored and black population seized the opportunity, with the whites on the defensive, to claim civil rights; and the slaves, in a tremor of conspiracies and rebellions that shook the whole British Caribbean, manifested their desire for freedom. It was in these circumstances that the Baptist and Wesleyan missionaries confronted the fact that their parent churches had given their full support to the abolition campaign.

Caught in these upheavals, the missionaries did not know which way to turn, how best to maintain a basis for mission work. In the event, they were transformed from reformers allied with planter patrons who saw their work as potential sacrifice to antislavery agitation, to reformers who actively benefited from the antislavery movement and opposed the slave owners. This transition was mirrored most completely in the correspondence of the Wesleyan missionaries, since their home church took a leading role in the antislavery agitation. The Wesleyans' dialogue with their home society, at times acrimonious, is analyzed in this chapter. It provides a unique insight into the tensions created and the hopes stirred by the antislavery movement in the period 1823–28, for both the missionaries and the society in which they worked.

The campaign confronted British church-goers with the key question: could a Christian condone slavery? It won a resounding negative in response. Wilberforce wrote the first campaign pamphlet, *An Appeal to the Religion, Justice, and Humanity of the Inhabitants of the British Empire, in behalf of the Negro Slaves of the West Indies,* and his chosen successor as parliamentary leader of the cause, Thomas Fowell Buxton, struck the opening blows in a House of Commons debate on May 15, 1823, with the resolution, "That the state of Slavery is repugnant to the principles of the British Constitution and the Christian Religion; and that it ought to be gradually abolished." Gradual abolition was to encompass the emancipation of all children born after a certain date and some immediate changes in slave conditions that would improve their status in law, remove obstacles to manumission, restrict the owners' right to punish, and, most important, provide them with religious instruction. Petitions, pamphlets, tracts, and newspaper articles as well as the Baptist and Wesleyan church magazines immediately manifested widespread support. "The country," Wilberforce commented, "takes up our cause surprisingly."[1]

The Wesleyan church had a long-standing antislavery association, and the hardcore antislavery group in the House of Commons, which never numbered more than a dozen dedicated men, included a prominent Wesleyan, Joseph Butterworth, M.P. for Dover, who was treasurer of the W.M.M.S. Association with the cause was turned into commitment, however, chiefly through the influence of Jabez Bunting and Richard Watson. Bunting, a founder of the W.M.M.S., was editor of the *Wesleyan-Methodist Magazine* from 1821 to 1824, and Richard Watson was secretary of the W.M.M.S. from 1816 to 1827. Both were profoundly convinced of the inhumanity of slavery.

Bunting was closely involved with the antislavery leaders; he took part in the discussion, held in the last months of 1822, that led to the new campaign and was a member of the committee of the Anti-Slavery Society.[2] His standing in the Wesleyan church and the influence he exerted as editor of the *Magazine* made him a valuable ally. Both Bunting and Watson were aware of the conflict between the missions' official neutrality and their own antislavery views; Bunting compromised by resigning from the W.M.M.S. committee and Watson by keeping his support anonymous. With stirring editorials by Bunting and anonymous articles by Watson, the *Wesleyan-Methodist Magazine* leaped to the support of Buxton.

Emancipation was defined as "a great act of national righteousness" and all Christians were urged to play their part in the cause. In case Buxton's resolutions had slipped by unnoticed in the newspapers, the *Magazine* reprinted them together with supporting speeches. A steady flow of articles followed up this initial commitment; each month's edition carried news of the activities of the African Institution or the newly founded Society for the Mitigation and Abolition of Slavery, and comments on West Indian events all pointed to the conclusion that emancipation was a necessity.[3] The Baptist commitment was similarly advertised in the *Baptist Magazine:* "It is high time for the British nation to awake from its slumber. . . . An abolition of slavery must not only be devoutly wished by the friends of humanity, but it is the imperious duty of all persons who have the least claim to benevolence to use every effort to accomplish it."[4]

While the missionaries' home churches trumpeted their allegiance to the humanitarian cause, Buxton's resolutions prompted the imperial government to outline a program of reform. The amelioration policy did not define a method of emancipation, but it aimed to prepare the slaves for the "civil rights and privileges which are enjoyed by other classes of His Majesty's subjects."[5] In the crown colonies the reforms were instituted by orders of council; in the representative colonies the assemblies were requested to act. The reform proposals included the abolition of flogging as a punishment for women and as a stimulus to work in the fields, and the regulation of all punishments; marriage was to be encouraged and the separation of slave families made illegal. The slaves were to have the right to purchase their freedom and to give evidence in court, as well as protection for their property and savings banks for their earnings.

Primary importance was given to the provision of religious instruction; Christianity was regarded as an "indispensable necessity . . . the foundation of every beneficial change in their character and future conditions." Funds were offered to the West Indian governments to promote this work, on condition that the slaves be assured time to attend religious services by the abolition of Sunday markets.[6] The implementation of this last reform would, of course, have been a mixed blessing for the slaves; the provision, however, translated the missions at a stroke from *ad hoc* charitable enterprises into semiofficial agencies of an imperial policy.

The amelioration policy roused the strongest resentment in Jamaica; as one newspaper commented, the island had exchanged the "blind and inveterate animosity of the anti-colonial party" for the "sly ensnaring policy of the King's ministers."[7] The Committtee of West India Planters and Merchants, which the government had closely consulted on the reform proposals, urged the planters to cooperate. The policy initiated under the stress of the initial attack on the slave trade was elaborated and defined:

> It is idle to disguise from ourselves that the various parties who from different motives are hostile to the West India interest, are at least as powerful, and act upon a more extensive system, and with greater means of influence on the public mind, than the Proprietors and Merchants connected with the Colonies . . . we cannot, therefore, beat them by influence—we must trust to reason—and the only way for getting that weapon into our hands, is by doing ourselves all that is right and reasonable to be done—and doing it speedily and effectually.[8]

But reason was urged in vain. The reform proposals were greeted by public protest meetings in the parishes, while the Assembly, meeting in October, 1823, would not consider what was right or reasonable and refused to make any changes in the existing slave code.[9]

At this stage the amelioration program did not focus hostility on the missions; rather, it exacerbated tension between the whites and the increasingly numerous free colored and black population. Encouraged by the antislavery movement's initial success in prompting a reform program for the slaves, they organized themselves, for the first time on an islandwide basis, to present a petition of grievances to the Assembly. Their demands, which included the rights to vote, to jury service, and to appointment as justices of the peace, amounted to a claim for equality with the whites. Both the scale of the agitation and the extent of the demands outraged and astonished the whites. They attributed the discontent to the influence of foreign subversives, in particular of the Haitian exile community established in Kingston since the 1791 revolution. Two members of this community, Louis Lecesne and John Escoffery, who had organized the campaign, were deported as aliens, one on the grounds that he had been born in Haiti and the other because his mother was Haitian. The Assembly, despite the fact that Richard Barrett argued eloquently the advantages of making an alliance with the free blacks and coloreds, refused to consider any further concessions.[10]

The missions attracted only the attention of a fanatic Anglican clergyman, the Reverend George Wilson Bridges, rector of St. Ann. Bridges, however, was a significant enemy. He had emerged as the ideologue of the Jamaican slave owners by responding to Wilberforce's campaign pamphlet with a riposte entitled *A Voice from Jamaica,* and he subsequently (1828) wrote a two-volume apologia for slavery, *The Annals of Jamaica,*[11] for which he was handsomely rewarded by the Assembly. He hated the missionaries as allies of Wilberforce, as sectarians, and as rivals to his authority; the Wesleyan mission in St. Ann's Bay, in his opinion, diverted support from his church. In July, 1823, almost as soon as news of the amelioration proposals reached the island, Bridges set about raising a "hurricane in a wash-hand basin" over the appointment, by the St. Ann vestry, of the Wesleyan missionary as visitor to the workhouse.[12]

Conflicts between the Anglican church and the Wesleyans over small public appointments of this kind reflected the antagonism traditional between establishment and dissent. Bridges argued his case to the vestry in the traditional manner, reading a long paper to prove, according to one listener, that Methodism was the root of all evil. But in a letter to the *Jamaica Journal* he made it clear that his opposition to the missionary was opposition to a political enemy. He appealed for war against "filth as deep as hell," those traitors in Jamaican society, the spies of the African Institution. Custos Henry Cox, who had encouraged the Wesleyan mission in St. Ann, had no high opinion of Bridges and was unwilling to take the case seriously; the workhouse supervisor testified to the good effects of the missionary's visits, but the vestry decided that Wesleyan ministrations must cease and a second curate be requested for the work.[13] The respect shown by the St. Ann's vestry for Bridge's protest was not respect due to a clergyman—Jamaican vestries enjoyed prolonged conflicts with their clergy—it was rather that, though Bridge's attitude was extreme and his manner of approaching the question unnecessarily ostentatious, the vestry was more sympathetic to his views than to justice for the Wesleyans.

Actually, general hostility focused on the missions only when the antislavery campaign stirred discontent among the slaves throughout the West Indies and the island was threatened with slave rebellion. The most striking manifestation at this stage was in Demerara; a rebellion in August, 1823, led the colonists to accuse the London Missionary Society's John Smith of instigating the disturbances and condemn him to death for treason.[14] In Barbados the planters, sensing slave unrest, acted to prevent a repetition of the Demerara affair; in October, 1823, they destroyed the Wesleyan mission in Bridgetown and drove the missionary, John Shrewsbury, to the neighboring island of St. Vincent for fear of lynching.[15] Two months later the Jamaican planters found evidence of slave conspiracies in both the eastern parishes of St. Mary and St. George and in the western parish of St. James.[16]

The conspiracy in St. James evidently consisted of nothing more than talk of freedom. The antislavery campaign had stirred excitement and prompted noisy, convivial meetings, but no organization was in evidence and no destruction of property had taken place. The seventeen slaves sent for trial were arrested when drinking and hurrahing for Wilberforce. Even the judges could not agree as to the seriousness of the slaves' intentions; the majority, which included Samuel Vaughan, one of the missions' patrons, thought there was a conspiracy but no specific plan. The minority, including Richard Barrett, thought there was no conspiracy, only "common amusement." The court agreed that the crime was rare; no slave had been punished for conspiracy in the parish since 1787, and the occurrence was attributed to "reports of what is going on in England." Three conspirators were transported and the rest given workhouse sentences.[17]

The conspiracy charges against the slaves in the eastern parishes were scarcely more substantial. The slaves on Frontier estate, St. Mary, base of the 1760 rebellion, excited suspicion, and guns were produced in evidence of conspiracy. The judges chose to believe the informers, and eight slaves were executed. The conspiracy was judged to reflect, however, not the influence of the antislavery campaign, or of the missionaries, but the lack of a garrison in the parish. And in St. George's the newly active and organized free colored and black population was blamed; the chief informer was Jean Baptist Corberand, a free black born in Haiti who claimed to have had dealings with Louis Lecesne, deported for his part in the free colored agitation. Seven slaves were hanged or transported as a result.[18]

Conspiracy or the fear of conspiracy was, however, a novel phenomenon by 1823. Signs of slave unrest had become so rare that the militia was no longer kept on stand-by during the Christmas holidays. For three plots to be discovered almost simultaneously was symptomatic of a changing situation, and the missionaries were fortunate that the slave court judges found other scapegoats: British politicians, the British military, and the free blacks and coloreds. The tensions the trials reflected, however, affected the reception of missionaries arriving in the island in the early months of 1824.

The Baptists, encouraged by the amelioration policy, sent three new men to join the four already established; two met with difficulties. Thomas Burchell landed at Montego Bay anticipating a warm welcome from their long-established patron, Samuel Vaughan, but he was not there to greet Burchell, and when they did meet a few days later, he was not encouraging. He claimed that all the planters felt the adverse effects of the emancipation campaign, which had reduced property values and made tenure uncertain. Vaughan himself seemed to want to cut down his commitment to the mission; on one estate the old mission house had been turned into a hospital, on another Sunday services had been discontinued. Burchell was required to attend only alternate weeks at one estate. Nevertheless, Vaughan used his influence on the bench of magistrates to obtain a license for Burchell, and a Baptist mission was founded in the town of Montego Bay.[19] At Spanish Town another new missionary, James Mursell Phillippo, met more determined opposition. His application for a license prompted one of the magistrates to refer to John Smith and declare that the missionaries were simply agents of the Anti-Slavery Society, while two others found fault with his credentials. Sir Francis Smith, the missions' established patron, used his influence to no avail and the documents were returned to England, Phillippo in the meantime being prevented from preaching.[20]

In more dramatic circumstances, two Wesleyan missionaries also were refused licenses at St. Ann's Bay. Stephen Drew, the mission's barrister friend, acted as chairman of the magistrates' bench in the absence of Custos Cox, but no sooner had he ordered the oaths administered than other magistrates, not then on the bench, took their places there and demanded a postponement. Confusion ensued. As in Spanish Town, the missionaries were accused of being agents of the African Institution and then openly threatened with the fate of Shrewsbury; the clerk of the peace, amidst threats and recriminations, refused to proceed. Stephen Drew urged Custos Cox to apply the 1812 English Toleration Act, which guaranteed Dissenters the right to preach. Cox, however, preferred to use his personal influence and promised to attend the next sessions, adding, "I am really ashamed at the conduct of our Magistrates." The real solution, Cox hinted, lay not in amending Jamaican law but in adjusting mission practice; the political atmosphere made it desirable for the Wesleyans to suspend their itinerant rule.[21]

Clearly, the missions in Jamaica did not, at this stage, focus white antagonism in the way the missions in Demerara and Barbados had done. There were good reasons for this. The Christmas plots were not as serious as the Demerara rebellion, and the mission in Barbados, the equivalent in size of St. Ann's parish, was comparatively new (established only for five years) and, as the only mission in the island, isolated. Jamaica, in contrast, had fifteen Baptist and Wesleyan missions, some of which had been founded the previous century.

The Jamaica missions' best protection, however, was the self-confidence of the planters. Richard Barrett, dismissing evidence of slave subversion as "nothing but common amusement," was expressing confidence in his own capacity to judge and adequately discipline the slaves. And even Vaughan, who showed graver concern, expected that the influence of a Baptist mission at Montego Bay would be absorbed by the slave system rather than undermine it. It was at this stage, nevertheless, that senior Wesleyan missionaries who had spent years cultivating planter patrons, watching the first repercussions of the campaign on mission work, began to feel betrayed. They not only attempted to placate the magistrates by closing the mission at St. Ann's Bay but also began, in private correspondence with the W.M.M.S., a barrage of protest against the antislavery commitment of the *Wesleyan-Methodist Magazine*.

Under Bunting's editorship the *Magazine* made a striking contribution to the chorus of humanitarian propaganda by its treatment of the case against John Smith. Month after month, from November, 1823, articles discussed some aspect of this affair. From the first, the Demerara rebellion was interpreted as pointing to the need for emancipation. The full facts were expected to show that "the notion of INTERMINABLE slavery is as incompatible with the *security* of the West Indians themselves, as with the righteous claims of our Negro Bondsmen on the justice and liberality of this professedly Christian Empire." And in April, 1824, *Missionary Notices,* the W.M.M.S.'s own magazine, despite its official neutrality, published the London Missionary Society's vindication of Smith. Even routine reports in the *Magazine* gained a new significance through the publicity they offered to the society's political associations; at the annual anniversary meeting in 1823, for example, the chairman was Joseph Butterworth, and Wilberforce moved a resolution and tribute was paid to James Stephen.[22]

The missionary committee tried to differentiate between society policy and the *Magazine*'s antislavery bias, and in January, 1824, it published a statement in the *Magazine* disclaiming all responsibility for the views expressed in Bunting's editorials.[23] The committee also reminded their missionaries that "at this time especially, when great anxiety prevails in the West Indies, you must *carefully attend* to your printed instructions . . . carefully guarding your words in and out of the pulpit that you may not be misunderstood. . . ."[24]

The missionaries, however, felt that the *Magazine* hopelessly compromised the committee's neutrality; it was read as reflecting the views of the missionary committee equally with those of the church, and Shipman warned the committee that if the *Magazine* fell into the hands of any Jamaican gentleman, it might be the means of upsetting the missions altogether. John Smith was repudiated; "nobody here thinks anything of him, but as a traitor and an incendiary."[25] Eventually, individual protests led to official action. Shipman, as district chairman, emphasized in a strong letter to Jabez Bunting the mission's delicate political position, and all the missionaries assembled for the May 1824 district meeting sent a formal remonstrance against the "un-Methodistical and un-Christian interference of our Editor with West India Politics at this most critical season," together with a copy of Shipman's letter to Bunting, over the heads of the missionary committee, to the annual conference of the Wesleyan church.[26]

The missionaries took this step at a time when hostility had been shown in the courts but their patrons were standing firm; they had met with obstruction but no persistent, effective opposition. Events in the months that followed, however, intensified their fears and drove some of the missionaries to take an extraordinary step. Setting aside the principle of neutrality enjoined on them by their instructions and in contradiction to the policy of their home church, they published in the Jamaican press a series of resolutions that directly repudiated the antislavery cause.

The circumstances were as follows. Within a month of the district meeting and just six months after the Christmas conspiracies, rebellion erupted on three estates in Hanover. Trash houses were fired and stock killed; it was said that the slaves had planned a strike, followed by a massacre of the white population.[27] Discontent, sharpened by news of the antislavery campaign in England, had continued to reverberate among the slaves. As in Demerara, the conviction grew that freedom had already been granted them. The governor, prompted by the Colonial Office, issued a royal proclamation to deny the fact and warn the slaves that acts of insubordination made them "undeserving of the King's protection." But belief in freedom was so strong that the slaves dismissed the proclamation as a forgery fabricated by the slave owners.[28] The convicted rebels from Golden Grove and Alexandria estates held this opinion to their deaths; one committed suicide declaring he was a free man and another announced at the place of execution that "the war has only begun." The Golden Grove slaves who heard him "were with difficulty restrained from interfering with the Execution of the Convicts." The "Argyle war" suggested the island was "on the brink of a volcano."[29]

This time events in Demerara were seen to provide a close parallel with the Jamaican situation, and rage and resentment against the missionaries were further heightened when the news reached the island of the English campaign to exonerate John Smith, who had died in prison the previous April. Wilberforce and his supporters were castigated by the Jamaican press for the zeal with which they defended "their agents, the instigators of Colonial rebellion." The imperial government was accused of using Smith's death to intimidate colonial governments into prostrating themselves "at the feet of every agitator who may call himself a Missionary." Throughout the summer months the local press harried the missionaries with the awful precedent of John Smith. The Assembly was called on to take some measure "to prevent that inundation of persons calling themselves Ministers of the Gospel, but who we are satisfied, in many instances, are wolves in sheep's clothing and through whom the schemes of our enemies are carried into effect." Correspondents urged that every sectarian missionary in the island should be examined by the Assembly and steps taken to prevent their chapels being used as rendez-vous for the conspirators.[30] The 1807 disallowance was recalled and attributed to the connivance of the imperial government with the Wesleyans. An investigation of the June rebellion was anticipated as soon as the Assembly met in October, and there seemed to the missionaries, relaying these threats in letters home, a real possibility that it would take steps to put an end to mission work.[31]

Friends of the Wesleyan mission underlined the need for great caution. One magistrate, James Seton Lane of St. Thomas in the Vale, warned a young missionary, "This is a period little calculated for too much active and prominent exertion," and other friends were equally pressing. At this juncture the mission once more faced the license problem. Despite the recommendation of Attorney General William Burge, Sir Francis Smith, and Sir M. B. Clare, a missionary with several years service in the island was subjected to hours of questioning before the custos of Kingston decided to give him a license, and the magistrates of Clarendon refused to license another missionary.[32]

There were two obvious courses of action for the Wesleyan mission-

aries to take at this point. They could batten down hatches and ride out
the storm in the expectation that once the panic roused by the rebellion
had died down, licenses would be distributed as usual; or they could take
legal advice. Given the disturbed political climate, the latter was a risky
course. The missionaries had accepted the practice that developed from
the 1802 act allowing them minimal rights, rights established in England
in 1689. A legal opinion at this time was unlikely to secure what they
needed, an advance on those minimal rights, a recognition that properly
qualified missionaries had a right to preach. The district committee,
nevertheless, decided to request the attorney general, William Burge, for
his opinion on the toleration law.

Predictably in the circumstances, the highest legal authority on the
island backed up the magistrates. Burge declared that only the Toleration
Act of 1689 was in operation in the island. The missionaries therefore
had to apply for a license in each parish. A properly qualified missionary
was entitled to a license and, if refused, could apply for a writ of *man-
damus,* but the magistrate's refusal would be upheld by a higher court if
it was proved that he professed antislavery sentiments or intended to
inculcate discontent. To underline the precariousness of the missionaries'
position, Burge went further and suggested that it would be "injurious,
no less to their own Interests, than to the tranquility of the Island, if they
involved themselves in controversy with the Magistrates, on any Rights
or Claims which were not sanctioned by the *Practice* or *Usage* of the
Island."[33]

The Wesleyan missionaries' public repudiation of the antislavery
cause was a direct response to the attorney general's opinion, which
suggested that the faintest trace of antislavery sentiment could keep them
silent indefinitely. A group of Wesleyan missionaries met in Kingston and
drew up a document designed to answer all the charges ever made against
the mission and, in particular, to define the missions' attitude to slavery.
The missionaries queried first the principle that slavery and Christianity
were incompatible and stated "*their decided belief* that *Christianity does
not interfere with the civil condition of Slaves,* as Slavery is *established*
and *regulated* by the laws of the British West Indies." The charge that
their doctrines promoted insubordination and that they aimed secretly at
the emancipation of the slaves was denied; emancipation would be a
"*general calamity—injurious to the Slaves—unjust to the proprietors—
ruinous to the Colonies—deleterious to Christianity, and tending to the
effusion of human blood.*"

It followed that the mission had no connection with the African Institution or with any enemies of the West Indians, since their own lives and property would also be destroyed in the event of emancipation. As if these statements were not definitive enough, two more resolutions condemned outright the antislavery party and expressed the mission's gratitude to their many kind friends in Jamaica. The party was accused of *"blending, most absurdly, religion with politics,* of interfering with other men's properties under the profession of christian philanthropy, and, whilst claiming to be disciples of the Prince of Peace, doing everything to spread dissension and anarchy, [they] are utterly destitute of honesty and justice. . . ." The "Wesleyan Body," the missionaries asserted, "have not participated in these proceedings."[34]

The resolutions identified the missionaries with the class interests of their patrons. It is clear, however, that the Jamaica district's protest to the conference in May, 1824, and the resolutions themselves reflected the influence of two particular missionaries, district chairman John Shipman and James Horne. Both represented the "old guard" of the Jamaica mission; Shipman had served since 1814, Horne since 1817. Both had pioneered mission work at a time when cooperation from the magistrates was a novelty, and both put all their reliance on maintaining good relations with their patrons. Shipman designed his special catechism for the slaves to teach Christianity by rote, not reading, out of respect for their prejudices. He restrained Stephen Drew's enthusiasm for introducing the 1812 Toleration Act in the island. He had been "unspeakably agitated" by the events in Hanover, and the mildest criticism of West Indian authorities made him fear for the safety of the mission. A single sentence, pronounced at the missionary society's 1824 anniversary meeting, embedded in paragraphs of praise for the planters, declared that the Demerara government's action over John Smith was unjustifiable; Shipman pounced on it and sent an angry protest to the committee: "We were going on well until the devil put it into the hearts of some to blend Religious and Political questions and God, perhaps, is about to chastise the church for this corrupt mixture."[35]

Shipman was a conscientious, hard-working missionary but an extremely cautious, even nervous man who was easily intimidated. He was strongly influenced by James Horne, who was in many ways his opposite. Horne was proud, ambitious, bad tempered, and contemptuous of his colleagues, whom he freely criticized to the W.M.M.S. committee. He was disappointed of the district chairmanship and did his best to find other claims to special status. Wesley chapel was largely his creation, and he made his work in connection with it a pretext for remaining on the Kingston station. Horne actively identified himself with the missions' patrons and made himself "the most powerful and influential man" among the mission's white friends.[36] Predictably, it was Horne who was found guilty by the district of flogging the elderly slave he hired as servant.

Both these men, as senior missionaries, were in a position to exert influence over their fellows. Nevertheless, the resolutions divided the district. The meeting that approved the initial protest to conference was attended by only six missionaries. No meeting at all was called to discuss the resolutions, and of the missionaries approached for signatures three refused to sign and another wanted alterations made. Shipman and Horne had the full support only of the junior men, John Crofts, Robert Young, and John Jenkins. They had been in the island only two or three years and all served on stations where there were friendly planters and magistrates. Young was strongly influenced by James Horne; anxious to make his own contribution to pacifying the planters, he preached and had printed a sermon on Philemon and Onesimus, the final pages of which delineated the comforts of slavery in the manner of a proslavery tract. There were no creditors, no lack of medical attention, no starvation, and none of the trials faced by English laborers.[37]

Of the missionaries who opposed the resolutions, Isaac Whitehouse, later a protagonist of religious rights for the missionaries and for the slaves, probably disagreed with the proslavery bias; all may have considered, correctly, that the resolutions contravened the neutral policy. The final version was entirely Horne's responsibility; he inserted the fifth resolution, expressing fulsome gratitude to the mission's gentlemen friends, and sent the document to the printers without checking even with the district chairman.[38]

The resolutions were immediately interpreted in the Jamaican press and in England as making the Wesleyan missionaries a strong party for the colonists: "these . . . missionaries on the spot, in the very centre of the system, publicly, in their official character . . . express their belief that Christianity does not interfere with the civil condition of the slaves as slavery is established and regulated by the laws of the West Indies," commented the *Glasgow Courier*.[39] The missionaries were chagrined. In their own eyes they had merely disassociated themselves from the anti-slavery cause for the good of the mission, without considering that this threw them into the proslavery camp. Even Shipman, after all his protests, found the newspaper articles distressing, and some missionaries, including one who signed the resolutions, refused to circulate Young's sermon.[40]

Their chagrin, however, was tempered by the more laudatory tones of newspaper references and the pleasure their patrons expressed. The resolutions were characterized as being "precisely what the advocates of the Wesleyan mission in the island require."[41] When the Jamaica Assembly's report on the rebellions was published in December, 1824, the missionaries were not, as they feared, held responsible. Discussions in Parliament were blamed for arousing among the slaves a "restless expectation of benefits of which they have no definite idea," and for spreading the notion that the king and Wilberforce had made them free. The Assembly committee, in these circumstances, held to their conviction that the chief threat to the island's security was not the influence of the missionaries but the influence exerted by the black republic of Haiti.[42] Not surprisingly, the resolutions were allowed to stand as an expression of Wesleyan mission policy.

The Wesleyan church was outraged by the Jamaica mission's undisciplined defiance and denial of principle. At the first official signs of opposition to the antislavery campaign, Shipman's letter to Bunting and the district's remonstrance against "un-Methodistical and un-Christian" interference in politics, disciplinary action was taken. The problem was discussed at the church's annual conference in July, 1824, which pronounced John Shipman responsible for the communications and determined that he should be recalled from duty.[43] Shipman eventually left the island in February, 1825, and James Horne was transferred to the Bahamas. The missionary committee told the missionaries remaining in forceful terms: "You are not sent to the West Indies to lose your Christian and English feeling on the subject of Slavery, nor to acquire the prejudices of caste and colour; nor to surrender in conversation, or by any act any principle of Christian truth and justice to obtain favour from any man. . . ." The only appropriate position was neutrality; ordinary citizens could take part in politics but missionaries must renounce all civil rights:

> Good men at home take a part . . . by writing, petitioning Parliament and speaking. . . . This they will and ought to do. . . . you . . . have given yourselves up to us to be employed entirely and altogether in making the Society as it there exists, better in morals and knowledge . . . [but] you are not to suppose that your being bound affects the

Liberty of the Christian public at home. . . . It is enough for you that
the Missionary Committee in every part of its public capacity ab-
stains . . . from all civil matters whatever.[44]

The Jamaican missionaries' resolutions, however, forced the
W.M.M.S. to reconsider the neutral policy, which, to this point, had
been the basis of mission work in the West Indies. The society could not
have William Wilberforce on its platform and the *Missionary Notices*
could not vindicate John Smith without contributing to antislavery propaganda. The Shipman resolutions confronted the missionary committee
with this fact. The committee, in response, was forced to define a new
basis for mission policy. This was done at a general meeting of the society
on January 5, 1825, in a series of counter-resolutions.

The meeting first condemned the district's definition of the relation
of slavery and Christianity as "equivocal." To maintain that "all slaves
brought under the influence of Christianity are bound by its precepts to
obey their Masters" was just, but "if it was intended as a declaration,
that the *system* of Slavery . . . is not inconsistent with Christianity, the
Committee, and the 'Wesleyan Body,' whose names the framers of the
resolutions have thus presumed to use without any authority whatever,
hold no such opinion." The meeting then officially endorsed the principles of the antislavery party and declared that it was "the duty of every
Christian Government to bring the practice of Slavery to an end . . . and
that the degradation of men merely on account of their *colour,* and the
holding of human beings in *interminable* bondage, are wholly inconsistent with Christianity." The committee, therefore, could never permit
any criticism of the "excellent and benevolent men" who took part in
the antislavery campaign, and censored "the very blameable language of
the 4th . . . resolution," which repudiated the anticolonial party.[45]

This definition of principle paved the way for a modification of
policy. The committee acknowledged that the campaign might increase
colonial hostility and might cause old friends to withdraw their protection; the counter-resolutions therefore invoked a new authority for the
defense of the missions. If subjected to persecution, the missionaries must
be prepared, when necessary, to suffer patiently for righteousness' sake,
but their suffering would not be without redress. Cases of persecution
would be brought to the attention of His Majesty's government, to whom,
the committee claimed, it had never looked in vain.[46]

This claim appeared to be soundly based. Not only did the amelioration program give primary importance in principle to religious instruc-

tion for the slaves, but the imperial government had appointed, at its own expense, bishops to the Anglican church in the West Indies, and there was even talk of financial assistance for the W.M.M.S.[47] The missionary societies were also aware that their affairs were the active concern of a large and very vocal body of public opinion. The John Smith affair had demonstrated that the fate of missionaries in the West Indies excited as much attention as the condition of the slaves. Smith's trial was reviewed in a lengthy debate in the House of Commons on a motion condemning it as a "violation of law and justice," and the governor was recalled to mark the imperial government's dissatisfaction with the treatment of Smith.[48]

Three months after the counter-resolutions were passed, the House of Commons again demonstrated its keen interest in West Indian missions. The threatened lynching of the missionary Shrewsbury in Barbados, and the destruction of the Wesleyan chapel there, led the Commons to declare its readiness "to concur in every measure which His Majesty may deem necessary for securing ample protection and religious toleration to all His Majesty's subjects in the West Indian colonies."[49] The feeling roused in the Commons and in the country on Shrewsbury's behalf demonstrated the number and influence of the missions' friends and gave the W.M.M.S. every reason to suppose that the imperial government would exert itself to avoid the embarrassment of another missionary martyr.

The Jamaica district was deeply shaken by the criticism to which it had exposed itself. This was more particularly so because other missionaries in the island had quietly continued their work throughout the period. In the case of the Moravians, working directly under the control of the planters, this was to be expected, but the Baptist missionaries, who were equally exposed by the events of 1824 to colonial hostility, had found that a traditional statement of aims was an adequate defense. An article disclaiming any connection between the Baptists and "parties accessory to the insubordination of servants," and emphasizing the mission's intention of teaching servants their duties, was published in the *Jamaica Journal* in September, 1824. A Baptist sermon on the text "Thy Kingdom Come," explaining that the laws of the heavenly kingdom were "calculated to exalt the lowest natures . . . to ensure the discharge of every duty . . . to secure, maintain and enforce the authority and dictates of every government," also received timely publicity.[50]

The recall of Shipman and the removal of Horne to the Bahamas, together with the appointment of a new district chairman from the Antigua station, Thomas Morgan, helped the Wesleyan mission to turn over a new leaf administratively. The key question, however, was ideological. To what extent were they concerned that their attitude to slavery, embodied in the resolutions, was mistaken? Three missionaries refused to sign in the first place; one had been critical. Evidently even the missionaries who signed did not altogether realize the full political implication of their action, and everything suggests that the counter-resolutions were accepted as a just chastisement. More important, as events unfolded, the Wesleyan missionaries proved capable of making the counter-resolutions the basis for a new departure in policy that led them to claim for themselves the right to preach and for their converts the right to religious instruction.

Initially, however, the missionaries were not prepared to take any action to change their position as planter protégés. Two developments prompted them to do so; the imperial government gave proof of its interest in protecting them from harassment, and the Wesleyan mission itself, together with the Baptist and the newly founded Presbyterian mission, was staffed increasingly after 1825 by young men who believed that to be a Christian was to be an abolitionist.

The imperial government's intervention followed an attack, at Christmas 1826, on the Wesleyan mission in St. Ann's Bay. The attack was instigated by the Reverend George W. Bridges and celebrated the fact that the Jamaica Assembly's revised slave code, which included three clauses restricting mission work, had received the governor's assent in the last days of the session. Bridges, eager to encourage the antisectarianism the new law reflected, used his Christmas sermon, on the sin of separatism, to point directly to the great harm done by the Wesleyan chapel and the "novel doctrines of those who, I am sorry to say, have political rather than religious reasons for their activity."[51] The spirit of these remarks did not escape the congregation, which included some of the militiamen on guard duty for the Christmas holiday. Late that night shots were fired into the Wesleyan mission at intervals over an hour.

The missionary, William Ratcliffe, and his family assumed the militia guard was making a nuisance of themselves by firing off blank cartridges, but the next morning seven bullets were found.[52] Custos Henry Cox hurried to St. Ann's Bay the following day to form a bench of magistrates, and witnesses were collected and examined. There was not enough evidence to make a charge, but in an effort to find more evidence the custos secured an offer of £100 reward from the vestry. The newspapers meanwhile had pointed out the connection between Bridge's sermon and the outrage, but the rector wrote an exonerating letter to the vestry, which was accepted. At the quarter sessions no further evidence was elicited and Attorney General William Burge advised that an indictment could not be prepared.[53] Once the attorney general had delivered his verdict, the case seemed closed. Stephen Drew, the Wesleyan's patron, died shortly after the first investigation, and the mission was deprived of his energy and influence in pursuing the matter.

The Wesleyan district endured the outrage in silence. Although an attack had been made, endangering the life of the missionary and his family, no petition was sent to the governor, and Ratcliffe did not even send an account of his experiences to the missionary committee until three months after the event.[54] As usual, the missionaries allowed gratitude for local efforts to find the miscreants to outweigh their sense of injustice, and they did not pursue the case. It was brought to the attention of the imperial government by the antislavery interest in the House of Commons. Dr. Stephen Lushington, who had taken up the cause of civil rights for the West Indian free blacks and coloreds, read the Jamaican newspaper accounts and presented the outrage to the Commons as an attack on Parliament's authority. He emphasized the similarity between the St. Ann affair and the destruction of the Wesleyan chapel in Barbados. The offenders there had gone unpunished and Parliament had been made to appear impotent; another Barbados must at all costs be avoided. The Jamaica district now reaped the benefit of the debates on Shrewsbury and Smith, whose cause they had denied; the House of Commons supported the motion, and the governor of Jamaica, the Duke of Manchester, was instructed to investigate.[55]

Manchester had no interest in defending the missions or promoting the amelioration program. He was concerned, however, that the outrage, as publicized in England, reflected badly on the routine efficiency of his government, and the instructions to investigate were promptly and thoroughly complied with. All the parties involved in the affair had to account for their conduct. Custos Cox had to explain his failure to take the case to the governor on the ground that he did not wish to trouble the executive with every breach of the peace. Bridges had to submit his sermon and the vestry the minutes of the meeting at which he was exonerated. Attorney General Burge pursued his investigations with more vigor. One of the suspects was subjected to a four-hour examination and, on the basis of the evidence extracted, an indictment was prepared against five of the militiamen on the Christmas patrol. At this point imperial authority ceased to operate. The indictment was laid before the grand court in June, 1827, but the grand jury found it *ignoramus* as to all parties; the Jamaican jury, like the House of Assembly, could defeat imperial purpose.[56]

Despite this inconclusive outcome, the investigations, which took place between May and June, 1827, afforded a striking vindication of the missionaries' importance; within three months a further blow was struck by the imperial government on their behalf. The new Jamaican slave code, passed in December, 1826, was disallowed primarily on the ground that it obstructed mission work.[57]

The Assembly's blanket opposition to the amelioration policy, manifested in December, 1823, by a refusal to revise the slave code, had been modified by imperial pressure and by the determination of a group of Assembly members, including a number of the missions' patrons, Cox, Clare, Robertson, and Stewart, to support the West India Committee's policy of cooperation with the imperial government. Their influence was greatly strengthened when in May, 1826, the imperial government sent out eight draft bills incorporating the reforms imposed in the crown colonies to demonstrate what was required of the representative colonies. Under this pressure the Jamaica Assembly set to work to revise the slave code on its own terms. The result was a code that made some minimal changes in favor of the slaves,[58] but expressed the majority's fundamental opposition to amelioration by retaining old restrictions and imposing new ones on mission work, the work the imperial government regarded as fundamental to the slaves' improvement.

The 1826 slave code continued in clause 83 to penalize, as the 1816 slave code had done, the practice of "ignorant, superstitious, or designing slaves" attempting to instruct others; any slave found guilty of preaching or teaching without the permission of his owners and the quarter sessions would be whipped or imprisoned. This clause, aimed against the use of slaves as lay preachers by the mission churches, as well as against the "Mammies" and "Daddies" of the Native Baptist sects, had made the missionaries cautious in using slaves as leaders. Clause 84 also re-enacted an 1816 regulation against night meetings, but where the 1816 regulation had been directed against persons attending the meetings, the 1826 clause condemned specifically "dissenters and others" who held such assemblies, and the penalty was a fine of £20 to £50. Though Dissenters' meetings were condemned, ministers of the Presbyterian Kirk, Jews, Roman Catholics, and "licensed ministers" were allowed to hold services until 8 P.M. This made the position of the missionaries particularly ambiguous; the regulation was evidently aimed against them, but as licensed ministers it also gave them a claim to exemption.

Clause 85 was entirely new and its implications not at all ambiguous: ". . . under pretence of offerings and contributions, large sums of money . . . have been extorted, by designing men professing to be teachers of religion, practising on the ignorances and superstition of the negroes . . . to their great loss and impoverishment. . . ." Dissenting ministers were therefore prohibited from demanding or receiving money under penalty of a £20 fine or a month in jail.[59]

These clauses, specifically directed against the Dissenters while not interfering with Anglicans, Catholics, or Jews, directly contravened the principle of religious toleration asserted in 1809. Manchester was authorized by his instructions to insist on a year's suspending clause for such a law. Had he been conscientious, the clauses would have been first criticized and contested and the law eventually suspended. But Manchester, concerned to praise and not to criticize and grateful for the concessions to the slaves, assured the Assembly that the code would be "highly satisfactory to His Majesty's Government."[60]

The imperial government, however, considered the religious clauses the most important element in the code, both because they controverted a long-established principle of religious toleration and because they challenged the policy to which the government was officially committed. The Colonial Secretary, William Huskisson, considered them in the nature of a "Jack," put in to provoke imperial opposition.[61] The challenge was accepted; in September, 1827, the slave code was disallowed and the offending clauses were criticized in detail.

The prohibition of money collections was described as humiliating and unjust to both missionaries and their converts; it prevented the slaves from obeying a Christian precept and was a "gratuitous aggravation" of the evils of their condition. The restrictions incorporated from the 1816 code were found unacceptable; mutual instruction by the slaves was defended as an established part of mission discipline, and the prohibition on night meetings was condemned. The disallowance concluded, after criticizing other aspects of the code, "Even were the law unobjectionable on every other ground it would be impossible to surmount the difficulty presented by the Clauses for restraining Religious liberty."[62] The principle asserted in 1809 was freshly endorsed, its terms extended and more specifically defined.

Reaction in Jamaica was hostile. The Assembly, after a brief debate on the disallowance, resolved that the doctrine of religious toleration was "utterly at variance with the institutions of Jamaica."[63] Mission patrons, already antagonized by the imperial government's investigation into the St. Ann's Bay mission affair, were further affronted.

The disallowance was a great boost, however, to the missionaries' self-confidence; it demonstrated in the most direct way possible that the missionaries and their work were under imperial protection. Its impact, moreover, was immensely strengthened by the growing number of missionaries recruited from churches wholeheartedly committed to the antislavery cause. These young men, though maintaining, like their predecessors, a nonpolitical stance on the slavery issue, were abolitionists at heart who feared that custom might dull their sense of the enormity of the system. "I pray God I may never view with indifference a system of so infernal a nature," wrote William Knibb in his shipboard diary.[64] Such missionaries, when confronted by obstruction and hostility from the magistrates, reacted not as men bent on placating their superiors but as men bent on winning privileges from them. The magistrates, as planters and slave owners, were their natural enemies and they reacted accordingly. One young Wesleyan, arriving in May, 1827, found his credentials questioned by the magistrates and promptly appealed to the attorney general;[65] the following month another Wesleyan, Josiah Grimsdall, spent ten days in jail at St. Ann's Bay rather than pay a fine for preaching at an outstation that the magistrates refused to license.[66]

The Wesleyan missionaries showed the effects of these developments when in the early months of 1828 the district meeting decided to challenge the magistrate's right to refuse a license to preach. Isaac Whitehouse, who had refused to sign the resolutions, was sent to the established trouble spot of St. Ann's Bay and instructed that if the magistrates refused to allow him to take the oaths, he was to preach without obtaining a special license for St. Ann. The Wesleyans had decided to provoke a test case on the toleration issue.

The issue was in fact taken up, as in the Grimsdall case, over the question of a license for the outstation at Ocho Rios. Whitehouse was summoned to court after preaching in St. Ann for about a month and challenged to take the oaths. He was prepared to comply, but then a petition from residents in Ocho Rios against licensing the missionary was laid before the court. The petition had previously been presented to prevent Grimsdall from preaching at Ocho Rios but had been set aside by Custos Cox. On this occasion Cox, who had hitherto lent all countenance to the missionaries, took part for the first time in efforts to restrain them; instead of laying the petition aside, he advised Whitehouse not to preach there. The missionary protested and was ordered to retire or be committed for contempt of court. Whitehouse persisted in preaching at Ocho Rios, and at the following quarter sessions he was charged, as an unlicensed minister, with preaching and teaching in and about the parish and was bound over to appear at the grand court, in the meantime being forbidden to preach.[67]

The Wesleyan missionaries took up the challenge with spirit and enthusiasm, and publicly attacked the magistrates at the mission's anniversary meeting in Kingston that July. Whitehouse's presence on the platform was attributed to their persecutions; the £100 contributed by the parish to the Wesleyan funds in the last year was proclaimed a triumph over opposition. The hostility of the St. Ann magistrates was a theme passed from speaker to speaker; one member of the congregation, A. H. Beaumont, editor of the *Jamaica Courant*, got to his feet, denounced the meeting as seditious, and left in protest. His newspaper gave these seditious proceedings full publicity next morning.[68]

The St. Ann magistrates, already attuned to respond to the slightest mark of disrespect, awaited Whitehouse's return. He was arrested, charged with preaching without a license, and committed to jail. The magistrate who committed him was Samuel W. Rose, who had taken the lead in opposing the license for the house in Ocho Rios and was one of the three magistrates involved in the Grimsdall affair. He had reacted very strongly against Grimsdall; "this man does nothing but defy us," he exclaimed on one occasion.[69] Having gotten away with one jail sentence, he was ready to repeat the method and, having done it twice, did not hesitate to seize a third opportunity.

The Wesleyan missionary Joseph Orton, from the neighboring parish of Trelawney, heard of the arrest and persisted, in accordance with a previous arrangement, in holding Sunday service in St. Ann's Bay. He, too, was arrested and taken before Rose and a colleague, Hemming. His license was declared invalid for the parish of St. Ann, the oaths refused, and bail offered only on condition that he discontinue preaching at the bay. Orton joined Whitehouse in jail. Two Kingston missionaries offered bail on their behalf, which Rose and Hemming again refused. Rather than compromise the license issue, Whitehouse and Orton remained in jail until writs of *habeas corpus* arrived from Kingston on August 25.[70]

The missionaries brought their case to issue in peculiarly favorable circumstances. The imperial government had occasion to stress once more to the island authorities the supreme importance of the toleration issue. The Assembly in December, 1827, had decided that they could not pass a new slave code without surrendering "their undoubted and acknowledged rights,"[71] and the 1816 slave code was put back into operation. The Colonial Office reviewed the situation, consulted the secretaries of the Baptist and Wesleyan missionary societies, and answered the Assembly's objections to further reform in a dispatch of March, 1828, that again gave supreme importance to the principle of religious toleration. Consultation with the missionary society secretaries focused attention for the first time on the license system; the question was raised as to what colonial statute it was based on, for the term "licensed minister," used in the disputed clause of the 1826 slave code, was nowhere defined.[72]

This reassertion of principle was backed up by executive action. Manchester left the island in July, 1827, and until the new governor arrived, Sir John Keane was in charge. Keane was a veteran of the Peninsular War and had been commander-in-chief in Jamaica since 1823. As lieutenant-governor he was lavish with entertainments but unwilling to embrace responsibility.[73] Fortunately for the missionaries, however, Keane had particular, personal reasons for displaying an interest in mission rights. He wished above all to avoid any trouble with the Assembly. When the Colonial Office reply to the re-enactment of the 1826 slave code came into his hands early in May, 1828, he so dreaded its possible repercussions that he withheld it from the Assembly, though at the same time he assured the Colonial Office that it would have a "most favourable effect" on that body. His expedient was exposed when the dispatch was printed in the parliamentary papers and sent out by the island agent in August, 1828.[74] Keane had just finished trying to justify his conduct in this matter to the Colonial Office when the Orton-Whitehouse case presented itself for attention, and he made use of this opportunity to demonstrate, as fully as he could, his concern for religious toleration.

Keane was informed of the case by the chief justice, William Anglin Scarlett, who commented that the conduct of the magistrates in refusing bail was "most unwarrantable." Keane took immediate action: Rose and

Hemming were erased from the roll of magistrates. Keane commented, "If ministers of religion are to be hunted like wild beasts and exposed to all the injustice and oppression which gentlemen clothed with the authority of magistrates may choose to exercise toward them, it is time that a stop should be put to such arbitrary proceedings."[75] Disciplinary action against the magistrates was extremely rare, and Sir John Keane became the first island governor to use his authority, independent of specific imperial instructions, on behalf of the missions.[76]

The missionaries' trial in October, 1828, thus took place in a context created by a clearly defined imperial policy supported by firm executive action; it is scarcely surprising that the new attorney general, Hugo James, displayed a more liberal approach to the toleration question than had his predecessor. James set the tone of his opinion by quoting Lord Mansfield, author of the Somerset judgment: "The Common Law of England (and of the island) . . . knows no prosecutions for mere opinion." He then briefly described English statute laws on toleration from 1779 to 1812, pointing out that on some occasions the St. Ann magistrate had licensed missionaries under the 1812 act. He concluded that the acts of 1689 and 1711 were enacted as laws of Jamaica by the act of 1728. The indictment against Whitehouse and Orton could not, therefore, be sustained; under the 1711 act a license for one parish entitled a missionary to preach in any other. The only justification for commitment was a refusal, on request, to subscribe to the oaths.[77] The license issue was settled; the magistrates had no discretion in administering the oaths, and a license, once issued, was valid for the whole island. The missionaries' effort was completely vindicated.

At first glance the missionaries owed their success in reducing the power of the magistrates to nothing more than a happy combination of circumstances. Their own efforts had coincided with Keane's need to restore his reputation with the Colonial Office. At every turn, however, the situation had been vitally influenced by the imperial government's response to the antislavery movement and the pressures that had consequently been brought to bear on the Jamaican administration. The missionaries' own action followed from the investigation, prompted by the antislavery party, of the St. Ann mission outrage and the strong line the imperial government had taken on the principle of religious toleration. Keane had been shamed into action by the publicity given to the imperial government's policy on this issue, and the law officers were clearly influenced by both the policy and Keane's energetic if belated response to it. In the upshot, the island judiciary had ruled in support of the amelioration policy by extending the rights of the slaves' teachers.

The missionaries who brought the test case were also responding to the antislavery politics of their home churches. Their action, like the slave conspiracies and the continuing struggle of the free coloreds and blacks for civil rights, demonstrated the new hopes stirred in Jamaican society by the existence in England of a party actively concerned to change the condition of Jamaica's nonwhite population. The missionaries' action as well as their success reflected the influence exerted by the antislavery movement.

The planters in the Assembly did their best to cancel out this victory for the missionaries and the forces supporting them. It was at this point that the Sectarian Committee, already mentioned, purported to find that the missionaries' principal object was to extort money from their congregations, and its report was accepted as justifying the much disputed clauses in the 1826 slave code.[78] The code was passed once more, unamended, in December, 1828. Sir John Keane refused his assent and, in the face of the Assembly's violent and determined opposition to imperial policy, ordered its dissolution.[79]

The missionaries, with the new ruling behind them, were at an interesting juncture. For the first time since the missions were founded, given the fulfillment of particular terms, they had a right to preach. Their rights, though more restricted than those of Dissenters in England, nevertheless secured their independence of the planter patrons. They were now in a position to align themselves as reformers with the government's amelioration policy and the antislavery forces promoting it. They could revive the tradition of political activism embedded in Dissent and reflect that, as a Baptist missionary expressed it, "Had our Protestant forefathers been indifferent about human rights . . . our souls . . . might now be bound in the chains of despair and darkness."[80] The question that finally drove the missionaries into action, religious freedom for the slaves, is addressed in the following chapter.

NOTES

1. Coupland, *Wilberforce*, p. 476, quoting diary.
2. Thomas P. Bunting, *The Life of Jabez Bunting, D.D.* (London, 1859) 2

vols., 2:202; minutes of the Anti-Slavery Society, Jan. 31, 1823, M.S. Brit. Emp. S/20 E2/1, Rhodes House, Oxford.

3. *Wesleyan-Methodist Magazine,* July, 1823, p. 464; Sept., 1823, passim.
4. *Baptist Magazine,* July, 1823, p. 278.
5. Circular dispatch, May 28, 1823, enclosing resolution of May 15, 1823, f. 134, C.O. 854/1.
6. Circular dispatch, July 9, 1823, ff. 160–64, C.O. 854/1.
7. *Jamaica Journal,* July 12, 1823, p. 193.
8. Hall, *Brief History of the West India Committee,* p. 9.
9. Manchester to Bathurst, Nov. 10, 1823, no. 51, enclosing Address to the Assembly; Manchester to Bathurst, Dec. 23, 1823, no. 62, enclosing Address from the Assembly, Dec. 11, 1823, C.O. 137/154.
10. Mavis C. Campbell, *The Dynamics of Change in a Slave Society, 1800–1865* (Rutherford, N.J., 1976), p. 100.
11. George W. Bridges, *A Voice from Jamaica* (London, 1823) and *The Annals of Jamaica,* 2 vols. (London, 1828).
12. *Jamaica Journal,* Sept. 6, 1823, p. 317, letter from "Drocensis."
13. Ibid.; p. 189, letter from "Quercus."
14. See the London Missionary Society's *Report of the Proceedings against the late Rev. J. Smith, of Demerara* (London, 1824).
15. See W.M.M.S., *Annual Report,* 1824, pp. 88–95.
16. Great Britain, Parliamentary Papers (Commons), "Papers relating to the Manumission, Government and Population of Slaves in the West Indies, 1822–1824, pt. 7, Copy of all Judicial Proceedings, relative to the Trial and Punishment of Rebels, or alleged Rebels in the Island of Jamaica, since the 1st of January 1823" (no. 66), 1825, 25 (hereafter cited as P.P. (Commons) (no. 66), 1825, 25).
17. Ibid., pp. 38, 45, 59–81, Manchester to Bathurst, July 31, 1824, enclosure 7, Vaughan to Bullock, Oct. 9, 1823; enclosure 10, Vaughan to Bullock, Dec. 23, 1823; enclosure 14, Vaughan to Bullock, Feb. 2, 1824, with the minutes of the St. James court.
18. Ibid., pp. 40–43, 44, enclosure 4, Cox to Bullock, Dec. 19, 1823, with minutes of the slave court; enclosure 6, Cox to Bullock, Dec. 25, 1823; pp. 86–90, enclosure 17, Gray to Bullock, Jan. 21, 1824, with minutes of the slave court.
19. Burchell, *Memoir of Thomas Burchell,* pp. 51–53.
20. Phillippo, "Personal History," p. 80.
21. W.M.M.S. Letters, Drew, Apr. 17, 1824, f. 155, Box 120; May 12, 1825, enclosing Cox to Drew, f. 18, Box 121.
22. *Wesleyan-Methodist Magazine,* Jan., 1824, "Christian Retrospect," p. 42; *Missionary Notices,* June, 1823, pp. 82, 88, 89.
23. *Wesleyan-Methodist Magazine,* Jan., 1824, p. 45.
24. Jackson, *Memoir of John Jenkins,* p. 72, quoting letter from J. Taylor, Jan. 13, 1824.
25. W.M.M.S. Letters, Shipman, Kingston, Apr. 24, 1824, f. 161, Box 120; Horne, Montego Bay, May 7, 1824, f. 12, Box 121.

26. Minutes of the District Meeting, Jamaica, May 17, 1824, Box 148, M.M.S. Archives.
27. Manchester to Bathurst, June 16, 1824, no. 96, C.O. 137/156.
28. Manchester to Bathurst, May 21, 1824, no. 90, acknowledging receipt of royal proclamation, Mar. 10, 1824; July 1, 1824, no. 99, C.O. 137/156.
29. Manchester to Bathurst, July 31, 1824, no. 104, C.O. 137/156; *Jamaica Journal,* July 3, 1824, p. 225, quoting *Montego Bay Gazette.*
30. *Jamaica Journal,* July 17, 1824, p. 294; Aug. 14, 1824, p. 394, quoting John Bull (Eng.), June 13, 1824; July 31, 1824, p. 353, quoting *Montego Bay Gazette,* Aug. 7, 1824, p. 366, "Letters from a Planter," and p. 368, "Cicero."
31. W.M.M.S. Letters, Shipman, Kingston, Aug. 2, 1824, f. 76; Crofts, Spanish Town, Sept. 13, 1824, f. 111, Box 121.
32. Jackson, *Memoir of John Jenkins,* p. 68, quoting Lane to Jenkins, Cool-Shade, July 16, 1824; P.P. (Commons) (no. 721), 1831–32, 20:407–8, evidence of Rev. J. Shipman; Duncan, *Narrative of the Wesleyan Mission to Jamaica,* p. 161.
33. Lipscomb to Hay, May 30, 1828, enclosing opinion of Attorney General W. Burge, Spanish Town, July 17, 1828, ff. 141–43, C.O. 137/268.
34. *Wesleyan-Methodist Magazine,* Feb., 1825, pp. 116–17, italics in original.
35. W.M.M.S. Letters, Drew, Bellemont, Mar. 7, 1825, f. 37, Box 122; Shipman, Kingston, Sept. 13, 1824, f. 110, Box 121; *Missionary Notices,* June, 1824, p. 276.
36. P.P. (Commons) (no. 721), 1831–32, 20:407, evidence of Rev. J. Shipman.
37. Robert Young, *A View of Slavery in connection with Christianity* (London, 1825).
38. P.P. (Commons) (no. 721), 1831–32, 20:405, evidence of Rev. J. Shipman.
39. *Jamaica Journal,* Feb. 26, 1825, p. 245, quoting *Glasgow Courier.*
40. Jackson, *Memoir of John Jenkins,* p. 144, quoting Shipman to Jenkins, Nov. 11, 1824; p. 145, quoting Young to Jenkins, Nov. 12, 1824.
41. P.P. (Commons) (no. 721), 1831–32, 20:407, evidence of Rev. J. Shipman, quoting letter from H. de la Beche, Oct. 14, 1824.
42. Manchester to Bathurst, Dec. 24, 1824, no. 129, enclosing Assembly report, C.O. 137/157.
43. Minutes of the W.M.M.S. Committee, Nov. 3, 1824, Box 547, M.M.S. Archives.
44. W.M.M.S. Committee to the District Chairman, Jamaica, Dec. 16, 1824, Box 24, M.M.S. Archives. This letter makes no reference to the September resolutions, and it is not clear whether the secretaries were following up conference action in August or providing an answer to the resolutions without referring to them. The resolutions were dealt with at a meeting of the general committee of the Missionary Society on Jan. 5, 1825. If the

decision had already been taken to place the resolutions before this meeting, the secretaries may have thought it better to deal only with general questions arising from them.

45. The whole tone of the counter-resolutions reflects the indignation the Jamaica district's action aroused. Six months after the February meeting, at the 1825 conference, feeling still ran high; one faction proposed that all the missionaries in Jamaica be tried for immorality. Jackson, *Memoir of John Jenkins,* pp. 148–49, quoting Shipman to Jenkins, Aberdeen, Sept., 1825.

46. *Wesleyan-Methodist Magazine,* Feb. 25, 1825, pp. 117–19; minutes of the W.M.M.S. Committee, Jan. 5, 1825, Box 547, M.M.S. Archives.

47. Butterworth to W.M.M.S. Committee, June 25, 1823, Box 662, M.M.S. Archives; Jackson, *Memoir of Richard Watson,* 1:593.

48. Ragatz, *Fall of the Planter Class,* p. 432.

49. Great Britain, *Parliamentary Debates,* 2d ser., 13 (Apr.–July, 1825): 1346–47.

50. *Jamaica Journal,* Sept. 25, 1824, pp. 56–57.

51. Manchester to Bathurst, June 1, 1827, no. 15, enclosing copy of Bridge's sermon, pp. 7–8, C.O. 137/165.

52. W.M.M.S. Letters, Ratcliffe, Port Antonio, May 28, 1827, f. 122, Box 124.

53. Manchester to Bathurst, June 1, 1827, no. 15, enclosing Cox to Bullock (governor's secretary), C.O. 137/165.

54. W.M.M.S. Letters, Ratcliffe, Port Antonio, Mar. 10, 1827, f. 47, Box 124.

55. Great Britain, *Parliamentary Debates,* 2d ser., 16 (Nov., 1826–Mar., 1827):1166–71; Bathurst to Manchester, Mar. 19, 1827, no. 50, pp. 203–4, C.O. 138/51.

56. Manchester to Bathurst, June 1, 1827, no. 15, enclosing (1) Cox to Bullock, May 16, 1827, (4) sermon, (5) vestry minutes, Jan. 10, 1827; Manchester to Goderich, June 9, 1827, enclosing (1) indictment before grand court, C.O. 137/165. None of this material was laid before Parliament.

57. Huskisson to Keane, Sept. 22, 1827, no. 3, pp. 235–63, C.O. 138/51.

58. Punishments were limited, slave evidence made admissible in some circumstances, and the method of trial modified. Manchester to Bathurst, Dec. 23, 1826, no. 72, C.O. 137/165.

59. Manchester to Horton, Jan. 8, 1827, enclosing "An Act to Alter and Amend the Slave Laws," printed by the *St. Jago Gazette,* pp. 32–33, C.O. 137/165.

60. Keane to Huskisson, Dec. 24, 1827, no. 16, enclosing (2) report from the committee appointed to consider the letter from Mr. Huskisson, p. 1, C.O. 137/165.

61. Huskisson to Keane, Sept. 22, 1827, private draft, f. 49, Add. Mss., British Museum 38751, ff. 44–58.

62. Huskisson to Keane, Sept. 22, 1827, no. 3, pp. 235–63, C.O. 138/51.

63. Keane to Huskisson, Dec. 4, 1827, no. 15, enclosing Address from the Assembly, C.O. 137/165.

64. William Knibb, "Journal of my voyage to Jamaica," Jan. 28, 1825, Box W.I./3, B.M.S. Archives.

65. The Wesleyan missionary Harrison had been sent out to Jamaica before he had been ordained. The magistrates at the Falmouth quarter sessions in May, 1827, claimed his credentials were inadequate and refused him a license. Harrison, nothing daunted, immediately had recourse to higher authority. His credentials were sent to the attorney general, who ruled that, providing Harrison signed an affidavit declaring himself to be a Dissenting minister, a license could be granted. The magistrates continued to procrastinate and the license was subsequently twice refused "on the determination of the Magistrate." When Harrison thereupon proceeded to behave as a licensed preacher and continued services until 8 P.M., he was charged under clause 84 of the 1826 slave code. The battle lasted five months; finally the attorney general's decision was accepted by the magistrates. Harrison had successfully sustained his right to a license and to the privileges of a licensed minister. W.M.M.S. Letters, Harrison, Falmouth, Nov. 7, May 14, 1827, f. 17, Box 126.

66. W.M.M.S. Letters, Grimsdall, St. Ann's Bay, June 4, 11, 1827, ff. 129, 140, Box 125; Nov. 23, 1827, f. 22, Box 126.

67. W.M.M.S. Letters, Whitehouse, St. Ann's Bay, Apr. 25, 1828, f. 153; July 10, 1828, f. 214, Box 126.

68. Jamaica: *Votes of the Assembly,* 1828, App. 60; Sectarian Committee report, pp. 460–61, evidence of A. H. Beaumont, C.O. 140/116; W.M.M.S. Letters, Morgan, Kingston, Aug. 4, 1828, f. 10, Box 127.

69. W.M.M.S. Letters, Whitehouse, common jail, Aug. 23, 1828, f. 24, Box 127; Grimsdall, St. Ann's Bay, Sept. 29, 1827, f. 7, Box 126.

70. W.M.M.S. Letters, Orton, common jail, Aug. 18, 1828, f. 19; Montego Bay, Nov. 15, 1828, f. 81, Box 127.

71. Keane to Huskisson, Dec. 4, 1827, no. 15, enclosing Message from the House of Assembly, C.O. 137/165.

72. Huskisson to Keane, Mar. 22, 1828, no. 16, C.O. 138/51; Lipscomb to Hay, May 30, 1828, f. 137, C.O. 137/267.

73. Gardner, *History of Jamaica,* pp. 265, 267.

74. Keane to Huskisson, May 9, 1828, no. 48; Keane to Murray, Aug. 26, 1828, Confidential; Keane to Murray, Nov. 21, 1828, no. 27, C.O. 137/167.

75. Great Britain, Parliamentary Papers (Commons), "Copy of all Communications made to the Colonial Department since 1st January 1826 by the Government of Jamaica, or by the Colonial Organs of the different Religious Societies employing Missionaries in Jamaica, respecting the obstacles alleged to be thrown in the way of their giving religious instruction to the Slaves, and the alleged persecution, imprisonment, or other punishment of the Missionaries employed by them in that Island" (no. 672),

1830, 21:185, Scarlett to Keane, Aug. 30, 1828, p. 186, Keane to Murray, Sept. 8, 1828, Keane to Cox, Sept. 6, 1828.

76. The immediate precedent for the Rose and Hemming case was the dismissal in 1823 of three magistrates in Hanover for hanging a slave on their own authority. Bathurst to Major General Conran, Feb. 16, 1822, C.O. 138/47; Major General Conran to Bathurst, Dec. 19, 1821, no. 13, enclosures, C.O. 137/152.

77. W.M.M.S., *Annual Report,* 1828, pp. 152–55; see also Chapter One.

78. Jamaica: *Votes of the Assembly,* Dec. 23, 1828, p. 236, C.O. 140/116. Hostile evidence was presented to the Sectarian Committee by a small group of dubious characters including A. H. Beaumont, editor of the *Jamaica Courant,* dissatisfied free black and colored leaders, one or two free colored members of the Anglican church, and a gentlemen debtor released from prison for the purpose. Five of these witnesses gave evidence relating to one Wesleyan service held in Spanish Town in 1825 where the elegantly attired free colored women in the congregation were invited to give their jewelry to the collection. This was given as an example of the Wesleyans' methods of extortion. See ibid., App. 60, pp. 466–68.

79. Keane to Murray, Dec. 11, 1828, no. 30, C.O. 137/167; Keane to Murray, Jan. 2, 1829, no. 38, C.O. 137/169.

80. Phillippo, "Personal History," p. 178.

CHAPTER FIVE

The Struggle for
Religious Freedom

Sᴌᴀᴠᴇ ᴄᴏɴᴠᴇʀᴛs ᴡᴇʀᴇ the readiest sacrifice to the antisectarianism of their managers. Yet as long as the missionaries depended on the protection of planter patrons, any references in letters home about the punishments inflicted on religious slaves had to be carefully filtered of names and dates and presented as exceptional. It is evident, however, that slave converts, under pressure from plantation managers, proved capable of far greater sacrifices for conscience's sake than were ever demanded by the magistrates from the missionaries. The slave martyrs joined a well-defined Christian tradition; in doing so, they extended the areas of conflict with their managers and claimed a new right, the right to save their souls. The missionaries, once their legal position was secured, assisted their converts in this struggle.

This development was facilitated by a new imperial policy that reflected the penetration of the Colonial Office itself by humanitarian influence. The Colonial Office in 1827, after four years of unsuccessful efforts to win support from colonial assemblies for the imperial government's amelioration program, in a desperate attempt to improve slave conditions, implemented a policy of investigating all complaints of cruelty and injustice to the slaves as were not "manifestly frivolous."[1] The investigations were intended to make crown officeholders at every level in the colonial administrations take their duties to the slave population seriously, and extend to the representative colonies the services provided in crown colonies by specially appointed law officers called protectors of slaves.[2]

Investigations became a regular feature of imperial policy during the administration of two notably weak and indecisive colonial secretaries, Sir George Murray and Lord Goderich; they allowed West Indian affairs to fall into the hands of two permanent officials with strong humanitarian interests, James Stephen, son of the leading abolitionist of the same name and official legal adviser to the Colonial Office, and Henry Taylor, senior clerk.[3] Stephen viewed the investigations as a last recourse. "There is no other method," he wrote, "of correcting public opinion, of vindicating justice, of showing the Government are in earnest, or of inducing the Governors to act with resolution."[4]

The missionaries both benefited from and contributed to the final discrediting of this policy. By demonstrating conclusively that the slave system denied the slaves religious as well as civil liberty, denied their right to be Christian, to save their souls, they fueled the conviction growing in England, at government as well as popular level, that attempts to reform the slave system were futile; the system itself had to be abolished.

Jamaican reaction to the Colonial Office's new policy initiatives created the circumstances that exposed slave converts, and more particularly slave officeholders, to special punishments. The first investigation[5] was set in train by a free colored resident of Falmouth who instigated a Colonial Office review of the conduct of two slave trials. The magistrates who comprised the slave court, including Custos James Miller, were strongly criticized as a result. The case created a furor throughout the island; the whole investigation process was considered more derogatory of the slave owners' authority than the disallowance of the 1826 slave code had been. Nevertheless, as Stephen and Taylor had hoped, it made some magistrates more conscious of their duties to the slaves. Custos Cox was one of them. When he was confronted by a woman domestic slave, Kitty Hilton, property of the Reverend George Bridges, who had had the flesh whipped from her back by the parson for killing a turkey without his authority, he called a council of protection to investigate the case.[6] He hoped no doubt to pre-empt imperial government action; in the upshot, however, the council exonerated Bridges, and a Colonial Office investigation ensued.

The spirit informing the council's decision inspired in the meantime a regular reign of terror over the slaves in St. Ann's parish. Rage and frustration against the imperial government, Wilberforce, and his allies were taken out on the slaves, and religious slaves who were members of Bridges's hated rival, the Wesleyan mission in St. Ann, attracted particular attention.

Isaac Whitehouse, who was still in charge of the mission there, found himself listening daily to reports of this persecution.[7] Whitehouse was especially sensitive to such information. During his imprisonment on the license issue he witnessed slave floggings and was moved to send the W.M.M.S. an account, unique in a decade of correspondence from the Jamaica district, of a routine slave punishment.

> My ear caught the sound of a whip, and, though I have now been in this country upward of four years and have always avoided being present at the flagellation of negroes, I now resolved to see what was going on. . . . I saw the driver flogging a young man with a large cart whip. After he had inflicted as many strokes as he thought proper he proceeded to renew the lash on his whip. When he had done this a female, apparently about forty years of age, was laid, her stomach upon the ground, her clothes were most indecorously turned up and whilst two persons held her hands and one her feet . . . the driver inflicted stroke after stroke until I was ready to ask whether it was a human being or a demon in human shape who inflicted the same. Gracious God! Is this humanity?[8]

Whitehouse knew that a report on cruelty to a slave would be used as antislavery propaganda; his own letters from jail were published in the *Anti-Slavery Monthly Reporter*.[9] He also knew that such information as the Trelawney case demonstrated might provoke a Colonial Office investigation. It was in these circumstances that from June, 1829, he kept the W.M.M.S. informed about the harassment and persecution of a slave leader of his church, Henry Williams.

Henry Williams belonged to Rural Retreat estate, for which a magistrate, James Betty, was the attorney.[10] As head driver, Williams, an intelligent and capable man, was virtually in charge of the estate. Like many others of this class of slaves, he was attracted to the Wesleyan mission where Whitehouse, impressed like Betty by his capabilities, appointed him as the first slave leader in the society. Under Williams's influence other slaves from Rural Retreat attended the Wesleyan mission. Attorney Betty, playing his part in the St. Ann campaign against chapel-going slaves, warned Williams in June, 1829, that he must give up his religious work and threatened, if he did not obey, to send him to Rodney Hall workhouse, notoriously the most severe in the island. He then called the rest of the Rural Retreat slaves together and ordered them not to attend the Wesleyan chapel.[11]

The slaves' reaction made clear to Betty their strong objection to this interference with their free time and their religion. One of the privileged slaves, Williams's sister, Sarah Atkinson, who had been housekeeper for the late proprietor and enjoyed a £10 a year pension, greeted the order with a sigh of such proportions that Betty took the unusual step of having her flogged. This degradation of a traditionally privileged slave was intended to cow the rest into subjection, but Betty evidently feared he had merely hardened resistance and called on the Reverend George Bridges to support his ban on the Wesleyan chapel.

Bridges did his best. The very next day he saw Williams and demanded to know why he did not support the Anglican church. Williams, by his own account, told the rector he had not known what sin was until he attended the Wesleyan chapel. Bridges tried to intimidate him by telling wild stories about Methodists being hanged by the hundreds in England and warned him that he must take the people to church or face the consequences.

That night Williams sought Whitehouse's advice; all the latter could do was warn him to be particularly careful of his conduct of plantation business lest a charge should be brought against him on that account. The following Sunday Williams, under Betty's orders, attended the Anglican church service; when questioned about the other slaves, he said, "The people had said that Sunday was theirs, and that some had gone to chapel and some in other directions." The following day Williams was sent to Rodney Hall workhouse.

To stamp out the possibility of further resistance by the Rural Retreat slaves, Sarah Atkinson was taken to the rectory and, in the presence of two white militiamen, one of whom had taken part in the attack on the Wesleyan mission at Christmas 1826, was told that if she did not attend the Anglican church she would be turned off the property. Recently flogged and with a brother in the workhouse, Sarah Atkinson yet remained defiant. She told Whitehouse, "I am a poor woman and Mr. Betty is a great fish and might swallow me up, but I will not leave my religion." Whitehouse commented of Bridges, "May I not say he is the mainspring in this machine?"[12]

At this stage Whitehouse was uncertain what to do. He understood the significance of Williams's incarceration in Rodney Hall; the previous year another church member had died there. He attempted first to appeal to Betty and called at his residence. Betty was out; fearing, no doubt, that an appeal might only make matters worse, Whitehouse did not repeat the call. Three months passed and then he heard from a white slave owner and church member, Mrs. Simpson, that Betty intended to charge Williams with holding night meetings in the house of one of her slaves[13] and that, if this failed, he would be charged with stealing pimento. By this time Williams was so sick from repeated floggings that the workhouse master had taken him out of irons and put him in the hospital. It was at this stage that Williams's wife came to Whitehouse, nearly distracted, in fear for his life.

Whitehouse confronted an acute version of a dilemma common enough in the round of mission work. "I hardly know how to act to have a conscience void of offence," one missionary had cried. Whitehouse more vividly wrote, "I myself was distressed beyond description. My instructions prevented my interference and yet I knew of a friendless individual who was literally butchered for no other offence than that of coming to our chapel." Customarily the missionaries had resorted to prayer; God was not only the final but the only authority open to appeal. Whitehouse, however, could rely not only on friends in England but on important allies in Jamaica. Significant elements of the free black and colored population, traditionally mission supporters and many identified with the antislavery cause, had founded a newspaper, the *Watchman and Jamaica Free Press,* to assist their fight for civil rights. Its editor, Edward Jordon, was a long-standing member of the Kingston Wesleyan church, and it was to the *Watchman* that Whitehouse turned. He wrote a letter detailing the case that Jordon made the basis of an able article. It had the desired effect; Williams was released to spend weeks lying on his stomach, "his poor back being a mass of corruption."[14]

If the Jamaican magistrates expected thereby to avoid any further publicity of the affair, their expectations were misplaced. The Williams case made the W.M.M.S. committee eager to invoke imperial action. The Anti-Slavery Society, with which the committee maintained close connections, had been able to promote an investigation of the Kitty Hilton affair in October, 1829, and the "martyrdom" of a slave for religious reasons was a more provoking case than the abuse of a domestic. The committee also had political incentives. The Jamaica Assembly had recently published its scurrilous Sectarian Committee report[15] and had, in addition, re-enacted the disputed slave code of 1826. The committee could feel real satisfaction in demonstrating the depth of the planters' hostility to their mission and the consequent brutalities inflicted on the slaves. The details were forwarded to the Colonial Office, and as a result the governor of Jamaica was requested in May, 1830, to investigate.[16]

Bridges and the attorney, James Betty, treated the investigation with contempt. Bridges, who had already survived both an imperial and a local investigation of his conduct (the St. Ann mission affair and the Kitty Hilton case) took the attitude that the island authorities (including the bishop, with whom he had quarreled) were "officially arraigned against me under the orders of the Colonial Office," and proudly projected himself as a lone defender of the slaves against the mercenary sectarians. Betty's reply, written no doubt with Bridges's advice, adopted the same defiant tone and protested the same desire to protect the slaves from sectarians. The Jamaican executive was hardly more respectful. The attorney general, Hugo James, credited these contumacious statements with the value of a cogently argued defense and advised the governor, the Earl of Belmore, that responsibility for any further action lay with the missionary, Whitehouse. As the accuser it was his duty to collect statements on oath to corroborate his story and lay them before the crown office.[17]

The Earl of Belmore, appointed governor early in 1829, had already proved himself unsympathetic to imperial policy and resentful of efforts to direct his executive power. He had refused to investigate the Kitty Hilton case when first instructed to do so, and he now displayed a less acute concern for justice than Custos Cox, whose response to the slave's complaint had provided the occasions for further investigations. Once the attorney general had pointed to Whitehouse as the party responsible for further action in the Williams case, Belmore was more than willing to consider his duty fulfilled.

Whitehouse was placed in a difficult position. The investigations roused great resentment in Jamaica; the Hilton case had been particularly well publicized by a local periodical, *The Christian Record,* run by evangelical clergy. For the defenders of Jamaica's constitutional privileges the practice had sinister implications; it was "inquisitorial," "unconstitutional," and, above all, symptomatic of a policy that "seems likely to be satisfied with nothing less than our absolute ruin."[18] The Henry Williams case, which also got full newspaper coverage, fueled this rage. Whitehouse himself was filled with all the customary apprehensions for the safety of the missions. He was, however, too deeply committed to withdraw; he accepted the challenge and pursued the case, even though the lawyers who advised him felt obliged to remain anonymous. The ensuing correspondence with the governor was conducted in a spirited manner.[19]

The challenge was flung back to the executive. Whitehouse declined the position as public prosecutor, but told the governor who could give evidence and suggested investigation by a council of protection or a magistrate. Belmore's reply, through his secretary, was clearly intended as a crushing rebuke to the upstart Methodist; it concluded, ". . . it is unnecessary to reply in detail to the diffuse and impertinent observations contained in your letter." But Whitehouse and his lawyers, in turn, rebuked Belmore for the term "impertinent" and commented, "Your letter seems to leave the case very much where my answer placed it . . . if, in the face of a direction from the Colonial Secretary and with the power of calling into exercise the judicial functions of the whole magistracy, it is thought consistent . . . to shift the task and responsibility of investigation to a private individual in the possession of no authority, it is clear inquiry must end."[20]

The Colonial Office found Whitehouse's arguments convincing; faced by this correspondence, Stephen and Taylor decided that further inquiries were unnecessary. There remained only the question of what action could be taken. There was no legal case against Betty, who had simply exercised his right to discipline a slave driver. Judgment, however, was guided by the consideration that, "as the only means of mitigating, in any degree, the evils inseparable from the existence of slavery, the Imperial Government will in no case consent to the authority of the magistrate . . . remaining in the hands of any person who cannot satisfactorily show that no grounds exist for imputing to him a want of humanity either . . . as a magistrate, or as a proprietor."[21] Belmore was instructed that if Betty continued to refuse an explanation of his conduct, he was to be erased from the roll of magistrates, and Bridges was to be reminded that only "gentleness and persuasion" could win back Dissenters to the church. Most important, Belmore was roundly criticized for his handling of the case and Whitehouse held up as an example of correct conduct. The Colonial Secretary Lord Goderich (following Stephen's draft) wrote, "I regret that the remarks of that gentleman, though very clearly and forcibly stated, failed to produce on your Lordship's mind a conviction of the unreasonableness of imposing on him the character of public accuser. . . . The arguments of Mr. Whitehouse upon each of these topics do not, I confess, appear to myself susceptible of any satisfactory answer."[22]

As a step toward imposing humanitarian standards on the Jamaican administration, the Henry Williams investigation was unsuccessful. Punishment was not meted out to the chief offender; Betty died before the order to erase his name from the roll of magistrates reached the island.[23] Nor did the advice sent to the governor serve any purpose; far from emulating the imperial government's critical attitude to Jamaican magistrates, Belmore, within a few months of receiving the Colonial Office's analysis of the Williams case, reinstated Rose and Hemming as magistrates in St.

Ann.[24] Belmore was not only incapable of giving constructive support to imperial policy but guilty of undoing the one constructive act the Jamaican executive had to its credit.

The benefits accruing from the investigation were reflected not in any immediate improvement in the Jamaican administration, or in the position of the slaves, but in the confidence of the Wesleyan and Baptist missionaries in their new role as protagonists of their converts. Whitehouse had so far left behind the anxiety in which he began the proceedings that he was ready, at the end, to accede to his lawyer's suggestion that his correspondence be published in *The Christian Record*.[25] When a comparable injustice was inflicted on a Baptist slave, Sam Swiney, the missionary William Knibb had no hesitation in pursuing the case.[26]

The slave whose punishment prompted Knibb into action was a tradesman, belonging like Williams to the slave elite, and was also an active church member, in this case a deacon. Swiney met with a group of members at the mission premises at Savanna-la-Mar on Easter Sunday evening, 1830, for a prayer meeting. They were disturbed by two "troublemakers," and the following day warrants were issued for the arrest of six slave and six free mission members who were charged with illegal preaching, teaching, holding a night meeting, and disturbing the peace. Swiney, who had been seen leading the group in prayer, was charged with illegal preaching and teaching.[27] The magistrates were evidently determined to intimidate church members and prevent meetings in the absence of a missionary.

William Knibb, pastor at Falmouth and responsible for Savanna-la-Mar, attended the court and for its benefit defined the difference between extempore prayer and preaching. The bench, led by the Honorable David Finlayson, custos of the parish and Speaker of the Assembly, insisted on finding Swiney guilty; he was sentenced to twenty lashes and two weeks in jail. Knibb proclaimed his support for Swiney by accompanying him when he was led, chained to another convict, the length of the town to the place of punishment; there he took his hand and said loudly, "Sam, whatever you want, send to me and you shall have it." Immediately afterward Knibb wrote a full account to a local newspaper, *The Struggler,* concluding with the observation that, having witnessed the "disgusting scene" of a "fellow creature, a respectable tradesman of his class ... lacerated with a cart whip, and immediately after chained to a convict and sent to work on the road ... I must consider, if the law sanctions such a conclusion, that that law is an abomination, a disgrace to a

Christian country." The account was prefaced by a letter to the editor in which Knibb declared he intended to invoke imperial action.[28]

Knibb, though following the pattern established by Whitehouse, reacted more positively. He protested at the courthouse and at the marketplace, he signed his letters, and, above all, he advertised his appeal to the Colonial Office. Publishing the letter in Jamaica was probably intended simply to add weight to the case in England. The paper Knibb chose was not the *Watchman and Jamaica Free Press,* the most popular radical newspaper in the island, but a little, quarto-size news-sheet *The Struggler,* published in Montego Bay and supported, like the *Watchman,* by the free colored population.[29] *The Struggler* put the case in print without exposing Knibb prematurely to islandwide publicity.

Belmore behaved in a characteristic manner, once more interposing his influence between the magistrates and justice. He forwarded, two months after receiving them, Knibb's account from *The Struggler* and a cryptic, blotched statement from Finlayson that Swiney had been punished under clause 50 of the 1816 slave code, commenting, "I think it is due to Mr. Finlayson to say, that he is a gentleman of remarkably mild disposition, and at a time of life not likely to lead him into any intemperate exercise of power." It was left to the Colonial Office to request the attorney general's opinion. Eighteen months thus elapsed before the sentence, quite apart from the justice of the charge, was declared illegal: the punishment for unlicensed preaching was *either* imprisonment *or* flogging. Goderich, once more on the advice of Stephen, though regretting the need to censure and disgrace "persons whom it would be my first wish to maintain in . . . enjoyment of respect," nevertheless insisted that "the principles of justice and toleration and the interests of humanity must not be compromised." Finlayson and his associate, Hardin, were erased from the roll of magistrates.[30]

As in the Williams case, arbitrary and unjust punishment was inflicted on a slave, on this occasion by magistrates in court who ignored the law; when called to question, the culprits defied imperial authority, and the governor was reluctant to pursue the case. The difference was that in this instance the guilty magistrates were removed from office. These investigations were typical of all the Jamaican cases. Other informants were a free colored doctor, a customs collector, and an attorney. The punishments included the flogging of an elderly woman with a wet cart whip for requesting money owed her and the imposition, over a period of six months, of a concentration camp routine on a mother and daughter for some domestic fault. Every case revealed a strong reluctance at every level of the Jamaican administration, from the magistrates to the governor, to make any attempt to punish those whose standards of justice and humanity toward the slaves were found wanting.

The significance of the missionaries' role in these cases is measured partly by the effect the investigations had on the Jamaican administration; not only were magistrates dismissed, but the governor himself, in February, 1832, was removed from office. The Colonial Office indictment of Belmore, the work of Stephen's close associate Henry Taylor, defined the main functions of a governor as that of "vigilantly supervising the conduct of the Island Magistracy, detecting and visiting with due censure the abuse of their powers or neglect of their duties . . . and thus imparting to the Slave Population all the protection . . . it is practicable for His Majesty's Government to afford them." Though there were other charges to lay against Belmore, including his acceptance in 1829 of the much disputed religious restrictions embodied in the 1826 slave code and his failure to fulfill the routine function of his office (the jail returns, for instance, were inadequate), the most weighty evidence against him was his conduct of the investigations. In the Williams case, by leaving responsibility for the prosecution to Whitehouse, Belmore had revealed "a fundamental and incurable difference" between his sentiments and those of His Majesty's government. And the Swiney case, though it involved a punishment "excessive, cruel and unlawful," had prompted no comment from Belmore. Following Taylor, the Secretary of State concluded, "Beyond the bare execution of His Majesty's commands, where that has been at length obtained, I am not aware that I have received from your Lordship any assistance towards the exercise of His Majesty's authority for the relief of persons who are injured or oppressed, or for any other of the more beneficial purposes for which His Majesty's authority is delegated to the Governor of Jamaica." Belmore's services were dispensed with.[31]

The missionaries' actions also contributed in a small but significant way to convincing their home churches, the antislavery movement, and the officials at the Colonial Office that efforts to reform the slave system were a waste of time: the only cure for slavery was abolition. The Jamaican cases were items in an accumulation of evidence, supplied by private individuals and officially appointed protectors of the slaves throughout the West Indies, which delineated both the barbarity of slavery and the sheer unreality of a policy that depended on making slave owners behave like humanitarians. If further evidence were needed to support this conclusion, it was provided by the slave code presented by the Jamaica Assembly to the Colonial Office in 1831. The suggestions for reform made in 1823 were barely acknowledged: punishments were limited, slave evidence was made admissible in some circumstances, and the method of trial was modified. All the Colonial Office had achieved in a prolonged struggle with the Assembly was the omission of the two clauses intended to restrict missionary work. In October, 1831, James Stephen concluded that "the evils of slavery are beyond the reach of legislation and can be remedied only by laws directly abolishing the relationship of master and slave."[32]

The investigations, fully publicized in the *Anti-Slavery Reporter,* kept people informed of the misdeeds of slave owners and magistrates and implied the inadequacy of the crown's representatives. This knowledge informed the annual meeting of the Anti-Slavery Society in the Freemason's Hall in May, 1830, when the society pledged itself to effect "at the earliest period the entire abolition of slavery throughout the British dominions" and founded a new activist group, the Agency Committee, to rouse the country. The Wesleyan church, whose missionaries had made their particular contribution to these developments, instructed its preachers at the 1830 annual conference to organize antislavery petitions to Parliament and told its members to reserve their votes in the election expected in the autumn for candidates pledged to abolition.[33] The missions' claim to religious rights for their converts had helped to promote the cause of immediate emancipation in England.

The Williams and Swiney cases are, however, primarily important as reflections of developments among the slaves themselves. Given the planters' uneasy tolerance of mission work, membership in the mission churches had always implied, for slave converts, an element of resistance to the system. The Williams case demonstrated how, under pressure, this element of resistance was transformed into outright defiance. Williams chose, when challenged, to put his God before his master and to claim for the slaves in his charge the right to do the same. He told Bridges, "The people had said the Sunday was theirs and that some had gone to chapel and some in other directions."

The reaction of the slaves on Rural Retreat suggested that such leaders enjoyed widespread support. Sarah Atkinson defined their attitude: "I am a poor woman and Mr. Betty is a great fish and might swallow me up, but I will not leave my religion." To the instances where the slaves took corporate action to maintain customary rights sanctioned by plantation organization—their right to allowances of particular food and to work the provision ground—was added an occasion demonstrating the slaves' determination, under dedicated leadership, to claim a new right. And they did so despite the penalties; Sarah Atkinson was flogged, Williams faced imprisonment and flogging in circumstances that, given the reputation of Rodney Hall workhouse, threatened death.

Williams made a conscious decision to defy authority; Swiney's position is less clearly defined. Given, however, the limitations imposed on the functions of slave converts by the 1816 slave code, restrictions emphasized by the missionaries, a slave leader who took a leading role in a prayer meeting held to celebrate one of the great festivals of the Christian church was certainly asserting the limited rights he had in a public manner. He exposed himself to the risk of punishment as a preacher.

Both cases indicated the emergence of a new type of religious leader among the slaves, leaders who were not content to compensate themselves entirely for the limitations imposed by their slave status within the missionary churches by becoming heads of sects that met surreptitiously, at night. These men were prepared to testify openly to their beliefs and take the consequences; they had translated religious conviction into political action. The examples set by the leaders of the Argyle war, by the free colored and black campaign for civil rights, by their sense of forces at work in England on their behalf, as well as by the missionaries' own example, worked in concert with their own interpretation of Christianity to prompt this development.

The emergence of such leaders and the defiant attitude of the Rural Retreat slaves, placed in the context of mission work throughout the island, suggest a new level of political consciousness among the slaves. Their links with the mission churches not only established fresh contacts for them beyond the boundaries of the plantation but assisted the formation of a cohesive sense of common rights and common purpose. Elements in the slave population had evidently resolved the contradiction at the heart of mission teaching, the insistence on due submission to authority and the insistence that each individual's primary responsibility was to seek salvation, by putting rights before duty. Bunyan's ideal Christian had overtaken Brother Anansi.

The slaves' action in these cases had one further significance: they achieved little and at great cost. Swiney maintained his position as deacon in the Baptist church; the slaves at Rural Retreat continued to attend the Wesleyan mission. Williams was lucky to be alive. The one immediate gain of any significance was in the slaves' relationship with the missionaries, whose exertions on behalf of their converts demonstrated that they were capable of aligning themselves with the slaves in opposition to their masters. The slaves' experience in pursuit of religious freedom within the system, however, simply underlined the fact that their primary need was freedom from slavery. It is not surprising to find that Williams and Swiney proved harbingers of ideological developments among the slaves that turned Christianity into a weapon to overthrow the system.

NOTES

1. Memo., Stephen to Taylor, Aug. 6, 1830, following Dyer to Murray, July 9, 1830, C.O. 137/173.
2. The appointment of protectors of slaves was suggested by one of the legal commissioners who was appointed to investigate the administration of justice in the British West Indies in 1822. Murray, *West Indies and the Development of Colonial Government,* pp. 104–5, 142.
3. Ibid., pp. 147–48, 166–67.
4. Stephen's minute, following Belmore to Goderich, Aug. 23, 1831, no. 82, C.O. 137/179.
5. Seven investigations were made in Jamaica from 1828 to 1832. The cases involving the unjust punishment of religious slaves are fully discussed in this chapter. The other cases were as follows: (1) Accusations of unjust punishment in two cases in the Trelawney slave court: Benjamin to Huskisson, Falmouth, Apr. 22, 1828; Benjamin to Twiss, Aug. 28, 1828, C.O. 137/168; memo., Stephen to Taylor, July 15, 1828, C.O. 137/170; Murray to Keane, June 19, 1828, C.O. 137/51. (2) Great Britain, Parliamentary Papers (Commons), "Copy of any information received from Jamaica respecting an Inquiry into the treatment of a Female Slave, by the Rev. Mr. Bridges, Rector of St. Ann" (no. 231), 1830–31, 16. (3) Great Britain, Parliamentary Papers (Commons), "Copy of all Correspondence relative to the Punishment of Two Female Slaves belonging to Mr. Jackson, Custos of Port Royal, and the Proceedings thereon" (no. 737), 1831–32, 47. (4) The ill-treatment of a slave sick with small pox: Goderich to Belmore, Feb. 18, 1832, draft, C.O. 137/179; Goderich to Belmore, Apr. 2, 1832, no. 87, p. 204, C.O. 138/54. (5) The ill-treatment of a female slave by an overseer: Belmore to Goderich, May 6, 1831, no. 40, enclosures, C.O. 137/178; Goderich to Belmore, Feb. 18, 1832, confidential, pp. 120–22, C.O. 138/54.

6. Under the 1816 slave code slaves were entitled to complain of improper punishment to the magistrates and vestry, whose duty it then became to constitute themselves a council of protection to investigate the complaint.

7. Whitehouse heard, for example, of four such cases in two days during June, 1829; in two instances owners refused permission to the slaves to marry and in two others slaves were flogged, one for attending chapel and one for reputedly visiting a neighboring estate to teach the slaves to pray. W.M.M.S. Letters, Whitehouse, June 13, 1829, journal, June 6, 7, f. 21, Box 128.

8. W.M.M.S. Letters, Whitehouse, St. Ann's jail, Aug. 23, 1828, f. 24, Box 127.

9. *Anti-Slavery Monthly Reporter,* Nov., 1828, Mar., 1829.

10. The owner, a Reverend Mr. Adams, was an absentee proprietor residing in Inverness. W.M.M.S. Letters, Whitehouse, Kingston, Nov. 12, 1832, f. 117, Box 132.

11. W.M.M.S. Letters, Whitehouse, July 1, 1829, f. 21a, Box 128; Great Britain, Parliamentary Papers (Commons), "Copies of all Comunications relative to the reported Maltreatment of a Slave named Henry Williams in Jamaica" (no. 91), 1830–31, 16:240 (hereafter cited as P.P. (Commons) (no. 91), 1830–31, 16).

12. W.M.M.S. Letters, Whitehouse, St. Ann's Bay, July 1, 2, 1829, f. 21a, Box 128; P.P. (Commons) (no. 91), 1830–31, 16:241–42.

13. Betty probably assumed that the slave, George, would be amenable to this arrangement. Earlier that year George had been taken up and flogged on some arbitrary charge by Bridges, and when Mrs. Simpson tried to bring the matter to court, George had settled out of court for a "trifling sum." W.M.M.S. Letters, Whitehouse, Bellemont, Nov. 16, 1829, f. 136, Box 128.

14. P.P. (Commons) (no. 91), 1830–31, 26:243, Whitehouse, Nov. 4, 1829; W.M.M.S. Letters, Whitehouse, St. Ann's Bay, Nov. 4, f. 136a; Nov. 16, 1829, f. 136, Box 128. Betty subsequently claimed Williams was moved because he was sick. The case has a characteristic coda: Betty, suspecting Whitehouse's part in the newspaper publicity, charged his servant with traveling without proper papers and kept him in St. Ann's workhouse with an iron collar for four days. Belmore to Murray, Aug. 27, 1830, no. 49, enclosing Betty to Bullock, St. Ann's, July 5, 1830, C.O. 137/172; W.M.M.S. Letters, Whitehouse, Nov. 4, 1829, f. 136a, Box 128.

15. Jamaica: *Votes of the Assembly,* 1828, App. 60, C.O. 140/116. See Chapter four, p. 126.

16. P.P. (Commons) (no. 91), 1830–31, 16:235–39, Townley to Murray, Feb. 12, 1830, pp. 239–40, Townley to Murray, Feb. 25, 1830; Twiss to Townley, Mar. 5, 1830; Townley to Twiss, Mar. 10, 1830; p. 246, Murray to Belmore, May 6, 1830.

17. Ibid., pp. 248–51, Bridges to Bullock, July 25, 1830; Betty to Bullock,

July 5, 1830; pp. 247–48, Belmore to Murray, Aug. 27, 1830; James to Belmore, Aug. 27, 1830.

18. *Royal Gazette,* May 2–9, 1829, pp. 9–10, 15, account of a meeting in St. Thomas in the East (the speaker quoted was Alexander Barclay, author of *A Practical View of Slavery),* C.O. 141/24; W.M.M.S. Letters, Kerr, Spanish Town, Sept. 30, 1830, f. 196, Box 129.

19. W.M.M.S. Letters, Whitehouse, Bellemont, Sept. 8, 1830, f. 190; Apr. 14, f. 82; Oct. 1, f. 187, Box 129. The firm was Whitehorne and Forsyth, regular advisers to the Wesleyan mission. Their part in the case was probably well known to interested parties.

20. W.M.M.S. Letters, Whitehouse, Kingston, Sept. 14, 22, 1830, enclosures, f. 191, Box 129; P.P. (Commons) (no. 91), 1830–31, 16:256, 258–60.

21. Memo., Stephen to Taylor, Aug. 6, 1830, following Dyer to Murray, July 19, 1830, C.O. 137/173.

22. Goderich to Belmore, Dec. 9, 11, 1830, nos. 3, 4, pp. 184–89, C.O. 138/53; P.P. (Commons) (no. 91), 1830–31, 16:19–21, 28.

23. Belmore to Murray, Oct. 6, 1830, no. 64, C.O. 137/172.

24. The governor judged them to be respectable persons and considered that "all the benefit to be derived from their example has . . . been obtained." Goderich commented, "I am bound to express my regret that more than two years experience of the state of affairs in Jamaica should have failed to impress your Lordship with the inexpediency of reversing a censure passed on two magistrates for an act of gross and unlawful oppression." Belmore to Goderich, Nov. 11, 1831, no. 113, C.O. 137/179; Goderich to Belmore, Jan. 9, 1832, no. 77, p. 92, C.O. 138/54.

25. W.M.M.S. Letters, Whitehouse, Bellemont, Oct. 26, 1830, f. 214, Box 129.

26. The Baptist Missionary Society had already approached the Colonial Office with the case of a free black allegedly punished for praying. The case was not carefully prepared and, although the governor was requested for information, it was not brought to issue. Belmore to Murray, Apr. 12, 1830, no. 19, C.O. 137/171.

27. Great Britain, Parliamentary Papers (Commons), "Copies of all Communications from Jamaica relating to the Trial of George Ancle and Samuel Swiney, Negro Slaves for certain alleged offences relating to Religious worship" (no. 480), 1831–32, 47:345, Finlayson to Bullock, Oct. 5, 1830 (hereafter cited as P.P. (Commons) (no. 480), 1831–32, 47).

28. Ibid., pp. 6–7; Hinton, *Memoir of William Knibb,* pp. 95–96, quoting Knibb to Dyer, Apr. 26, 1830.

29. All the advertisements in *The Struggler* were taken by John Manderson, a prominent free colored merchant and land owner.

30. P.P. (Commons) (no. 480), 1831–32, 47:344, Belmore to Murray, Dec. 1, 1830; pp. 348–49, Goderich to Belmore, Apr. 25, 1831; p. 350, Belmore to Goderich, Aug. 23, 1831; James to Bullock, Spanish Town, Aug. 9, 1831; pp. 354–56, Goderich to Belmore, Nov. 15, 1831.

31. Goderich to Belmore, Feb. 18, 1832, confidential, pp. 130, 131, 132, C.O. 138/54.
32. Murray, *West Indies and the Development of Colonial Government,* p. 193, quoting 3d Earl Grey's Papers, C.O. Slavery.
33. Jackson, *Memoir of Richard Watson,* 1:509–10.

CHAPTER SIX

The Baptist War

ON TUESDAY, DECEMBER 27, 1831, a fire on Kensington estate in St. James, one of the most important sugar-growing parishes in Jamaica, marked the outbreak of the largest slave rebellion in the history of the island. All the western parishes were involved, the sugar harvest was destroyed, and more than £1 million of damage was done.[1] The rebellion was organized by Christian converts who used the established network of mission meetings and their connections with the Native Baptists to promote political action, took their inspiration from the Bible, and claimed the missionaries as their allies. The missions, founded by the churches, advocated by the antislavery party, and fostered by the imperial government simply to afford the slaves means of salvation within the existing social structure, had proved, as the slave owners had always suspected, subversive of the slave system.

The rebellion took place in the western parishes where the missions were most numerous and independent religious meetings proliferated. The Baptists were particularly popular among the slaves in St. James; Thomas Burchell, who had been in charge of Montego Bay since 1824, was a familiar and much-loved figure throughout the parish. Wesleyans and Presbyterians also were well represented in the north, while the Moravians dominated Manchester, St. Elizabeth, and Westmoreland.

Christianity became a political force when rumors of emancipation created political excitement while epidemics and economic distress threatened despair. These stresses forced the emergence of new ideas, and new leaders to put them into action. The slaves used Christianity as their revolutionary ideology and, in doing so, identified the missionaries as their allies. None of the missionaries, in fact, were aware that their teaching was inciting political action, and all lent their influence to restoring law and order, to the point in one case of turning informer. The slaves, however, fully exposed the ambiguity of their position. The missionaries had served the slaves in a society geared to exploit them, taught that no man could serve two masters, and made it possible for the slaves to perceive them as representatives of the friends in England who clamored for abolition. It is not surprising that, after the rebellion, the Baptist and Wesleyan missionaries were not allowed to continue work within the slave system and were forced, finally, to become active abolitionists.

The 1831 rebellion took place in a society under pressure both internal and external. A six-month drought gripped the island in 1831, the most severe since 1796. Rivers and springs dried up, and the harvest of ground provisions was badly affected. The people were hungry and exposed to infection; in the wake of the drought came heavy rains, followed by epidemics of smallpox and dysentery.[2]

The hardships induced by these special circumstances increased the tensions associated with new labor problems that were affecting the whole slave population and were particularly acute on the sugar estates. By the 1830s slave workers were in short supply. On the sugar estates, where the rate of natural decrease was the highest for any section of the slave population, numbers had declined to the point that in some cases it was no longer possible to carry out the spring planting while the crop was being taken off. Pressures on the estate labor force, particularly on the first gang of field hands, increased, and their numbers had to be supplemented by workers accustomed to being in the second gang where the tasks were lighter. The shortage in numbers of workers was aggravated by demographic developments; in the rebellion area by 1832 there were only 92 men to every 100 women.[3] Increasing numbers of the first and second gang, the cream of the estate labor force, were women.

The difficulties created by a dwindling and increasingly female labor force were further compounded by the fact that an increasing proportion of the slaves was of mixed ancestry. The tradition that colored slaves were superior to blacks and had a right to positions of privilege and authority within the estate structure was an important element in stabilizing the slave system. Gradations of color synchronized with gradations of rank, and expectations helped to keep the slaves divided among themselves. As the slave population diminished, the growing demand for field hands undermined the colored slaves' claim to privileges. The immediate hardships and miseries induced by drought and hunger deepened the slaves' disillusion with a system that was increasingly unsatisfactory to black field hands and colored artisans, supervisors, and domestics. Both categories were under pressure: more work, harder work, and the loss, or threatened loss, of privilege gave the slaves first-hand knowledge of the incipient breakdown of the traditional estate regime and made the news from England in 1831 more than a novelty to excite animated discussion at the weekly market or stir a small-scale riot. Their experience made freedom a necessary alternative to the reality they knew.

Political developments within the island had also broken the whites' exclusive monopoly of political power. In December, 1830, the Assembly was forced to concede the demands of the free colored and black population in alliance with the imperial government for equal rights with the whites. It was in these circumstances that news of the emancipation campaign, launched in 1831, reached the slaves.

It stirred an unprecedented level of hope and excitement. The Colonial Office, mindful of the impact of the 1823 debates on slavery in the British West Indies, supplied West Indian governors in June, 1831, with a royal proclamation to quiet signs of unrest. But the Jamaican whites, by the force of their reaction to the threat of abolition, magnified and intensified for the slave population the significance of the 1831 campaign. The 1823 proposals for the reform of the slave system had roused fierce resentment, but the reactions of 1823 among whites already smarting from concessions to the free blacks and coloreds paled into insignificance compared with the rage created by the threat of abolition. The whites held a series of public protest meetings throughout the island between July and November. Inflammatory speeches were made and duly published in the newspapers; armed revolt was advocated, and the possibility of securing assistance from the United States was openly discussed.[4] Plans were made to set up a new governing body, independent of the crown, consisting of delegates from the parish meetings to meet concurrently with the Assembly in November, 1831. This scheme had no immediate results,[5] but the Assembly, meeting in November, marked its unrelenting opposition to any mitigation of the slave system by refusing almost unanimously to discuss a proposal to abolish flogging for women, a reform introduced in the crown colonies in 1824. The governor, the Earl of Belmore, commented that the public meetings seemed calculated "to disturb the minds of the slaves,"[6] but he made no effort to restrain them, and the royal proclamation was not published until December, after the rebellion had virtually begun.

The intensity and extravagance of the whites' reaction to abolition conveyed the promise of freedom more clearly to more of the slaves than were ever affected by the 1823 campaign. Comparatively few of the slaves understood the precise nature of political developments in England and Jamaica, but the gist of the political situation was translated into easily remembered and amended anecdotes, which circulated endlessly among the population. One slave heard his master say, "The king is going to give us free: but he hoped that all his friends will be of his mind and spill their blood first." It was rumored that James Grignon, well-known St. James attorney, and his friends were "making a studiation" to keep the women and children in slavery while they took out the men and shot them like pigeons. Reports of the intentions of the "high buckra" were confirmed by the conduct of their underlings; Baptist members told Knibb, "When Busha [i.e. overseer] and bookkeeper flog us they say we are going to be free and before it comes they will get it out of us." The missionaries reported in July from Kingston that "the expectation of the slaves has been raised to the very highest point with references to freedom." The same month, on the other side of the island, Knibb wrote from Falmouth: ". . . the slaves believe they are soon to be free, and are anxiously waiting till King William sends them their free paper."[7]

Political discontent was expressed in the network of independent religious meetings and, in the last months before the rebellion, overflowed into the mission churches. In the north coast parishes there was what the missionaries called "a great outpouring of the Spirit"; the chapels were crowded and membership figures swelled.[8] But the numbers included members of the independent sects drawn by the promise of freedom to listen to the white men expected to announce it. The missionaries, in their conflict with the planters, had begun to emerge not only as teachers, chapel builders, and leaders of their congregations but as men in contact with forces in England capable of giving freedom to the slaves. It seems probable that some missionaries had themselves drawn the slaves' attention to the abolition campaign and in such a way as to convey their sympathy with it. William Knibb had voiced a question in the minds of many when he wrote to the B.M.S. in July, 1831, "While you are exerting all your energies at home, ought we to sit all day idle?"[9] It is certain that in the atmosphere of excited expectation in which rebellion plans were made, even customary texts quoted by the missionaries were given added value and interpreted as manifestations of support. After the rebellion the tide receded, and the missionaries concluded that "many churches and congregations had been swelled by a host anticipating freedom, who, now that their hopes were disappointed, fell away. It was common for a backslider to answer an exhortation thus: 'It is no use minister; what can church and prayers do for we again? . . . ' "[10]

Out of this political ferment leaders emerged who directed the widespread excitement and discontent into action. The most outstanding rebel leader was Sam Sharpe. Sharpe's development reflected fully the political impact of mission teaching. He was one of the small minority of urban slaves, a domestic highly regarded by his owners, working in Montego Bay. Intelligent, ambitious, and not overworked, Sharpe made himself literate and found in the mission church both an outlet and a stimulant for his ambition. He was an eloquent and passionate teacher and became a leader, entrusted with the spiritual care of a class of converts. Sharpe was not content to remain a subordinate in the mission church and became a "Daddy," or "Ruler," among the Native Baptists. Sharpe was convinced from his own reading of the Bible that the slaves were entitled to freedom; this conviction, together with his knowledge of the emancipation campaign in England, led him to believe that the slaves must organize to overthrow the system.[11]

Sharpe naturally turned to associates in the Baptist church and among the Native Baptists, men of his own stamp: George Taylor, like Sharpe, was a town worker, a saddler in Montego Bay, and a member of the Baptist church. The rest were headmen or skilled workers on the estates, predominantly creoles rather than Africans, who combined attendance at the Baptist chapel with leadership positions in the independent sects. John Tharpe was head driver at Catadupa; he attended the Baptist chapel and as Father Tharpe held his own night meetings.[12] The other leaders included Dove of Belvedere, a large estate in Hanover, Johnson of Retrieve Pen, St. James, and Gardner of Greenwich in Westmoreland, recruited from one of the centers of independent preaching reported in 1825, which included Seven Rivers and Hazelymph estate.[13]

These leaders were based on properties that had been exposed to missionary preaching and its informal offshoots for more than a generation. There were the Baptist and Wesleyan chapels in Montego Bay, the Moravian mission at Irwin Hill nearby, and Presbyterian missions at Hampden and Cornwall. Attached to the missions was a round of out-stations and estates, the most important of which were the Baptist stations to the southeast at Crooked Spring (first established by Moses Baker) and Salters Hill and the Wesleyan station at Ramble, over the border in Hanover. In the interior the independent sects were established at Seven Rivers, Greenwich, and Hazelymph, where Sharpe himself, though based in Montego Bay, was a familiar figure.[14] These were the "Baptist people on the mountain" who spread the belief that freedom had come.[15]

The network of religious connections gave the rebels contacts with the headmen, drivers, and skilled workers on some of the largest estates in St. James and Hanover, including Bellfield, Adelphi, Moor Park, Crooked Spring, Unity Hall, Hazelymph, Duckett Spring and Cambridge in St. James, and Argyle, Alexandra, Golden Grove (scenes of the 1824 disturbances), Great Valley, Flint River, Welcome, and Knocklava in Hanover. The whites were chagrined to observe that "the head and confidential slaves, and consequently the most intelligent, have been the most active rebels."[16]

Contemporaries labeled the rebellion "the Baptist War," a title that pointed the finger at the Baptist missionaries as agents provacateur and reflected the predominance of Baptist connections among the rebel leaders and consequently among the rebel body. Of ninety-nine slaves eventually court-martialed at Montego Bay, no less than twenty-five were allegedly connected with the Baptist mission or the Native Baptists. The Baptist war, however, was essentially the Native Baptist war; its leaders shaped mission teaching to their own ends and used mission organization for their own purposes. The Baptist missionaries as such, like colleagues in other denominations, were ancillary to the development of the rebel cause. The Baptists' historic connection with the Black Baptist churches founded by Leile and Baker in the eighteenth century had meant that, throughout the slavery period, there was a stronger tendency for the Baptist mission members to enjoy, like Sharpe, dual status as mission members and as Native Baptists. Arguably, therefore, the slaves had higher expectations of active assistance from Knibb and Burchell than from any other missionary. But it was primarily the historic connection that identified the Baptist missionaries in particular with the rebellion, rather than any significant difference in what they taught. Missionaries of all denominations were both essential to the rebel cause and ancillary to it; leadership lay with the slaves they inspired and trained.

General Ruler Sam Sharpe, "director of the whole and preacher to the rebels,"[17] claimed in the account he gave the Wesleyan missionary Henry Bleby, who had several conversations with him in jail, that he planned not armed rebellion but what would today be called mass passive resistance. After the Christmas holidays, when the cane harvest was due to begin, the slaves were to sit down and refuse to work until their masters acknowledged that they were free men and agreed to pay them wages. Sharpe expected that the whites would try to intimidate the strikers by shooting hostages as examples, but the slaves were not expected to fight back, simply to continue passive resistance.[18] Sharpe, however, had evidently also made plans for armed revolt. Some of his aides, the Baptist leaders Johnson, Gardner, and Dove, took the title of colonel, and lesser ranks were captains. Sharpe was said to have timed the rebellion for Christmas so that, with the whites away in the towns, the slaves could easily collect guns from the estates[19] to supplement the machetes used normally for cane and grass cutting. Certainly the Black Regiment was formed, equipped with guns, and, some observers claimed, distinguished by a blue and brown uniform, and the military found caches of arms in slave huts on Ginger Hill estate in St. Elizabeth and on Catadupa between Lucea and Montego Bay.[20]

The rebellion plans were promulgated at religious meetings wherever the leaders had contacts among mission members of all denominations and among the Native Baptists. The practice was to invite likely supporters to one of the regular prayer meetings on the estate; after the meeting a selected few were asked to remain behind, and Sharpe or one of his aides explained the plan and tried to persuade all present to swear on the Bible not to work after Christmas. Sharpe himself was a speaker who had "the feelings and passions of his hearers completely at his command"; when he spoke against slavery, they were "wrought up almost to a state of madness."[21]

The arguments included the notion, current during the Jamaican disturbances in December, 1823, and June, 1824, and in the 1823 Demerara rebellion, that freedom had already been granted and was being withheld by the whites. Sharpe, though too well informed to believe this himself, was said to have told his followers that the legislation had passed in March, 1831. As a natural extension of this idea, it was also said that, since the slaves were claiming their legal rights, the king's troops would not fight against them and might even lend support. During the rebellion some of the slaves believed that the "black sand," or gunpowder, landed from a naval ship at Savanna-la-Mar was for their use.[22]

The main body of arguments, however, related to religion; Christianity became a positive justification for action. Sharpe and his aides proclaimed the natural equality of men and denied, on the authority of the Bible, the right of the white man to hold the black in bondage. The text "No man can serve two masters," persistently quoted by Sharpe, became a slogan among the slaves. To protest against slavery was a matter of "assisting their brethren in the work of the Lord . . . this was not the work of man alone, but they had assistance from God."[23] The protest seemed to the slaves to be sanctioned by the authority of the missionaries themselves, for they believed that the missionaries favored freedom and had no problem interpreting what they were told in their own way. Sharpe's pastor, Burchell of the Montego Bay Baptist mission, who had left for England in May, 1831, was made in his absence a political leader. Messages attributed to him circulated among the slaves: that he would be a pillar of iron to them, but they must shed no blood, for life was sweet, easy to take away, but very hard to give. The more determined believed he was bringing out boatloads of arms.[24]

Preparations for the Christmas rebellion probably followed on the white population's parish meetings and started in the autumn of 1831, in the interval between the arduous work of cane holing and the cane harvest. Given the network of religious meetings and a readymade following among the slaves, Sharpe and his aides were able during that time to spread their influence through St. James, parts of Hanover and Trelawney, and into Westmoreland, St. Elizabeth, and Manchester, an area of 600 square miles.

The missionaries learned of the rebellion plans when they met their congregations for the Christmas services and, at the eleventh hour, made every effort to keep the slaves from any form of violence or disobedience. George Blyth, a Presbyterian who had just returned from England, strove to convince his congregation at Hampden that he had the latest news on abolition and argued against rebellion on grounds of principle and policy, pointing to "the bloodshed, anarchy and injury to religion which would be the consequence of insurrection . . . I also described to them the great improbability of the slaves obtaining their liberty by such means on account of the want of unanimity, arms, etc." On December 27, at the opening of a new Baptist chapel at Salters Hill, St. James, Knibb warned the people: "I learn that some wicked persons have persuaded you that the King has made you free. Hear me, I love your souls.—I would not tell you a lie for the world. What you have been told is false—false as hell can make it. I entreat you not to believe it, but go to your work as usual. . . . If you have any love to Jesus Christ, to religion, to your ministers, to those kind friends in England who have given money to help you build this chapel, be not led away by wicked men." A day-long Wesleyan meeting at Ramble in Hanover, on December 26, admonished the people that religion meant to love God and men.[25] The slaves were profoundly disappointed. When it became clear that the missionaries did not identify themselves with the cause, could in no way be regarded as allies, and were solely concerned with law and order, they became sullen, resentful, and then openly furious. Blyth's congregation was "not only disappointed, but offended" with him; at Salters Hill the Baptists were "perfectly furious and would not listen to . . . dissuasions from engaging in such a perilous enterprise. . . . They accused their ministers of deserting them, and threatened to take revenge upon them."[26]

The slaves' rage against the system and their hopes of freedom in fact betrayed them into giving the white population warning of their intentions. A week before Christmas there was a labor dispute on Salt Spring near Montego Bay. The attorney for the estate, James Grignon, well known among the slaves as an opponent of abolition and who later proved an incompetent and cowardly military commander, prompted the trouble. On his way to the estate he met one of the slave women on the road, accused her of stealing sugar cane, and flogged her on the spot. On reaching the estate he ordered the head driver to flog her again, but the woman was the driver's wife and he refused. The second driver backed him up and Grignon sent for two constables from Montego Bay to discipline the offenders. When the constables arrived, "the whole body of slaves on the plantation resisted the constables, menacing them with their cutlasses"; they removed the constables' pistols and then, when the militia arrived, absconded to the woods.[27]

Corporate action by the slaves was extremely rare, and to challenge the whites and remove their weapons was almost unprecedented. The magistrates immediately recalled the Argyle war, mobilized the militia, and sent for troops from Falmouth. Belmore, confronted by news of this disturbance and similar reports from other parts of the island, sent warships to Montego Bay, Port Antonio, and Black River and belatedly issued the proclamation from England received the previous June. On December 23, in Trelawney, the trash house was fired on one estate and the slaves went on strike on two others. Receiving this news on December 28, the governor in council decided to send two companies of the 84th Regiment to Montego Bay. These troops were ready to embark when news of the rebellion reached Spanish Town. A further 300 men and artillery were allocated to the rebellion area, and martial law was immediately declared.[28]

The signal for the rebellion was the firing of Kensington, St. James, on the evening of December 27, 1831. That morning the owner of Kensington had been warned by a neighbor of the slaves' plan; the properties to be fired were said to be numbered and Kensington was first because, set on a hill, it would serve as a beacon.[29]

As the estates went up in flames, the western interior militia retreated from their barracks at Shettlewood to Old Montpelier estate. There, on December 28, they confronted the rebels' military core, the Black Regiment, about 150 strong with fifty guns among them, assisted by slaves recruited from the surrounding estates and under the command of the self-styled Colonel Johnson of Retrieve estate. The militia was forced to retreat to Montego Bay. The Black Regiment lost Johnson, but a new leader, Colonel Gardner, took over. Elated with success, the slaves carried rebellion into the hills, rousing support, burning properties, and setting off a trail of fires through the Great River Valley in Westmoreland and St. Elizabeth. The country between Montego Bay, Lucea, and Savanna-la-Mar was in rebel hands.

Colonel Robert Gardner made his estate, Greenwich, the established center of Native Baptist preaching, one of the headquarters of the rebellion. From Greenwich a sketchy organization held sway over the surrounding country. On rebel estates slaves were organized into companies, each responsible for guarding its boundaries and holding allegiance to Gardner at Greenwich. Other rebel leaders, also Baptist members, notably Captain Dehany operating in the Salters Hill area and Captain Tharpe in the interior, created similar centers. Their work was supplemented by self-appointed leaders who organized their own estates, or roamed the country collecting recruits to resist the whites, destroying property, proclaiming freedom, and blocking roads against the military.[30]

There appears to have been no cooperation among these various groups; they were short of arms, they had no experience in military operations, and in their contacts with the soldiers they showed none of the skill in guerrilla warfare that had characterized the Maroon wars. The scene of a typical skirmish between the rebels and their trained opponents was described by the Wesleyan missionary Bleby: "The insurgent slaves, with little judgement had posted themselves on the side of a hill commanding the narrow mountain road; and when the soldiers came in sight, they discharged upon them a volley of musketry and stones. . . . They then ran and attempted to gain the brow of the hill, but in so doing exposed themselves fully to the unerring aim of the military. . . . Sixteen bodies, dragged into the road, were putrefying in the sun when we passed by . . . carrion crows were feeding upon them."[31] The troops sent to Montego Bay found little difficulty in clearing the roads, re-establishing communications, and dispersing the rebel forces; by the first week in January armed rebellion was virtually at an end.

Strike action was effectively organized in some areas; in Trelawney, for example, the slaves on Carlton estate "sat down" firmly after Christmas. The Presbyterian missionary Waddell went to the estate to persuade them they were not yet free, but they accused him of being paid by the magistrates to deceive them. The strikers were equally firm in dealing with a gang of rebels who invaded the estate; they did not allow them to burn the property or plunder the stores, arguing that if they were to be free, they would want rum and sugar for themselves.[32] Successful strike action demanded the cooperation of large numbers of estates, but it proved impossible to organize widespread passive resistance with the help of only a few aides and a proliferation of meetings where the converted kissed the Bible and swore allegiance. A strong nucleus of strike leaders working with the headman or one of the drivers on each plantation, with weeks of careful instruction for all the slaves on the precise form the strike was to take, would have been necessary before there was hope of success. In the circumstances the authorities, instead of being confronted by thousands of slaves over a wide area refusing to work, had to deal only with isolated groups; pacification consisted of forcing the slaves to choose between martyrdom and submission. On Georgia estate, Trelawney, there was determined and well-disciplined opposition under the leadership of the head driver, Edward Grant. The slave village was subjected to a daybreak attack by the militia using a fieldpiece; when the people still refused to move, they were dragged out one by one, and one man was shot as an example.[33] Sharpe had warned his followers that the whites would try to intimidate them by shooting hostages, but only the consciousness of being part of a solid strike resistance involving hundreds of estates could have given the slaves the confidence to accept the necessity of such martyrs. In the circumstances they were intimidated and returned to work.

The rebels' rudimentary organization did not reach all the estates in the area, and many slaves simply joined in the rebellion spontaneously after the fires had started. On these properties conflict developed between the law-abiding slaves and those who claimed their freedom, a conflict that reflected the divisions institutionalized among the slaves by estate organization. On Burnt Ground Pen, St. James, for example, the head driver tried to prevent the buildings from being burned, but the slaves followed the lead of a man fresh from three months' punishment in the workhouse and lit the fires. At Moor Park, however, the headman was with the rebels, and the slaves there prevented the house women from defending the property.[34] On estates where the rebel cause found no representative, confusion reigned. The slaves were intimidated by the fires and by the appearance of rebel bands wanting to loot and burn their property. Some left their homes and went into hiding in the woods; others kept their nerve and organized guards to keep out the rioters, and in some cases, like the estates observed by a missionary in Hanover, they carried on with the cane harvest, "making sugar and rum as good as they usually do without any white supervision."[35]

A small minority of the slaves seized the opportunity to distinguish themselves by faithful service in the hope of reward. Henry Plummer of Anchovy Bottom, an estate with 239 slaves, was promoted to head driver for conducting himself with "great propriety" while his fellows burned the house and works. A slave from Leyden estate was even more fortunate; having saved the overseer's furniture and given the lead to a group who "fought boldly against the rebels," he was exempted from labor. There were even a few slaves who joined the militia. But such shining examples of fidelity were rare; in the whole county of Cornwall, embracing St. James, Hanover, Trelawney, Westmoreland, and St. Elizabeth, contemporaries calculated that the proportion of faithful slaves rewarded by the Assembly was one in every 1,465 of the population.[36]

In St. James and Hanover the proprietors claimed that more than £1 million of damages had been done. The destruction engulfed a high proportion of the largest properties with the greatest number of slaves. In St. James, of twenty-seven properties with 201 slaves or more, twenty-one were destroyed; of fifty-one properties with 101 to 200 slaves, almost half, twenty-four, were destroyed. Losses in St. James amounted to forty-five estates, fourteen pens, and fifty-three plantations. The destruction involved in almost every case the great house and, on the estates, the sugar works; the slave villages in many cases were destroyed by the militia in the aftermath of the rebellion.[37]

For the slave population as a whole the rebellion, though sketchily organized and rapidly suppressed, raised their hopes and their confidence to the very highest pitch. The rebels recruited the energetic and daring wherever they went; the advice of the old, the cautious, and the frightened, who remembered the price of rebellion, was ignored. For the first time the slaves felt their strength and rejoiced in it. "We have worked enough already," they cried on one estate to a proprietor and a missionary who tried to persuade them slavery was not ended. "The life we live is . . . the life of a dog. We wont be slaves no more; we wont lift hoe no more; we wont take flog no more. We free now, we free now; no more slaves again."[38] In that moment, when they held freedom in their hands, their hope for the future was unbounded and their confidence in themselves was total.

The failure of the rebellion left the slaves exposed to white vengeance. The rebels had behaved with restraint; they had fought only the whites who attacked them, while whites who offered no opposition met with no harm. At the fringe of the St. Elizabeth rebellion the overseer of Ginger Hill estate, though threatened with death, was required only to sign his own resignation.[39] Throughout the whole rebellion there were only two acts of violence against the whites. The slaves' conduct was remarked on by contemporaries; a Presbyterian missionary wrote, "Had the masters when they got the upperhand been as forbearing, as tender of their slaves' lives as their slaves had been of theirs, it would have been to their lasting honour, and to the permanent advantage of the colony."[40]

The military authorities, represented by Sir Willoughby Cotton at the official level, also showed restraint. On his arrival at Montego Bay, Cotton issued a proclamation that gave free pardon to all slaves who returned voluntarily to their estates and released a hundred rebel prisoners to circulate it.[41] For the overseers and attorneys turned militiamen, however, as the missionary's comment suggests, pacification involved not only restoring order but vengeance for their losses and humiliation. The militia, after the defeat at Old Montpelier, had been pinned in Montego Bay waiting for the military to arrive, watching estates go up in flames, anxiously patrolling the streets for fear of rebel incursion, their women and children bestowed for safety on ships in the harbor. Pacification took place amid the charred and blackened ruins of a countryside that, a few days before, was ripe for harvest.

The militia were bent on vengeance, and among them were individuals whose rancor approached insanity. All the blacks were their enemies and they raided the estates bent on killing and destroying. On the rebel estates the slaves' houses, gardens, every vestige of their property, were destroyed; when the militia approached an estate the slaves took to the woods, and "their flight was regarded as sufficient proof of guilt and they were shot at and often shot down."[42] Suspected ringleaders were shot out of hand, despite the proclamation. On an estate in Trelawney all the slaves had been pardoned by Cotton in person just an hour before, when a militia detachment under the command of the estate's attorney, John Gunn, arrived. The slaves were again called out, and the attorney turned lieutenant ordered the second driver of the gang shot. On this occasion the attorney was court-martialed, though acquitted; the court-martial was unique, the execution not unusual. The Wesleyan missionary Bleby witnessed the militia arrive at an estate where the slaves, in accordance with the proclamation, were at work. Two men, a boy, and a woman were taken from their work and sent for trial in Montego Bay, where the men were condemned and shot.[43] Such activities make nonsense of the official figure for slaves killed in the rebellion, 307 compared with fourteen whites. As a Presbyterian missionary commented, "In the rage for making examples [the colony] lost many able hands it could ill spare."[44]

The courts-martial, hastily constituted of militiamen on the warrant of the commander-in-chief, were equally ruthless. At Montego Bay ninety-nine slaves were tried, of whom eighty-one were executed; in the slave courts, which operated when martial law was lifted, eighty-one were tried, of whom thirty-nine were executed. In all, 626 slaves were tried, of whom 312 were executed.[45] The trials at Montego Bay, where the greatest number of slaves were tried, followed a regular pattern; it was established that the slaves on a particular estate were rebellious, the prisoner was proved to belong to this estate, and a witness was found to claim the prisoner had been seen to commit a rebellious act or even to have heard him claim to have committed one. Witnesses were occasionally condemned by interested attorneys and owners as "great rascals," "liars," or "notorious runaways," and the trial records suggest they often had private grievances to pay off or were turning witness to keep themselves out of the dock. Prisoners were executed for killing and hamstringing estate stock, offenses usually punished by whipping and workhouse sentences.

The courts made no attempt to assess the degree of guilt, or even to distinguish between prisoners who had taken some sort of leading role in estate disturbances and those merely caught up in events. The missionaries knew of cases where slaves had acted under provocation or were condemned apparently to settle private grievances. Blyth exerted himself to save a Presbyterian candidate who had complained bitterly before the rebellion of the overseers' harsh conduct, but he was found guilty of helping to cut a bridge and breaking into the estate stores and executed. The Wesleyan missionary Murray saw a church leader executed because he believed his religious convictions made him "obnoxious to those over him."[46]

The executions bore final witness to white vengeance. In Montego Bay

> the gibbet erected in the public square in the centre of the town was seldom without occupants, during the day, for many weeks. Generally four, seldom less than three, were hung at once. The bodies remained, stiffening in the breeze, till the court martial had provided another batch of victims. . . . [The executioner] would ascend a ladder and with his knife sever the ropes by which the poor creatures were suspended and let them fall to the ground. Other victims would then be . . . suspended in their places and cut down in their turn . . . the whole heap of bodies remaining just as they fell until the workhouse negroes came in the evening with carts and took them away, to cast them into a pit dug for the purpose, a little distance out of town.

Some of the prisoners were sent home to be hanged; at Lucea the condemned men were put into an ox cart, their arms pinioned, ropes around their necks, and white caps on their heads. "In this way they were carried up, under a strong guard, into the midst of the burned properties, distances of twelve to thirty miles, and the sentence was carried into effect on the estates as they successively arrived at them. On each of the melancholy occasions the unfortunate men met their death with a fortitude and cool deliberation that astonished all who beheld them."[47]

The executions bore witness not only to white vengeance but to the spirit that informed the rebellion. The blacks were courageous and confident of their cause in the face of death. Every rebel, leaders and led, walked to the scaffold "calm and undismayed . . . as if they had been proceeding to their daily toil . . . with the dignified bearing of men untroubled as to the justice of their cause they yielded themselves to their doom." Sharpe himself earned the highest accolade possible for a rebel leader; it was said, "He was such a man . . . as was likely, nay, certain, had he been set free, to commence another struggle for freedom,"[48] and it was certain the slaves would have joined him.

The rebellion, though unsuccessful, marked a significant stage in the political development of Jamaica. The slaves did not rebel, as their predecessors had done, in the hope of escaping from the plantations to build a new society for themselves in the mountain recesses of the island.

Nor did their religious inspiration lead them to expect a new society founded by divine revelation. They rebelled to change the society they knew and claim for themselves the right to wages for work on the plantations. They wanted freedom not as outlaws, not as the grateful recipients of a gift from supernatural forces, but as individuals whose rights were sanctioned by law.

To achieve this end, they undertook to redefine the authority of the planters and defeat the forces that protected them. Organized repression had to be met by organized resistance. The network of mission stations and their attendant satellites of sectarian groups became the mechanism for such mobilization. The rebel leaders developed two tactics: armed resistance to the militia and the military, and strike action against plantation management.

The aims and methods of the slave rebels brought to fruition the complex stresses to which they had been exposed. Sam Sharpe, his aides, and many of his supporters represented those elements among the slave population whose concept of their rights, rooted in plantation organization, had been expanded by experience in the mission churches. They transposed the claim to religious freedom, staked by Henry Williams, into a claim to free status. This development, latent with threat to the established order, was encouraged not only by the ambiguities of mission teaching and organization but by the living example of the missionaries as men introducing changes into slave society and claiming new rights for themselves and their converts. The missionaries' example was reinforced by the activities of the free colored and black population, whose campaign for civil rights eventually succeeded. Then, in the difficult economic circumstances of 1830–31, news spread of powerful friends in England who demanded from the Assembly changes in plantation discipline and proclaimed the necessity of abolition.

These circumstances made it conceivable that the slaves could achieve, in the teeth of white opposition, legally sanctioned rights. The idea gained immediacy from the connection the slaves assumed between the missionaries and the abolitionists, an idea encapsulated in the pleasing and plausible expectation that the Baptist missionary Thomas Burchell, expected to return from England at Christmas 1831, would bring the free paper with him. The claim to freedom, formulated by rebel leaders and communicated to the mass of the slaves in the western parishes through the network of religious meetings, generated such a spirit of solidarity that preparations for the rebellion spawned no informers.

The aims and methods of the slave rebels pushed Jamaica into the revolutionary mainstream of the time, the struggle for individual liberty sanctioned by law. They made the first step on the long, devious road to universal suffrage and national independence. In so doing, they took their place with the slaves who made the Haitian revolution, marking the point in the history of the Caribbean where its subject populations made the principles embodied in the ideology of their oppressors into a weapon to use against them.[49]

The rebellion, of course, confirmed the whites' oldest and deepest suspicion of the missions, that they undermined the slave system. Connections between the missions and the rebels were quickly established. The first captured rebels claimed to be Baptists. Burchell was named a leader, or was quoted to justify the belief that they were free. The Baptists' practice of giving tickets to "inquirers," as well as to members of their churches, meant that Baptist influence was traced to many slaves killed by the militia and to many rebel estates where tickets were found in the slave huts.[50] Extremists were convinced that the missions were guilty of direct complicity with the rebels. The newspapers, in particular the traditionally antisectarian *Courant,* kept up a barrage of accusations and threatened lurid vengeance on them; they were to be hanged rather than shot: shooting was "too honourable a death." The missions' traditional supporters like Richard Barrett, custos of St. James, and Henry Cox, custos of St. Ann, considered them free from "intentional guilt" but believed their teaching had been "perverted by ill-disposed slaves" and that mission organization, by creating islandwide connections among the people, exposed the country to periodic rebellions. These patrons also concluded that there was no place for the missionaries in the island. They did not deserve to hang, but they were expected to leave.[51]

While the whites united in opposition, important elements in the free colored and free black population rallied, in their customary way, to the missions' support. At this juncture, however, their support carried new political weight, since they had achieved political parity with the whites. To this point their political dividends had been limited to victories in two bye-elections. The crisis created by the rebellion, however, gave them a unique opportunity to demonstrate, as fully fledged Jamaican citizens, their power and importance in the society. Under the leadership of Edward Jordon, an informal, pro-mission, antislavery party played a significant role in the struggle to reopen the missions and, as will be seen in the following chapter, to make possible the peaceful achievement of emancipation. In the immediate aftermath of the rebellion they rallied in numbers to save some of the chapels from destruction, and Edward Jordon used the *Watchman* to counter the antisectarian *Courant*. John Manderson, free colored planter, merchant, and magistrate of Montego Bay, stood bail for the missionaries under arrest and exerted himself in every way on their behalf.[52]

In the immediate aftermath of the rebellion the missionaries needed all the moral and physical support they could get. Enmity focused primarily on the Baptists and Wesleyans, whose missions dominated the north coast rebel area; the Moravians, with numerous missions in the southwest parishes, also fell under suspicion. Only the Presbyterians, whose supposed connection with the Church of Scotland had always won them more respect from the planters than other sects enjoyed, were able to retain the confidence of the white population. The Baptists in charge of missions at Falmouth, Lucea, Stewart Town, and Savanna-la-Mar, Knibb, Abbot, Whitehorne, and Gardner, were arrested in the first week of January and then released on bail. The Reverend Thomas Burchell, who arrived in Montego Bay harbor from England on January 7, 1832, was confined to ship on the orders of Commodore A. Farquahar, commander of *H.M.S. Blanche*. Baptists at stations outside the rebellion area were also kept under surveillance; at St. Ann's Bay the missionary reported daily at the courthouse throughout martial law, and at Anotto Bay in St. Mary the missionary, Barlow, was arrested and kept in confinement under threat of court-martial until January 20. The Wesleyan missionary from Falmouth, Box, was arrested in Spanish Town on his way to the district meeting and sent to jail on January 9.[53] The Moravian missionary Pfeiffer, from New Eden in Manchester parish, was arrested on January 7.[54]

The missionaries' first reaction to the rebellion, as their lectures and sermons to the slaves at the Christmas services demonstrated, was to identify themselves with the forces of law and order and give them what assistance they could. Some served in the militia and the Wesleyan and Presbyterian missionaries in Lucea even took part in an expedition pacifying the estates.[55] The missionaries out on bail at Montego Bay helped the rectors of Westmoreland and St. James to collect confessions from slave prisoners, and one Baptist missionary, Francis Gardner, turned informer on the rebels. Gardner set out from Savanna-la-Mar on January 3 to meet Burchell, who was daily expected at Montego Bay, and on the borders of Westmoreland he was captured by rebels and held prisoner for several hours. His captors made it clear that, as a missionary, he enjoyed a special status among them and claimed they had only stopped his chaise because they mistook him for a "buckra." They told him, "This no parson hat, this 'busha' [overseer] hat. You should travel in black hat, and gown and then we know you and let you pass."[56] On the orders of Colonel Gardner at Greenwich estate he was allowed to return home, but his first concern on arrival was to go straight to the courthouse and lay all the information he had picked up before the magistrates.

The association of church members with the rebellion was generally established, and every mission had some members caught up in the trials and executions; at Montego Bay, for example, six Wesleyans were executed.[57] But there was no proof of the missionaries' direct complicity with the rebels; the only missionary tried under martial law, the Moravian Pfeiffer, charged with enticing and persuading "sundry slaves to join and engage in a traitrous rebellion," was triumphantly acquitted.[58] The other arrested missionaries, the Wesleyan Box and the Baptist Barlow, were released without trial. The missionaries, however, were warned by Richard Barrett that neither legal exoneration nor demonstrations of loyalty would placate Jamaican opinion;[59] his assessment proved accurate. Once the rebel slaves were crushed and order was restored, the whites turned on them in vengeance. A wave of antisectarian violence swept the western parishes; chapels were destroyed, leading Baptist missionaries were put on trial, and an antisectarian, anti–British government party, the Colonial Church Union, was founded to drive them off the island.

The destruction of the chapels began in Montego Bay on February 6, 1832, the day after the militia returned from pacifying the estates and martial law was withdrawn. The magistrates were warned by John Roby, an English customs collector and friend of the missionaries, that the chapel was threatened, but no protection was given. Within a few hours the chapel, situated within 300 yards of the courthouse, was ripped to pieces. The mob was composed of a cross-section of white society; bookkeepers and overseers took their place beside attorneys and proprietors, some of whom were magistrates.[60] It was augmented by free colored small cultivators from the countryside driven to take refuge in Montego Bay, whose crops and property had been destroyed like the planters', either by the rebels or by the militia, who suspected their complicity with the slaves. While the Baptist chapel was being destroyed, free colored church members and sympathizers rallied to protect the Wesleyan chapel and, with the permission of the custos, formed an armed guard.[61] The mob's violence suggested that the missionaries' lives were in danger, and, again through the good offices of the customs officer John Roby, they were given refuge aboard a naval ship.

On the following day the Wesleyan and Baptist chapels in Falmouth and Stewart Town were destroyed by a mob led by St. Ann militiamen. From these two centers destruction spread: the Baptist chapels at Lucea, Savanna-la-Mar, and Ridgeland were destroyed by the militia. In St. Ann's parish, Brown's Town and Rio Bueno Baptist chapels were destroyed, followed by the Baptist and Wesleyan chapels in St. Ann's Bay, where effigies of the missionaries were hung in the chapel yard. The St. Ann's Bay mob moved on to Ocho Rios, burning the house used by the Baptist mission and the Wesleyan chapels there and at Oracabessa and Botany Bay. Subsequently, two more Baptist chapels, at Green Island in Hanover and at Hayes Savannnah in Vere, were burned.[62] In small towns and country districts the free population was not numerous enough to provide a defense; but in Kingston, the largest free colored and black community in the island, which formed more than half the membership of the Wesleyan church, rallied in such numbers that they not only saved the chapels but deterred the whites from forming a branch of the C.C.U.

While the destruction of the chapels was taking place, fresh efforts were made to convict Burchell and Gardner of direct complicity in the rebellion. Elements in the white population were desperate to find a focus for their enmity, scapegoats for the real political problems the rebellion presented; Burchell, the minister of Sharpe's church whose name had been widely used by the rebels, made a particularly appropriate sacrifice. The Baptist missionaries, realizing Burchell's danger, arranged that on his release from bail on February 10 he should leave for America, simply transferring himself from the British naval vessel to an American ship. The rumor that he was to leave prompted the attempt to convict him. A warrant was issued for his arrest on the strength of a deposition by a free colored man, Samuel Stennett, who claimed to be a leader in the Baptist church in Montego Bay and swore that Burchell had told the church leaders to tell the country slaves they must fight and pray for freedom. Burchell was taken ashore and sent to jail. The scene that greeted him as the boat landed showed how wise his decision to leave had been: "Had I never been in Montego Bay before," he wrote, "I must have supposed myself among cannibals, or . . . the uncivilized tribes of Central Africa. Some cried out, 'Have his blood:' others, 'Shoot him:' others, 'Hang him.' " The Baptist missionary Francis Gardner, whose contact with the rebels, in spite of the fact that it was dutifully detailed to the magistrates, exposed him to suspicion, was arrested on the strength of the same deposition.[63]

It was this white backlash that the Reverend George W. Bridges, crowning his career as an ideologue with a burst of political activism, organized into the Colonial Church Union. Bridges was keenly aware of the direction of political events in England; the elections of December, 1831, threatened parliamentary reform and a Whig government committed to the abolition of slavery. Bridges attempted to use the antisectarianism roused by the rebellion as the basis for mobilizing the whites to oppose abolition, if necessary, by force.

The C.C.U., formed as soon as the rebellion was suppressed, identified three enemies; first were the missionaries, "the rifles of the assassin brigands who are so expert at picking off our best men," referring to the magistrates dismissed as a result of the investigations. The union was to expel the missionaries and coerce its second enemy, the free colored and black pro-mission party, into relinquishing their support; unionists were expected to give no money or employment to any "press or person who shall advocate the hateful cause of the dissenters," meaning Jordon's *Watchman and Jamaica Free Press*. The third enemy was the imperial government whose "unnatural conduct" threatened the slave system, and unionists had to be prepared for armed resistance; "let every member of the Colonial Church Union think that as in battle, the field may be won by his own arm, so in the present."[64]

The union in St. Ann, which was the model for the rest of the island, demonstrated the extent to which the rebellion had united the white ruling class. It had the support of all the leading men in the parish. These included James Lawrence Hilton, magistrate, militia officer, and Assembly member, who was identified with the most vociferous opposition to efforts to reform the system and was widely regarded as Bridges's mouthpiece there; Hamilton Brown, another magistrate and Assembly "die-hard"; and Samuel W. Rose, removed from the magistrate's bench for illegally imprisoning the Wesleyan missionaries. Hilton shared the honor of the presidency with Custos Henry Cox, traditionally patron of the missions and supporter in the Assembly of proposed reforms. These men led the overseers and bookkeepers, the second-rank whites whose position was threatened both by the collapse of the sugar market and by the threat of emancipation. Clutching the coattails of these white "gentry" was Benjamin Scott Moncrieffe, one of the few really wealthy free coloreds, whose family, by special privilege act, had enjoyed civil rights for two generations. The St. Ann's union was quickly imitated in other parishes; by March, 1832, there were eleven parish unions, and a Grand Island Union composed of delegates from the parishes was projected.[65]

The missionaries might reasonably have expected that the governor, Belmore, with whom responsibility for the maintenance of law and order ultimately lay, would have made some effort to restrain white violence. Belmore, though as yet unaware that he was under notice of dismissal,[66] took no effective action. Arriving in Montego Bay a few days after the destruction of the Baptist chapel there, his only reaction was to issue a proclamation, published on February 13, 1832, calling on the magistrates to restrain the chapel breakers, though it was well known that magistrates had formed part of the mob. The proclamation was treated with the contempt it deserved; the copy outside the Montego Bay court-house was torn down.[67]

Belmore condoned not only mob violence but legal chicanery. Within a few days of the arrest of Burchell and Gardner on February 10, 1832, it became known that they had been arrested on a perjured statement. Samuel Stennett swore before a free colored magistrate, John Manderson, that he had been persuaded to accuse Burchell and Gardner by a group of young men, leading lights in the St. James Colonial Church Union, by the promise of £50 annuity, of which £40 would be subscribed by one of the conspirators, George Delisser. The case against Gardner was supported by other witnesses; the case against Burchell, however, rested solely on Stennett's statement. These circumstances gave Belmore an excellent opportunity to show official concern for the missionaries, by either granting Burchell's release or at least affording him bail with military protection if necessary. He had taken an interest in the court-martial proceedings against Barlow and Pfeiffer; he did nothing, however, for Burchell.[68] He seemed to regard antisectarian outrages not so much as a challenge to the authority of the government as a proof that the missionaries were a public liability.

This was demonstrated beyond reasonable doubt when Burchell, despite the fact that he was acquitted at the Cornwall assizes, was forced to leave the island. None of the cases against the Baptist missionaries stood up in court. A case against Knibb, of which the missionaries themselves were kept in ignorance until the assize opened, was not proceeded with. Attorney General Fitzherbert Batty gave up the case against Gardner when the witnesses contradicted one another, and advised the grand jury to dismiss the case against Burchell. Burchell's acquittal, however, prompted an attempt to lynch him. As soon as he was released, a mob of several hundred people collected before his lodgings. One of the magistrates and the chief justice himself, G. L. Tuckett, attempted unsuccessfully to disperse them; finally, the landlord of the premises swore an affidavit that a great mob was assembled, "for the purpose of doing bodily injury to the person of the Rev. Thomas Burchell," and the soldiers were brought in. Burchell was escorted to a naval vessel for safety; the following day, pressured by strong arguments from the chief justice, the attorney general, and a leading magistrate, he agreed to leave the island.[69]

Anarchy provoked by the rebellion made it clear to the Baptist and Wesleyan missionaries that they could not hope to re-establish their work on the old basis of concession, compromise, and neutrality. The slaves had finally cut the neutral ground from underneath their feet and irrevocably identified them with the enemies of slavery. The identification was not entirely unwelcome. The critical spirit in which some of the missionaries had viewed the working of the slave system during the previous five years had been sharpened by their experience in the rebellion. They had always been aware of the brutality and coercion that underpinned the slave system; assisting the whites in the suppression of the slaves had made them eyewitnesses to a demonstration, on a massive scale, of the viciousness and inhumanity inherent in a society where class differences, reinforced by distinctions of race and legal status, branded one section of the population as inferior. They had always been aware that, as missionaries, serving the slaves in a society geared to exploit them, the values implied by their teaching and their lives ran counter to the values of a slave society. To the missionaries the slaves were souls to be saved, people to be won to a new faith, a new morality; they were men and not chattels. The rebels, by identifying the missionaries as their allies, by projecting Burchell as their deliverer from bondage, had made explicit the values implied in their teaching and challenged the missionaries to take action on their behalf. The Baptists and Wesleyans did not care to define this challenge, but they were forced to acknowledge that the future of mission work depended on the destruction of the slave system. The rights of the slaves and the needs of the missions were indissolubly linked. To secure both the future of mission work and freedom for the slaves, they became abolitionists.

The missionaries did not discuss their decision in political terms, but they took a step that implied commitment to the antislavery cause: they sent delegations to England. The Wesleyan district made this decision in February, 1832, and Peter Duncan and John Barry left the island on March 14, 1832, two days before Burchell was expelled; the Baptists' delegate, William Knibb, left in April. The deputations were charged simply with explaining events in Jamaica to their home societies. The Baptists resolved: "Considering the present distressed state of our mission . . . the manifest improbability of obtaining redress here, we deem it expedient, for the just representation of our wrongs, and the advancement of the Society's funds that . . . a deputation . . . proceed forthwith to England, to act under the direction of the Committee."[70]

The Baptist and Wesleyan churches had been committed since 1824 to the cause of freedom for the slaves, and their accounts of the desperate efforts of the Jamaican whites to deprive the slaves of religion could only serve as antislavery propaganda. Moreover, the Wesleyan Methodist Missionary Society itself had finally abandoned its officially neutral position on slavery; the society's magazine, *Missionary Notices,* was at one with the church's *Wesleyan-Methodist Magazine* in condemning the slave system. As the Wesleyan deputation traveled to England, readers of *Missionary Notices* were told: "Such are the timid and worldly principles which usually govern men in power, what ever party they may be, that it is in vain to expect that they should go on in the straightforward course . . . unless they are impelled by the constant and unrelaxed pressures of the conscientious part of the public at large."[71]

The Baptist Missionary Society was not yet officially committed to support the campaign; the Baptist missionaries in Jamaica, however, sent as their representative William Knibb, instigator of the Sam Swiney case. Once in England, Knibb took the lead in committing the Baptist Missionary Society to the cause. At the society's annual meeting in June, 1832, ignoring the secretary tugging his coattails in a plea for caution, Knibb excited his audience with an eloquent description of the sufferings of Jamaica and declared that the mission "could no longer exist without the entire and immediate abolition of slavery."[72] The audience's response swept the Baptist Missionary Society into the campaign.

The missionaries arrived in England at a crucial juncture in the abolition campaign. The Anti-Slavery Society had been committed to immediate emancipation since May, 1830, and the following year a new activist group, the Agency Committee, was formed to organize a countrywide campaign to rouse national support. Its campaign took place in the context created by the struggle for parliamentary reform. The Whig government that took office in November, 1830, pledged to reform, was defeated at the committee stage of the bill in April, 1831. Elections ensued, a great Whig victory was secured, and the parliamentary battle lines on the emancipation issue were defined. The West India interest organized for defense and in the first months of 1832 secured the appointment of a select House of Lords committee, officially concerned to investigate the condition of the slaves, unofficially intended "to confute the calumnies of the Abolitionists."[73] As a countermeasure, Buxton moved in the House of Commons in May that year for a select committee to consider the abolition of slavery "at the earliest period compatible with the safety of all classes in the colonies." The motion won substantial minority support, and an amended version secured the appointment of a committee to consider such measures "in conformity with the resolutions of 1823." Clearly, abolition of slavery had the support of a considerable body of the Commons; the question was, could that body be expanded, could the demand for abolition become so vociferous that the Whig government would feel impelled to promote it? Fortunately for the abolitionists the reform bill was finally passed in June, 1832, Parliament was dissolved, and elections for members recruited under the terms of the new act were held. The elections presented the antislavery party with a splendid new opportunity to promote abolition, an opportunity which the Agency Committee eagerly grasped. Up and down the British Isles, to the remotest corners of Scotland and Ireland, their speakers went, exhorting electors to demand from the candidates pledges of support for immediate abolition.[74]

The missionaries from Jamaica made a tremendous contribution to this work. The Committee of West India Planters and Merchants, active to the last in defense of slavery, hired speakers to counter the Agency Committee's propagandists. The missionaries provided the Agency's team with two immense advantages: expert knowledge and moral kudos derived from lives dedicated to the betterment of the slaves. William Knibb, in particular, made an outstanding contribution. He became one of the Agency Committee's strongest drawing cards; his presence secured large crowds in all the principal towns for discussion and debate on the abolition issue.[75] Thomas Fowell Buxton "frequently adverted to the overriding hand of Providence which had turned the intolerance of the system to its own destruction."[76]

The missionaries also made a direct impact on the government: it was Knibb's evidence to the Commons committee on the extinction of slavery which convinced Lord Howick, parliamentary undersecretary at the Colonial Office, of the need for immediate abolition.[77]

The missionaries served, in effect, as spokesmen for the rebel slaves. They testified to their confidence in the Negro population. They proclaimed that Negroes were intellectually the equal of any man, that their ambition for freedom was legitimate and could not properly be restrained by Christianity. They threatened that delay might promote further rebellion. With passion and conviction they urged emancipation; "I firmly believe," said one, "that [the difficulties] are more in theory than they would ever be found to be in practice."[78] Prompted by Sam Sharpe and his supporters, the missionaries made their commitment explicit: humanitarian values had at length completely triumphed over the pious neutralism of Dr. Coke.

NOTES

1. Estimate of the losses sustained as taken by the commissioners appointed by the House of Assembly, totaled by parish: St. James, £606,250; Hanover, £425,818; Westmoreland, £47,092; Manchester, £46,270; St. Elizabeth, £22,146; Trelawney, £4,960; St. Thomas in the East, £1,280; Portland, £772; grand total, £1,154,589. Great Britain, Parliamentary Papers (Commons), "Copy of the Report of a Committee of the House of Assembly of Jamaica, appointed to inquire into the Cause of, and Injury sustained by, the recent Rebellion in that Colony" (no. 561), 1831–32, 47:182 (hereafter cited as P.P. (Commons) (no. 561), 1831–32, 47).
2. W.M.M.S. Letters, Edney, Grateful Hill, Sept. 22, 1831, f. 203; Duncan, Kingston, June 7, 1831, f. 119, Box 130; Higman, *Slave Population*, p. 11.
3. Higman, *Slave Population*, p. 72, Table 10.
4. P.P. (Commons) (no. 285), 1831–32, 47:263, 266–68, Petitions of Freeholders and others; Burn, *Emancipation and Apprenticeship*, p. 49.
5. Belmore was advised that such a meeting would only be unconstitutional if it had a seditious intention. Belmore avoided any direct action by letting it be known that if the Assembly corresponded with the delegates, he would dissolve it. Belmore to Goderich, Dec. 17. 1831, no. 130, C.O. 137/179.
6. P.P. (Commons) (no. 285), 1831–32, 47:263, Belmore to Goderich, July 20, 1831.
7. Hinton, *Memoir of William Knibb*, pp. 112, 113, 115, quoting letter to Dyer, July 6, 1831; Henry Bleby, *Death Struggles of Slavery* (London,

1835), pp. 111–12; W.M.M.S. Letters, Pennock, Kingston, July 11, 1831, f. 144, Box 130.

8. W.M.M.S. Letters, Edney, Grateful Hill, Sept. 22, 1831, referring to Guys Hill, f. 203; Wood, St. Ann's Bay, Oct. 1, 1831, f. 216, Box 130. W.M.M.S., *Annual Report*, 1831, 1832–33, records annual increase in membership for 1830–31 as follows: St. Ann's Bay, 901 to 1,356; Falmouth, 566 to 821; Montego Bay, 766 to 883. Revivals of this sort occurred periodically; in 1826 and 1828 the mission churches had benefited in a similar way. Such movements might reflect an outburst of purely religious enthusiasm, but there seems no doubt that the revival of 1831 represented political interests. W.M.M.S. Letters, Ratcliffe, Bellemont, Nov. 10, 1826, f. 258, Box 123; Orton, Montego Bay, July 15, 1828, f. 220, Box 126.

9. Hinton, *Memoir of William Knibb*, p. 114, Knibb to Dyer, July 6, 1831.

10. Waddell, *Twenty-nine Years in the West Indies*, pp. 70–71.

11. Bleby, *Death Struggles of Slavery*, pp. 116, 120.

12. King vs. Tharpe, Courts Martial, Montego Bay, 2: ff. 171–73, C.O. 137/185.

13. P.P. (Commons) (no. 561), 1831–32, 47:211, confession of Ed. Morrice; p. 214, confession of T. Dove; Bleby, *Death Struggles of Slavery*, p. 110.

14. King vs. Sharpe, Special Slave Court, Montego Bay, ff. 304–13, C.O. 137/185.

15. P.P. (Commons) (no. 561), 1831–32, 47:219, confession of S. Cunningham to Rev. MacIntyre.

16. Ibid., p. 204, examination of Rev. T. Stewart, rector of Westmoreland.

17. P.P. (Commons) (no. 285), 1831–32, 47:284, report from Major General Robertson to Belmore, Jan. 2, 1831.

18. Bleby, *Death Struggles of Slavery*, pp. 113, 116–17.

19. P.P. (Commons) (no. 561), 1831–32, 47:217, confession of R. Gardner; p. 210, confession of J. Davies.

20. P.P. (Commons) (no. 285), 1831–32, 47:284, Robertson to Belmore, Jan. 1, 1832.

21. Bleby, *Death Struggles of Slavery*, pp. 110–12, 114, 115, quoting R. Gardner.

22. P.P. (Commons) (no. 561), 1831–32, 47:215, confession of T. Dove; (no. 285), 1831–32, 47:286, confession of W. Anand.

23. P.P. (Commons) (no. 561), 1831–32, 47:218, confession of R. Gardner; (no. 285), 1831–32, 47:295, deposition of W. Anand; Bleby, *Death Struggles of Slavery*, p. 111.

24. P.P. (Commons) (no. 285), 1831–32, 47:286, deposition of W. Anand; (no. 561), 1831–32, 47:188, evidence of H. R. Wallace; p. 211, confession of Robert Morrice; Bleby, *Death Struggles of Slavery*, pp. 2–3.

25. *S.M.R.* 13 (Mar., 1832):98, Blyth, Falmouth, Jan. 2; Thomas F. Abbott, *A Narrative of certain events connected with the late Disturbances in Jamaica and the charges preferred against the Baptist Missionaries in that*

Island (London, 1832), p. 29; W.M.M.S. Letters, Murray, Montego Bay, Mar. 10, 1832, f. 62, Box 131.

26. *S.M.R.* 13 (Mar., 1832):98, 101, Blyth, Falmouth, Jan. 2.
27. Bleby, *Death Struggles of Slavery*, pp. 3–4; P.P. (Commons) (no. 285), 1831–32, 47:272, Belmore to Goderich, Jan. 6, 1832.
28. P.P. (Commons) (no. 285), 1831–32, 47:272–73, Belmore to Goderich, Jan. 6, 1832. Detachments of thirty to fifty men were also dispatched to Black River, Morant Bay, and Port Antonio to deter further outbreaks.
29. P.P. (Commons) (no. 561), 1831–32, 47:200, evidence of J. H. Morris; Bleby, *Death Struggles of Slavery*, p. 118.
30. Courts Martial, Montego Bay, 1: f. 109, evidence of Philip; 2: ff. 171–72, trial of Tharpe; 3: ff. 213–15, trial of Dehany, C.O. 137/185; brief on behalf of Francis Gardner, pp. 5–6, Box W.I. uncatalogued, B.M.S. Archives.
31. Bleby, *Death Struggles of Slavery*, p. 18.
32. Waddell, *Twenty-nine Years in the West Indies*, p. 56–57.
33. Courts Martial, Trelawney, ff. 803–4, trial of Edward Grant, C.O. 137/185.
34. Courts Martial, Montego Bay, 1: f. 102, trial of James Guy, ff. 108–9, trial of Alick Gordon; 2: ff. 35–36, trial of Henry James, ff. 158–59, trial of Thomas Linton; 3: ff. 220–21, trial of Jinny, C.O. 137/185.
35. *S.M.R.* 13, (May, 1832):198–99, Watson, Lucea, Feb. 7, 1832.
36. *Christian Record*, July 1832, pp. 172–73, 178. The calculation was based on the 1831 estimate of the slave population of the county at 108,424; seventy-four slaves were rewarded by the Assembly.
37. There were four exceptions in St. James: on Lima, Guisboro, and Palmyra estates only the trash houses were burned; on Adelphi, early scene of Moses Baker's work, only the slave village. *Royal Gazette*, Feb. 18–25, 1832, C.O. 141/26; Higman, *Slave Population*, p. 70, Table 9.
38. Waddell, *Twenty-nine Years in the West Indies*, p. 59.
39. P.P. (Commons) (no. 285), 1831–32, 47:286, deposition of W. Anand.
40. Bleby, *Death Struggles of Slavery*, p. 43; Mulgrave to Goderich, Dec. 14, 1832, no. 45, enclosing "Return of Persons Killed; Total of White casualties, 14," C.O. 137/183; Waddell, *Twenty-nine Years in the West Indies*, p. 66.
41. P.P. (Commons) (no. 285), 1831–32, 47:288, Proclamation, Jan. 2, 1832: "Negroes, You have taken up arms against your masters.... Some wicked persons have told you the King has made you free.... In the name of the King I come amongst you to tell you that you are misled.... All who are found with the rebels will be put to death without mercy. You cannot resist the King's troop.... All who yield themselves up, provided they are not principals and chiefs in the burnings that have been committed, will receive His Majesty's gracious pardon, all who hold out will meet with certain death."
42. Bleby, *Death Struggles of Slavery*, p. 20.

43. Courts Martial, Trelawney, ff. 863–66, trial of Lieutenant John Gunn, C.O. 137/185; Bleby, *Death Struggles of Slavery*, p. 48–54, 17.
44. Return of the number of slaves killed and wounded in the rebellion, ff. 53–58, C.O. 137/185; Waddell, *Twenty-nine Years in the West Indies*, p. 66.
45. The courts-martial at Montego Bay were ordered by Colonel George Mc'Farquhar Lawson of the St. James Regiment of Foot Militia on Sir Willoughby Cotton's warrant. Abstract of the Courts Martial at Montego Bay, p. 1, C.O. 137/185; ibid., Parish Returns:

Parish	Total Tried	Total Executed
Hanover courts-martial	58	27
Hanover civil courts	82	60
Trelawney courts-martial	70	24
St. James courts-martial	99	81
St. James civil courts	81	39
Westmoreland courts-martial	26	12
Westmoreland civil courts	52	20
St. Elizabeth courts-martial	73	14
Portland courts-martial	23	7
Portland civil courts	5	5
St. Thomas in the Vale courts-martial	9	—
Manchester courts-martial	15	13
Manchester civil courts	16	7
St. Thomas in the East courts-martial	12	1
St. Thomas in the East civil courts	5	2
	626	312

46. Courts Martial, St. James, 1: f. 6, trial of James Guy; 2: ff. 20–21, trial of Thomas Linton; *S.M.R.* 13 (Apr., 1832):149, Blyth, Jan. 10; W.M.M.S. Letters, Murray, Montego Bay, May 28, 1832, f. 141, Box 131.
47. Bleby, *Death Struggles of Slavery*, pp. 29–30, 118; Waddell, *Twenty-nine Years in the West Indies*, p. 66, quoting letter from Watson, Lucea, May 8, 1832.
48. Bleby, *Death Struggles of Slavery*, p. 118.
49. For a full discussion of this thesis, see Eugene D. Genovese, *From Rebellion to Revolution: Afro-American Slave Revolts in the Making of the Modern World* (Baton Rouge, La., 1980).
50. P.P. (Commons) (no. 285), 1831–32, 47:275, Belmore to Goderich, Jan. 6, 1832; (no. 561), 1831–32, 47:195, evidence of H. G. Groves; p. 196, evidence of A. Whitelock.
51. Bleby, *Death Struggles of Slavery*, p. 140, quoting *Courant*, Jan. 6, 1832; P.P. (Commons) (no. 561), 1831–32, 47:187–88, evidence of R. Barrett.
52. Duncan, *Narrative of the Wesleyan Mission to Jamaica*, p. 295; Abbott, *Narrative*, pp. 37, 42–43.

53. Abbott, *Narrative*, pp. 37, 43, 91–93, 101–8; W.M.M.S. Letters, Box, Spanish Town, Jan. 7, 1832, f. 11, Box 131.

54. Buchner, *Moravians in Jamaica*, p. 90.

55. Bleby, *Death Struggles of Slavery*, p. 16.

56. Brief on behalf of Francis Gardner, pp. 13–14, statement of P. Green, servant, Box W.I. uncatalogued, B.M.S. Archives.

57. W.M.M.S. Letters, Murray, Montego Bay, Mar. 10, 1832, f. 62, Box 131.

58. Pfeiffer was arrested on the accusation of some Moravian "helpers," the equivalent of the Baptists' "leaders," who claimed he had told them that if they worked after Christmas, they would be slaves forever. The prosecution proved a trumped-up affair; the prosecution witnesses were two slave women, one of whom had been excluded from the Moravian church six years earlier, and two free colored men, one of whom joined the rebels after the trial and was captured and executed. Each claimed to have heard Pfeiffer tell of freedom but contradicted each other's testimony as to when he had said it. The defense, on the other hand, had thirteen free colored witnesses who denied the charges and gave evidence that Pfeiffer had urged obedience on the slaves. Slave witnesses also described his visits to two estates in the first days of the rebellion encouraging them to continue work. The weight of evidence secured Pfeiffer's acquittal, even in a court composed of militia officers. P.P. (Commons) (no. 561), 1831–32, 47:206, evidence of A. Hogg; Buchner, *Moravians in Jamaica*, p. 95.

59. W.M.M.S. Letters, Box, Kingston, Jan. 14, 1832, f. 15, Box 131; Abbott, *Narrative*, pp. 56, 101–8.

60. The following magistrates are named in the Baptist Abbott's *Narrative*, pp. 115–16, as being "on the spot, most of them very actively engaged in demolition": "John Coates, B. H. Tharpe, George Gordon, Wm. Mitchell Kerr, James Gordon, John Cleghorn, Alexander Campbell, Joseph Bowen, Charles O'Connor, Wm. Heath."

61. W.M.M.S. Letters, Murray, Montego Bay, Mar. 10, 1832, f. 62, Box 131.

62. Abbott, *Narrative*, pp. 58–59, 100, 114–18; W.M.M.S. Letters, Bleby, Montego Bay, Mar. 27, 1832, f. 87, Box 131; Wood, Kingston, July 4, 1832, f. 6, Box 132; *S.M.R.* 13 (May, 1832):200, Watson, Montego Bay, Feb. 14; Duncan, *Narrative of the Wesleyan Mission to Jamaica*, p. 294.

63. Abbott, *Narrative*, pp. 46–49.

64. Duncan, *Narrative of the Wesleyan Mission to Jamaica*, pp. 287–89, quoting the *Jamaica Courant*, Mar. 3, 1832.

65. Ibid., pp. 283–84, 287–88; Duncker, "The Free Coloured and . . . Civil Rights," p. 105.

66. Belmore to Goderich, Apr. 9, 1832, no. 185, acknowledging receipt of dispatch of Feb. 18, 1832, C.O. 137/182.

67. P.P. (Commons) (no. 561), 1831–32, 47:252, proclamation of Feb. 13, 1832; Abbott, *Narrative*, p. 62.

68. The authorities in St. George had been requested for a report on Barlow's case, and this sign of official interest had helped to terminate proceedings

against him. The authorities in Manchester were ordered to withhold execution on Pfeiffer pending a review. The order probably reached Mandeville too late to influence the court's decision to acquit him. Abbott, *Narrative*, pp. 106–8; Belmore to Goderich, Jan. 16, 1832, no. 143, C.O. 137/181; Mulgrave to Goderich, Dec. 14, 1832, no. 44, enclosing Major General Yates to Colonel Jacquet, Jan. 14, 1832, C.O. 137/183.

69. Abbott, *Narrative,* pp. 64–68; Belmore to Goderich, Apr. 9, 1832, no. 103, C.O. 137/182.

70. Abbott, *Narrative*, p. 153.

71. *Missionary Notices,* Nov., 1831, p. 792; Mar., 1832, pp. 226–27.

72. *Missionary Herald,* July, 1832, p. 325.

73. Burn, *Emancipation and Apprenticeship,* pp. 89–90; William L. Mathieson, *British Slavery and Its Abolition 1823–1838* (London, 1926), p. 222.

74. Burn, *Emancipation and Apprenticeship,* pp. 97–98.

75. Ragatz, *Fall of the Planter Class,* pp. 447–48.

76. Charles Buxton, ed., *Memoirs of Sir Thomas Fowell Buxton, Bart.* (London, 1849), pp. 305–6. The popularity achieved by the Wesleyan and Baptist missionaries and the publicity given to their sufferings in Jamaica provoked a widespread feeling in Scotland, gradually revealed in the *S.M.R.,* that the Presbyterian missions had been "less faithful" than those of other denominations in discharging their duties to the slaves. Various charges were brought against them including "blinking at colonial vices" and, in particular, not enforcing Sunday observance and having connections with the Colonial Church Union. The discussion, conducted in the *S.M.R.* during May, 1832, and Sept. and Oct., 1833, is important chiefly because of the light it throws on the appetite of church-goers of all denominations for some missionary heroes, if not martyrs, in the atmosphere created by the last stages of the abolition campaign.

77. Murray, *West Indies and the Development of Colonial Government,* p. 194, Howick to Mulgrave, June 21, July 5, 1832, 3d Earl Grey's papers.

78. P.P. (Lords) (no. 127), 1831–32, 306:430–31, evidence of Rev. J. Barry; pp. 636, 637–38, 668, evidence of Rev. P. Duncan; P.P. (Commons) (no. 721), 1831–32, 20:75–76, evidence of Rev. J. Barry; pp. 117, 124, evidence of Rev. P. Duncan.

CHAPTER SEVEN

Emancipation Achieved

W HILE THE MISSIONARIES in England campaigned for abolition, the antislavery struggle in Jamaica launched by the slaves continued in a different form, between the Colonial Church Unionists and the free colored and black supporters of the missions. The immediate issue was the missionaries' right to preach; the underlying issue was emancipation. For the unionists, to admit the missionaries' right to preach was to admit the slaves' right to freedom. The free blacks and coloreds who mobilized to defend the missionaries did so both as supporters of the mission churches and as loyal citizens convinced of the justice and necessity of the emancipation act. The conflicts created by the abolition issue, therefore, were brought to a head before the emancipation act was passed in Britain and in terms of the missionaries' right to preach. The missionaries acted as catalysts, crystallizing out the pro- and antiabolition forces, the loyal and rebel elements in Jamaica's free population. By focusing the support of the otherwise unorganized and amorphous loyal free colored and black population, they enabled the imperial government to swiftly suppress the rebel whites and prepare for a peaceful transition from a slave to a free society.

The battle lines between free black and colored mission supporters and the C.C.U., first drawn in Montego Bay when the Wesleyan chapel was saved from destruction, were re-established whenever the missionaries attempted to begin preaching. The unionists' resisted with violence, threats of violence, and legal action; mission supporters fought back, but without success. The Wesleyans challenged the unionists on Bridges's doorstep at St. Ann's Bay and stirred up such animosity between the whites and the freedmen in the militia that they considered it prudent to leave. The Baptists, equally bold, sent a man to preach in Montego Bay and licensed the house of a free colored member at the bishop's office in Spanish Town for the purpose. Twenty magistrates, including leading members of the St. James C.C.U., assembled in court to find him guilty of preaching in unlicensed premises and subsequently fined the landlady. A lynching party was only prevented by the number of mission supporters in the town.[1]

At Falmouth a lynching was actually attempted. A gang of about a dozen men went after the Wesleyan missionary, Henry Bleby, a few days after his arrival. They broke into his house and proceeded to tar and feather him in front of his family. He was saved by free black and colored friends, but the custos gave him military protection for only twenty-four hours and he had to leave. Antisectarian fervor manifested itself even in St. Thomas in the East, a parish where the missionaries had worked untroubled since the death of Sir Simon Taylor. A Baptist missionary and the owner of the house where he was staying were arrested, and the missionary was charged with illegal preaching.[2]

The missionaries and their allies, however, were not easily intimidated. With great courage and persistence the Wesleyans found enough evidence to prepare a court case against Bleby's attackers and against union members responsible for the destruction of the chapels at St. Ann's Bay and Oracabessa. The courts, however, were in the hands of unionists and their sympathizers, and in each case the juries found no true bill.[3]

These victories, secured across the island, were discussed at union meetings in the parishes as a preliminary to a C.C.U. conference held in July, 1832, at Falmouth, scene of the unionists' most violent outrage. The conference delegates, who represented all the north coast parishes and Westmoreland, demonstrated that the rebel whites included most of the magistrates in the area, the lowest but in many ways the most vital rank in the hierarchy of imperial authority and, in recent years, the most persistently criticized by the Colonial Office.[4] The C.C.U. clearly reflected the antagonism to the imperial government created by the investigation policy as well as by the threat of emancipation.

The proceedings were managed by the Assembly member for St. Ann, James Lawrence Hilton, an old ally of Bridges, and addressed the central problem confronting the union, how to deal with their free colored and black opposition. The C.C.U., as previously mentioned, had attracted the support of a minority of wealthy, well-established free colored slave owners who, as the *Watchman* put it, were "whitewashed," identified with the whites. Without the assistance of the bulk of the free colored and blacks, however, the C.C.U. could not realistically either get rid of the missionaries or organize resistance to abolition. And developments in England made it clear that this is what they must prepare to do. The passage of the Reform Act in June, 1832, promised the election of a strengthened Whig government and a distinctly antislavery House of Commons. The threat to the slave owners was more immediate than ever. The unionists' attempt to win free colored and black support by applying economic pressure had evidently not succeeded. With typical racist arrogance, however, the conference decided on new coercive measures. This time they addressed themselves to the free coloreds and blacks as militiamen. A solemn declaration was drawn up, to be signed on militia muster days, to pledge resistance to emancipation by force of arms.[5] The armed free colored and black militiamen evidently were to become unionist supporters under the guns of the whites.

To lend some reality to this ploy, the unionists proceeded to demonstrate once more their power in the courts. The conference demanded that the Wesleyan chapel in Montego Bay, saved from destruction by the free colored population, be closed. Within three days the Wesleyan missionary in Montego Bay was summoned before fourteen magistrates, fault was found both with the license for the chapel as a preaching place and with his own license, and he was threatened with arrest if he continued to preach. The chapel was closed.[6] The union's new success again spread its influence to the eastern parishes, and the Wesleyan missions in Port Maria and in Manchioneal, which had been undisturbed during the rebellion, were closed; in each case the missionaries were charged with illegal preaching and sent to jail.[7]

At this point, however, the imperial government began to bring its authority to bear. The violence of the Jamaican whites in the aftermath of the rebellion had not taken the Colonial Office entirely by surprise. Nonviolent resistance had been stirred in 1831, throughout the West Indian islands, by its efforts to speed up reform of the slave system; the November order in council prompted mass meetings in St. Lucia and a strike by merchants and planters to prolong the slaves' working day.[8] The formation of the C.C.U. and the destruction of the Montego Bay Baptist chapel marked the transition in Jamaica from constitutional to violent opposition, and the imperial government demanded immediate action to restore law and order.

Detailed and strict instructions were immediately sent to the governor for the prosecution of the chapel breakers. In the event that the culprits, for want of evidence or because the grand jury proved obstructive, could not be brought to justice in the courts, the attorney general was to make an investigation and any crown officeholders found guilty were to be dismissed. The governor, at this point the Earl of Belmore, was supplied with a list of persons named as responsible for the destruction of the chapel by the Baptist Missionary Society. To stir the whites' sense of responsibility, the governor was further instructed to find means of "re-imbursing the missions for their losses, either through the Assembly, or the parishes."

The Colonial Office attributed the rebellion entirely to the conduct of the slave owners, who had provoked the slaves by their public opposition to reform of the system. The colonists' notion that the missionaries were to blame was regarded simply as the product of "heated and prejudiced" minds. In light of the rebellion, in fact, the Colonial Secretary regretted that, for the whole of the previous decade, "from . . . an anxious desire to exhibit the most studious respect for the local legislature the discussion [of reforms] was prolonged after every reasonable hope of prevailing by mere persuasion had been disappointed."[9] The Colonial Office clearly understood that the restoration of mission rights was a necessary component of the restoration of imperial authority, which would demonstrate to the rebel whites that they must acquiesce, should the need arise, to the emancipation of the slaves.

Belmore, under notice of dismissal, did not exert himself to carry out Colonial Office instructions.[10] The arrival, however, of the new governor, the Earl of Mulgrave, put new spirit into the executive. Mulgrave, a young Whig reformer on his first colonial appointment, was well aware that the imperial government expected action.[11] He was appalled by the conditions he found in Jamaica and despaired of conveying to the Colonial Office "an adequate idea of the helpless state as to the exercise of legal authority into which I found that the events of the last few months had brought a Government that, from its very nature, can never be a strong one."[12] From the outset of his administration he displayed the energy, intelligence, and vital concern needed to implement imperial policy.

Mulgrave was prompted into action almost immediately. The C.C.U.'s efforts to force free colored and black support greatly exacerbated hostility between the two classes, and in Savanna-la-Mar civil war erupted. Political battle lines between the white ruling class and the free colored and black population had been sharply drawn in Savanna-la-Mar before the rebellion. Sam Swiney, publicly prosecuted and flogged on the ruling of Custos Finlayson, was the property of a free colored merchant, Aaron de Leon. Finlayson's subsequent removal from office as a result of Knibb's intervention, after thirty years' service in the Assembly, represented a significant victory for the newly enfranchised free coloreds and blacks. After the rebellion they actively encouraged the reopening of the Baptist chapel and, as a result, John Kingdon was sent to Savanna-la-Mar in June, 1832. Lodgings were provided by the de Leons. They were well aware that they were defying the Colonial Church Union and did so on clearly political grounds, since they were Anglicans by persuasion and not Baptists.[13]

The unionists responded to the challenge; on the July militia muster day a mob of thirty invaded the de Leon house and told Kingdon to leave the parish. Kingdon, confident of his support, refused to do so and the mob dispersed. But on the muster day following the Falmouth conference more inflammatory speeches were made, antisectarian resolutions were passed, and armed unionists got together to drive the de Leons out of town. Shots were fired and an attempt was made to set fire to the premises. The free colored population rallied to defend the beseiged de Leons embattled in the house, and by the time two magistrates arrived on the scene, a regular battle had taken place.[14]

The magistrates resolved their problem by putting the de Leon family in jail. They were joined there the next day by Kingdon, who had escaped from the house during the attack only to be arrested on a warrant issued by the president of the Westmoreland Colonial Church Union in his capacity as a magistrate. The unionists went about for the following week destroying free colored property and exposing the town to the danger of widespread fires. At this point some of the white population became frightened at the turn events had taken; the new custos, J. H. Williams, who had remained independent of the union, informed the governor of the situation.[15]

Mulgrave sent his adjutant general and the deputy clerk of the crown to investigate, in person, affairs in Savanna-la-Mar. As a result, the de Leon family and Kingdon were released on bail after twenty-four days in jail, and some of the men involved in the attack on the de Leon house were arrested.[16] The unprecedented promptness of Mulgrave's reaction and the sudden, astonishing mobility of the governor's aides did not, however, immediately quell the Westmoreland unionists. The "martyrs," charged for their part in the riot, refused bail and went to jail, depending on friends to release them. The custos, anticipating that September muster day for the militia would occasion another riot, again appealed to the governor for help. Mulgrave, who was touring the western parishes, went himself to Savanna-la-Mar on muster day and addressed the militia. He emphasized that in their military capacity they had no right to indulge in politics and threatened, if they persisted in using the militia for political purposes, to use the military to restore discipline. At the jail, finding the rioters installed in triumph with the union banner waving overhead, surrounded by their insignia, and cheered by friends, Mulgrave instantly dismissed the jailer and his assistant. As an earnest of the seriousness of his threat to the militia, a detachment of troops was installed in the town to secure law and order.[17]

Mulgrave's summary treatment of the Westmoreland C.C.U. passed without protest from other parish unions: no resolutions expressed fraternal support, or proclaimed patriotic aims, or threatened defiance of the governor. One small, supplementary riot took place; on Mulgrave's return to Montego Bay the house of a wealthy free colored man was attacked and the mob had to be dispersed by the troops.[18] But the union movement, confronted for the first time by active opposition, gave no sign of united resistance. The circumstances seemed opportune to attack the movement as a whole, beginning with the dismissal of crown officeholders who publicly declared themselves unionists. It seemed as if the missionaries could look forward to starting work again.

At this point, however, the unionists scored a notable victory; they succeeded in temporarily depriving the free colored and black community of its outstanding leader, Edward Jordon, who was sentenced to six months in jail on a libel charge. An attempt had been made in April of that year to dispose of Jordon permanently by charging him with treason. The case was inadequately based on an article in the *Watchman* that had called on all classes to assist in achieving emancipation, and it failed to convince the jury.[19] The libel case was based on a new sedition law, enacted in the wake of this acquittal in May, 1832, and evidently intended to facilitate restriction of press freedom. Jordon was arraigned for an accusation, in the columns of the *Watchman*, that Dr. Wordie of the Kingston kirk was the author of some violently antisectarian articles in the *Jamaica Courant*. He was sentenced to twelve months in jail and a £100 fine. The sentence was quashed on appeal to England, and the free coloreds and blacks reaffirmed his leadership by electing him, despite the sentence, as city alderman,[20] but the unionists could consider that their defeat in Savanna-la-Mar was matched by the humiliation in the courts of their enemies' political leader.

And more serious problems ensued. Mulgrave, the missionaries' young crusader, put down his lance and chose at this juncture to set aside imperial policy. Inexperienced in government, Mulgrave proved susceptible to the urbane insinuations of the Jamaican gentlemen he met during his tour of the island. They managed to impress him with the extreme dangers of emancipation, the disorder and ruin that would attend freedom for the slaves, and the liberal and humane attitudes that informed slave management. Gentleman spoke to gentleman amidst the lavish hospitality traditional in the island and in an atmosphere of apparently loyal deference to the crown. Lacking the Colonial Office's long experience of colonial recalcitrance, Mulgrave took the verbalisms for reality and began to think that the Colonial Church Union, despite occasional excesses as at Savanna-la-Mar, was an organization representing a justifiable viewpoint. He told the Colonial Office he was unwilling to resort to "a strong act of authority" against the C.C.U.[21]

Mulgrave's change of attitude was made apparent in October, 1832, when the St. Ann union passed a series of resolutions, evidently intended as a policy guide for the approaching session of the Assembly.[22] The resolutions reflected unionist response to political developments in England, since it was clear that, after years of hysterical protest against any reform of slavery, the island was in imminent danger of having the whole system swept away. Elections for the newly reformed House of Commons were due to take place in December, and the abolitionists, under the able leadership of the Agency Committee, were hard at work persuading prospective members of Parliament to pledge their support for slave emancipation. Abolition seemed on the verge of becoming imperial policy.[23]

The resolutions constituted the strongest verbal challenge the unionists had yet made to imperial authority. The C.C.U. declared "united resistance" to imperial policy and resolved that since the king's ministers, "at the instigation of an unprincipled and treacherous faction" (i.e. the Anti-Slavery Society) and supported by a majority of the House of Commons, were bent on destroying the constitutional rights of the island and robbing colonials of their property, and since "spies and incendiaries in the garb of religion were employed and authorised to preach 'Rebellion, Murder, Arson and Rape,' " there was no course left to the colonists but a firm and united resistance to tyranny and oppression. The statements libeled the House of Commons and exposed Custos Cox, as president of the meeting, to criminal proceedings. Mulgrave, instead of using Cox as an example, chose to try to win his loyalty to the crown. Numerous letters were exchanged for several weeks, and only Cox's extreme obstinacy finally drove Mulgrave to remove him from office. Even this move proved temporary; when the custodes of two other parishes intervened on his behalf, Cox was reinstated without so much as apologizing for his activities.[24]

Mulgrave had to learn by hard experience, as the Colonial Office had done, the real nature of Jamaica's ruling class. He was pushed from the path of conciliation by the Jamaica Assemby, which he met for the first time in November, 1832. He was astonished to find that the gentlemen who sounded so reasonable in private conversation displayed, when gathered together in the House of Assembly, complete contempt for imperial authority. In response to Mulgrave's opening address, the Assembly denied the right of the House of Commons to investigate island affairs and denied ever having accepted the amelioration policy defined in the resolutions of 1823. Mulgrave promptly asserted "the Transcendental Power of the Imperial Legislature, regulated only by their [sic] own discretion and limited only by restrictions they may themselves have imposed." The Assembly, well versed in tactics, moved in reply resolutions declaring themselves loyal to the crown but independent of Parliament.[25] Mulgrave's faith in conciliation was rudely shaken. He ordered a dissolution of the Assembly in the hope that the newly enfranchised black and colored voters, who had managed to capture two seats in bye-elections the previous year, would increase their influence. In the event, his hopes were disappointed; only one more free colored member was elected.[26] In the meantime the Colonial Office in dispatch after dispatch consistently urged him to take strong action against the Colonial Church Union.

The news from Jamaica of riots, the breakdown of the courts, and the harassment of the missionaries—detailed by both the governor and the missionary societies—reflected a society on the brink of disintegration. Mulgrave's accounts of events in Savanna-la-Mar, received in the Colonial Office early in December, 1832, finally made it clear that free society in Jamaica had divided for and against the missionaries, abolition, and imperial authority. The question of mission rights and the issues it encompassed had become what Lord Goderich defined as "an affair of caste and colour" that threatened not only insuperable problems in the event of abolition but, more immediately, further revolt of the slaves. The Colonial Office was convinced that "the peace of the whole island" was at stake.[27]

Mulgrave was initially instructed in October, 1832, to present the magistrates with an ultimatum: they must either retract, "distinctly and publicly," from all connection with the union, or they must be dismissed. At the same time he was to investigate and report fully on all the missions' grievances. To establish missionary rights, the attorney general was immediately to supply the magistrates with a ruling on the toleration law and facilitate the reopening of the missions. To underline the need for action, Mulgrave was urged to supplement these instructions with his own zeal.[28]

Mulgrave's attitude, however, was far from zealous. He complained: "Your Lordship . . . can have no idea of . . . the extent to which almost the whole Community is made up of only different degrees of Opposition to the Authority of the King's Government."[29] Nevertheless, he felt bound to demonstrate that his government was not simply lax, and at the first manifestation of union activity following his receipt of these dispatches he took action. On December 20, 1832, the union in St. John, one of the smallest parishes in the island, published a series of resolutions that, unlike the St. Ann resolutions of October, offered no direct challenge to imperial authority but simply pledged its members to expel sectarians. Mulgrave immediately demoted the two militia officers who had signed the resolutions, and on December 27 he sent out a general order to the militia condemning the Colonial Church Union as an illegal association and warning militia officers who took part that their commissions would be canceled.[30] The St. Ann union hastily identified itself with the St. John's branch; it passed three resolutions that regretted the demotion of the officers and asserted that the militia and the union served the same purpose. Mulgrave was forced to discipline the chairman in charge of these proceedings, James Lawrence Hilton, one of the founders of the union movement. Hilton was removed from his position as magistrate and also from his militia command.[31]

At this point the authority of the imperial government was brought directly to bear on the movement. Fear of civil war prompted the Colonial Office in December, 1832, to take the unusual step of using a royal proclamation to define imperial policy. The proclamation, which arrived in Jamaica in January, 1833, was a succinct public statement of the policy that had been pressed on the Jamaican executive for the previous year. Judges and magistrates were enjoined to "give full effect to the Law of the maintenance of toleration in matters of Religion and to co-operate in bringing offenders to justice."[32] Mulgrave, having begun his attack, was grateful for imperial support; he praised the proclamation as "timely" and made every effort to give it full effect. It was sent out to the custodes on January 25, 1833, so as to appear simultaneously in every parish, and was accompanied by a circular letter ordering that all violations of the proclamation were to be reported directly to the governor. Officeholders, particularly magistrates, who interfered with mission work were threatened with demotion, "that all others concerned in similar proceedings may perceive that neither actual violence, nor a Repetition of Illegal acts, will be allowed to pass unpunished."[33]

The royal proclamation, by publicizing imperial policy, was clearly intended not only to force Mulgrave's hand but to clarify imperial policy to the whole population and, more particularly, to the free blacks and coloreds. Mulgrave's hesitations, his anxiety to placate Cox and his colleagues, demonstrated a thorough appreciation of neither the nature of the unionists' opposition nor the capacity of the crown's free black and colored allies to become officeholders. It was, in fact, the existence of a loyal free black and colored population from which alternative magistrates could be recruited that made the royal proclamation an effective method of asserting imperial authority.

The proclamation induced a final flurry of defiance from the unionists. Custos Cox resigned his civil and militia commissions in protest against the imperial government's policy not merely to tolerate but to support "the Itinerant Baptists and Wesleyans in preaching to the Negroes, notwithstanding the strong evidence of their pernicious effects; and the open Professions of their leaders now escaped to England." Cox's transition from a liberal Jamaican, ready to protect and help the missionaries, into an obdurate, antisectarian, anti-imperial defender of slavery was complete. The union in St. Ann followed his example and declared that all its members preferred the union to their commissions and projected a union congress.[34] The St. Ann unionists, however, the founders of the movement and the most ardent defenders of slavery, were brought to order by the method Mulgrave had used at Savanna-la-Mar. Two hundred troops were sent to St. Ann's Bay, and the governor himself inspected the militia. The parade passed off without incident. Mulgrave had succeeded in crushing Jamaica's proslavery party before the news that the imperial government had decided to emancipate the slaves reached the island.[35]

The reopening of the mission stations, however, the first practical test of imperial authority, was delayed for a few months because of legal complications. The conduct of the magistrates after the rebellion had brought the legal basis of toleration in Jamaica into question once more. The new attorney general, Dowall O'Reilly, whose appointment coincided with Mulgrave's, was pressed from the time he took office by the governor, the Colonial Office, and the missionaries themselves to make a ruling on the law. O'Reilly never undertook this task seriously, but a cursory examination of the missionaries' legal position led him to cast doubts on the validity of their licenses. He pointed out that the Toleration Act of 1711 (10 Anne c.2), under which missionaries in Jamaica were supposedly licensed, required Dissenters to subscribe to the Articles of the Church of England. Jamaican practice, however, had allowed them to subscribe to a scriptural declaration as authorized by the Toleration Act of 1779 (19 Geo. III c.44).[36] The Wesleyan missionaries, unwilling to accept O'Reilly's ruling, brought a test cast against the magistrates in St. Mary for illegal imprisonment of a missionary, Greenwood, basing their case on the argument that the English toleration laws had never been effective in Jamaica, and in the absence of legislation no restraints could be imposed on Dissenting preachers. They lost the case[37] but obtained from the chief justice, Sir Joshua Rowe, a definite ruling on the toleration question. Rowe, like his predecessor Hugo James, held that all the English toleration acts passed before the Jamaican act of 1728 were in force, and he again emphasized that under the act of 1689 the magistrates "are positively called on to administer the oaths."[38]

On the strength of the new ruling in July, 1833, a Wesleyan missionary was sent to reopen the mission in St. Ann's Bay. His appearance in court to take the oaths prompted ex-unionists, led by the demoted militia officers, to drive him out in a scene which, in the judgment of the new custos, Samuel M. Barrett, was "seldom exceeded in the annals of brutality." Mulgrave took immediate action. A military detachment was sent to the town, and under its protection the missionary took the oaths and a mission church in the very heart of unionist country was reopened.[39]

Imperial intervention on behalf of the missionaries had by 1833 taken every form, from additional instruction to the governor, disallowances, and investigations to military protection. Each assertion of imperial authority had enabled the missionaries to survive and develop. The interventions took place, however, in the overall context of a policy for the reform of slavery in which the imperial government was prepared to rely on the slave owners themselves to define and implement reforms. It was a policy that for a decade treated the Jamaica Assembly's obstructive maneuvers with respect, inflated its constitutional pretentions, and, arguably, fostered the illusions on which the C.C.U.'s grandiloquent assertions of independence were based. Only persistent pressure from the antislavery party in Parliment, strongly supported by public opinion, had made the government take practical steps to promote the principle of religious toleration and provide religious instruction for the slaves. Mission rights were restored and imperial authority re-established, however, because the government enjoyed substantial free black and colored support and was prepared, in order to preserve its authority, to replace rebel white officeholders with loyal free blacks and coloreds. The fact that white dominance in all branches of island government was jeopardized guaranteed that, when the abolition act was passed, the whites, to preserve themselves in power, would come to heel.

The reopening of the St. Ann's Bay mission proved a true measure of Jamaican receptivity to abolition. News of the emancipation plan reached the island at the end of May, 1833, and, despite the provisions for compensation, provoked a good deal of hostile comment. The whites, however, had no means of resistance and, the better to preserve their remaining privileges and political status, the Assembly convening in October proved cooperative.[40] The role it had played for a decade, as the West Indian legislature that took the lead in obstructing imperial policy, was reversed; Jamaica became the first of the West Indian colonies to agree to the emancipation scheme.

Freedom for the slaves and rights for the missionaries were achieved only when a new balance of political forces won power in England. The old alliance of Tory landlord and West India interest, which had limited the influence of the antislavery party, was weakened by the reform of Parliament. The Reform Act reflected the great economic and social developments that had taken place in England since the antislavery movement started in the 1780s. It destroyed the rotten boroughs, the basis of the West Indians' parliamentary influence, enfranchised the manufacturing towns, and gave the antislavery party unprecedented strength. The abolitionists had the support of all the members of Parliament who saw the planters as bankrupt, inefficient, and oversubsidized, an obstacle in the way of a properly economic policy of free trade and a symbol of all the old, redundant, expensive, and reactionary vested interests the new Parliament was to sweep away. Under Buxton's leadership they pressed the Whig government into action, and the two problems of slavery and religious toleration were settled by the same stroke of imperial authority. The Toleration Act of 1812 was incorporated into the act for the abolition of slavery and, to circumvent obstruction in the representative colonies, the act was declared law by royal proclamation on September 4, 1833. The victims of imperial authority had become, briefly, its beneficiaries.

NOTES

1. Duncan, *Narrative of the Wesleyan Mission to Jamaica,* pp. 315–16; Abbott, *Narrative,* pp. 132–36.
2. W.M.M.S. Letters, Bleby, Montego Bay, May 1, 1832, f. 119, Box 131; Duncan, *Narrative of the Wesleyan Mission to Jamaica,* pp. 305–7; Bleby, *Death Struggles of Slavery,* pp. 198–207.
3. Duncan, *Narrative of the Wesleyan Mission to Jamaica,* pp. 320–23.
4. Ibid., p. 324; Bleby, *Death Struggles of Slavery,* p. 222.
5. Gad J. Heumann, "Between Black and White: Brown Men in Jamaican Politics and Society, 1823–1865" (Ph.D. thesis, Yale University, 1975), p. 97; Bleby, *Death Struggles of Slavery,* pp. 222–23.
6. Bleby, *Death Struggles of Slavery,* p. 225; W.M.M.S. Letters, Murray to Pennock, Montego Bay, July 31, 1832, f. 26, Box 132. The chapel, originally licensed in 1819, had subsequently been rebuilt on the same site, but no new license had been obtained. Murray's own preaching license had been issued in Spanish Town, and the magistrates, ignoring the ruling established by the Orton-Whitehouse case, claimed this-was unsatisfactory and refused to administer oaths.
7. At Port Maria the Wesleyan missionary, Greenwood, was arrested on July 30, 1832. His license, issued in a neighboring parish, was found inadequate; he was fined £10 for illegal preaching and, on refusal to pay, was committed to jail by the vice-president of the St. Mary C.C.U. Greenwood accepted bail after three weeks in jail. W.M.M.S. Letters, Greenwood, Kingston, Sept. 8, 1832, f. 61, Box 132.

    At Manchioneal the Wesleyan missionary was requested to vacate his house to accommodate a military officer or lose his license. He was duly arrested for illegal preaching and jailed briefly before being bound over. W.M.M.S. Letters, Rowden, Kingston, Nov. 10, 1832, f. 111, Box 132; Duncan, *Narrative of the Wesleyan Missions to Jamaica,* pp. 330–31.
8. Ragatz, *Fall of the Planter Class,* p. 442.

9. P.P. (Commons) (no. 482), 1831–32, 47:254, Goderich to Belmore, May 19, 1832.
10. The dispatch of Feb. 13 was received in the first week of Apr., 1832.
11. Son of a high Tory family, Mulgrave entered Parliament at twenty-two and distinguished himself by supporting the Whigs. He divided his time between politics and literature, spending some years in Italy writing novels before succeeding to his title in 1831. He was appointed to Jamaica by the Whig government in 1832.
12. Mulgrave to Goderich, Oct. 7, 1832, no. 25, C.O. 137/183.
13. Kingdon to Steane, July 28, 1832, no. 97, Letters to Rev. E. Steane, B.M.S. Archives.
14. Mrs. Kingdon to Steane, Aug. 21, 1831, no. 81, Letters to Rev. E. Steane, B.M.S. Archives; Abbott, *Narrative,* pp. 142–43.
15. Mulgrave to Goderich, Aug. 24, 1832, no. 15, enclosing deposition of L. H. Evelyn and Williams to Yorke, Aug. 14, 1832, C.O. 137/183; Abbott, *Narrative,* pp. 141, 143–44.
16. Mulgrave to Goderich, Aug. 24, 1832, no. 15, C.O. 137/183; *Narrative Account,* p. 145.
17. Mulgrave to Goderich, Oct. 5, 1832, no. 23, C.O. 137/183. So far as bringing the rioters to justice was concerned, the governor's efforts were unavailing. At the Cornwall assizes in December the grand jury, in face of the strongest evidence, found *ignoramus* all capital indictments against the C.C.U. party and most charges of misdemeanor. Inquiry revealed that a customs officer, Fawcett, had been involved in the disturbances, and he was dismissed for conduct unbecoming to a king's servant, but six months later he was reinstated when the governor was convinced he had never been a member of the C.C.U. and had acted in the excitement of the moment. Fawcett apologized fully to the custos. Mulgrave to Goderich, Dec. 17, 1832, no. 51, C.O. 137/183; Mulgrave to Goderich, Feb. 1, 1833, no. 74, C.O. 137/188; Mulgrave to Stanley, July 26, 1833, no. 14, C.O. 137/189.
18. Mulgrave to Goderich, Oct. 6, 1832, no. 24, C.O. 137/183.
19. Campbell, *Dynamics of Change in a Slave Society,* pp. 163–64. Attorney General Fitzherbert Batty encouraged the jury to acquit Jordon by handing the case to his assistant.
20. Ibid., pp. 165–67; Duncan, *Narrative of the Wesleyan Mission to Jamaica,* pp. 326–28.
21. Mulgrave to Goderich, Aug. 28, 1832, confidential, C.O. 137/183.
22. Mulgrave to Goderich, Nov. 12, 1832, no. 39, enclosing Yorke to Cox, Oct. 13, 1832, and copy of resolutions, Oct., 1832, C.O. 137/187.
23. Burn, *Emancipation and Apprenticeship,* p. 98.
24. Mulgrave to Goderich, Nov. 29, 1832, no. 42, C.O. 137/183.
25. Mulgrave to Goderich, Nov. 13, 1832, no. 40, enclosing (1) address to the Assembly, (2) address of the Assembly, Nov. 2, 1832, (3) reply of the governor to the Assembly, (4) resolution of the House of Assembly, Nov. 8, 1832, C.O. 137/183.

26. Heumann, "Between Black and White," pp. 106–7, 121.

27. Goderich to Mulgrave, Dec. 7, 1832, no. 47, p. 392, C.O. 138/54.

28. Goderich to Mulgrave, Oct. 2, 1832, no. 28, pp. 334, 335; Oct. 1, 1832, no. 27, pp. 330–31, 340, 341, C.O. 138/54.

29. Mulgrave to Goderich, Oct. 7, 1832, no. 25, C.O. 137/183.

30. Mulgrave to Goderich, Dec. 31, 1832, no. 55, enclosing general order, Dec. 27, 1832, and resolution of St. John's C.C.U., C.O. 137/183.

31. Mulgrave to Goderich, Feb. 4, 1833, no. 80, enclosing Hilton to Yorke, Jan. 28, 1833, C.O. 137/188.

32. Goderich to Mulgrave, Dec. 7, 1832, no. 47, pp. 392–94, proclamation, p. 448, C.O. 138/54.

33. Mulgrave to Goderich, Feb. 4, 1833, no. 79, enclosing circular, Jan. 25, 1833, C.O. 137/188.

34. Mulgrave to Goderich, Feb. 21, 1833, no. 86, enclosing Cox to Yorke, Feb. 3, 1833, and resolutions of Feb. 9, 1833, St. Ann's Bay, C.O. 137/188.

35. Mulgrave to Goderich, Feb. 21, 1833, no. 87, C.O. 137/188. Two magistrates were subsequently dismissed in St. Thomas in the Vale for attending a C.C.U. meeting in Mar., 1833. W.M.M.S. Letters, Wedlock, Grateful Hill, June 27, 1833, f. 118, Box 133.

36. Mulgrave to Goderich, Aug. 24, 1832, no. 14, enclosing opinion of Attorney General O'Reilly, C.O. 137/183; W.M.M.S. Letters, Pennock, Kingston, Aug. 20, 1832, f. 116, Box 132.

37. Mulgrave to Stanley, July 7, 1833, no. 9, enclosing judgment of Sir J. Rowe, Greenwood vs. Livingstone et al., Grand Court, June 20, 1833, and the dissenting judgment of Justice Bernard C.O. 137/189. Greenwood vs. Livingstone et al. was an attempt by the Wesleyan district to repeat the triumph they had scored in the Whitehouse case by obtaining a favorable definition of the Jamaican toleration law. Greenwood, the Wesleyan missionary, imprisoned at Port Maria in Aug., 1832, claimed he was legally entitled to preach and charged the magistrate, Livingstone, with illegal imprisonment. Since the attorney general had already given his opinion that none of the missionaries in the island were duly qualified under 10 Anne c.2, Greenwood's case was argued on the basis that the English toleration laws had never been effective in Jamaica and that, in the absence of any Jamaican statute, no restraint could be imposed on any Dissenting preacher. The chief justice ruled that all the English toleration acts passed before the Jamaica act of 1728 were in force in the island, including the Conventicle Act; Mr. Justice Bernard gave a strong dissenting judgment. He pointed out that when the island was originally settled, every encouragement was given to Dissenters to settle there, that the circumstances prompting the English laws had long since passed away, that the 1689 act itself when originally enacted applied specifically to England, Wales, and Berwick-on-Tweed, and that the restrictions of that act applied in his opinion to Dissenters, not to ministers of Dissenters.

Bernard's opinion is sound and compares very favorably with the chief justice's.

38. W.M.M.S. Letters, Pennock, July 9, 1833, f. 11, Box 132, enclosing minutes of extra district meeting, July 3, 1833, quoting Rowe's address to the Cornwall assizes.

39. Mulgrave to Stanley, Aug. 4, 1833, no. 16, enclosures. The four chief rioters, including the notorious Samuel W. Rose, were arrested and put on trial. Characteristically, the grand jury refused to find them guilty. Mulgrave to Stanley, Nov. 23, 1833, no. 40, C.O. 137/189.

40. Mulgrave to Stanley, July 6, 1833, no. 8; Oct. 24, 1833, no. 31, C.O. 137/189.

Conclusion

Emancipation day, August 1, 1834, marked the moment when chattel slavery throughout the British empire ceased to exist. Severe limitations were initially imposed on the ex-slaves' freedom—forty hours of unpaid labor a week were extracted from the Jamaican "apprentices" until 1838—but emancipation immediately established full religious freedom and transformed the missionaries' relation with their converts. It allowed them to develop full-fledged church organizations complete with Jamaican lay preachers, ministers, and even missionaries. Mission schools expanded with the help of an education grant from the British government, and the missionaries, freed from all political constraints, could openly engage themselves in all issues concerning their converts. They could, and did, intervene in wage disputes, attack the apprenticeship system, condemn racism, promote the development of an independent peasantry, and encourage the peasants to claim their share of political power by putting themselves on the electoral register.

The ex-slaves, to whom emancipation restored a measure of the hope and confidence generated by the rebellion, responded massively. They gave an "astonishing impulse" to the development of mission work; the destroyed chapels were replaced by larger buildings that were still too small to contain the congregations they attracted, and the number of mission churches and missionary societies represented in the island multiplied.[1] "It was all happiness—almost unmingled joy—wherever we went multitudes came flocking to hear the good men," wrote a Baptist missionary retrospectively. So great was the influence the missionaries enjoyed in the decade following abolition that their old ally at the Colonial Office, James Stephen, predicted that the government of the island would fall into their hands.[2] The freedmen's enthusiasm for the missionaries was justified; by 1834 they had proved to be agents in the destruction of slavery, contributors to the powerful conjunctions of internal and external pressures that brought the system to an end.

The history of the missions in Jamaica was shaped primarily by their association with the antislavery movement. Though the missionary societies adopted a neutral attitude to slavery as a political issue, they shared with the antislavery movement the conviction that the slaves were part of the brotherhood of man, capable of choosing salvation, and that religious instruction was the most important immediate benefit to bestow on them. This connection was deepened in 1823 when the campaign to free the slaves won the support of the Baptist and Wesleyan churches and prompted the imperial government to make religious instruction a top priority in its official program for the reform of slavery. From first to last, however, the missionaries in Jamaica were associated with the forces in Britain demanding improvements in the slave system and, eventually, its abolition.

Missionary work was consequently a divisive issue among the slave owners. The planters mistrusted the missionaries, as they mistrusted, to a degree, the American Black Baptist preachers, as innovators disturbing their chattels' established routines. It was, however, as the implementer of a reform advocated by the antislavery party, and from 1823 by an imperial government responsive to its influence, that mission work had political significance for the planters. One group was prepared, along the lines advocated by the Committee of West India Planters and Merchants, to compromise on the issue of religious instruction for the slaves and, on their own terms, to tolerate the missionaries in order to discredit their enemies and maintain good relations with the imperial government. Their opponents believed in outright opposition to the antislavery party, the reform program it inspired, and the missionaries who implemented it.

The balance between the militant and the moderate proslavery factions in the Assembly rocked back and forth in response to internal and external threats to the security of the slave system. The depth and extent of the militants' influence in the backlash created by the abolition of the slave trade made imperial government intervention on behalf of the missionaries necessary. And antisectarianism as a political force was reactivated by the repercussions of the 1823 attack on slavery, which prompted the Assembly to thwart the reform policy and attack its agents by incorporating new restrictions on mission work in the 1826 slave code.

These developments heightened the political controversy surrounding mission work. The imperial government disallowed the slave code and brought pressure to bear outside the Assembly to combat antisectarianism. The Jamaican executive, the judiciary, and the magistrates were pushed into action in an attempt to discipline persons suspected of illegal acts or abuses of authority in relation to both slaves and missionaries. The Baptist and Wesleyan missionaries themselves became active participants in this process. In the context created by imperial policy, and the warm concern it reflected in Britain for the missions to the slaves, they claimed their right to a legal basis for their work; when this was conceded by the judiciary, they took up the cause of religious freedom for their converts.

The missionaries' success in the courts and their activities on behalf of the slaves were symptomatic of the stalemate the imperial government, ultimate arbiter of the planters' property rights, created between the moderate and militant proslavery factions.

The slave rebellion, however, united planter opinion in opposition in the missionaries, and even long-established mission patrons, in a flurry of militant opposition to the imperial government, joined the Colonial Church Union. In the final act of the drama the nonwhite population was consequently treated to the spectacle of British troops being used to cow the rebel whites and restore the missionaries to their churches.

The fact that the missionaries excited varying levels of hostility from the planters, modified at best by a guarded tolerance, and were associated with policies inimical to them, vitally influenced their relationship with the nonwhite population. Both the Black Baptists and the first Wesleyan missionaries necessarily attracted support from freedmen and slaves conscious of the oppression they suffered and anxious to find new compensations for their disabilities and new outlets for frustration. Discontent as well as religious interest and curiosity assembled their first congregations. The intense hostility displayed to Black Baptists and Wesleyans over the following decades made continued support of these churches, for any motive, a form of opposition to the system, a tradition periodically refreshed over the years by the opposition the missionaries continued to encounter. It was the stubborn resistance of slave and free colored and black church members in the first years of mission work that ensured the survival into the 1820s of Black Baptist congregations and encouraged the Wesleyans to maintain a presence in the island and persistently pursue licenses to preach, though their Kingston chapel was closed for seven years. And it was with the assistance of free lodgings, preaching places, gifts of land, and interest-free credit from the free colored and black supporters that the missions spread throughout the island after 1815.

The freedmen's alliance with the missionaries, while it represented opposition to the planters who denied them full civil rights until 1830, allowed this element in the population to retain the social values slave society inculcated and identify themselves culturally with the whites and aspire to the social and political privileges they enjoyed. The mission churches, staffed by British missionaries, sent out by British organizations, and associated with the party that had abolished the slave trade, could both immediately fulfill some of the freedmen's social aspirations (they exchanged the side seats and galleries of the Anglican church for the front pews in the chapel) and legitimize their aspirations to take their place as part of Jamaica's ruling class. At the same time, however, the mission churches afforded this element of the population, divided by wide disparities of income and skin shade, opportunities to develop their skills as preachers and church organizers, and to practice sustained cooperation, factors which assisted them to take advantage of the new political possibilities opened up by the 1823 campaign for abolition.

The islandwide organization created then to claim political parity with the planters produced a form of partnership between the Baptist and Wesleyan missionaries and the free colored and blacks. Linked by a common ally, the antislavery party, dependent on the imperial government for the promotion of their interests in face of planter opposition, and sympathetic to emancipation, missionaries and freedmen together combatted antisectarianism. The partnership was personified by Edward Jordon, long-standing member of the Kingston Wesleyan church and cofounder and editor of the abolitionist *Watchman and Jamaica Free Press,* and was demonstrated by the crucial support the free colored's press gave to the missionaries' efforts to claim religious freedom for the slaves. This partnership was the basis of the pro-mission party, which, in the crisis conditions that followed the rebellion, demonstrated by its loyal support of the imperial government the existence of a social basis for the peaceful transition to a free society.

The missionaries' most important contribution to the disintegration of the slave system, however, derived from their relationship with the slaves, a connection that both undermined slavery from within and contributed to the external forces legalizing its destruction. The terms laid down for mission membership invited the slaves to make a radical break with the traditional moral, sexual, and social mores of plantation life, to divorce themselves, in pursuit of salvation, from their families, friends, and customary pleasures and to repudiate their tried and tested religious beliefs and practices. To take up the Cross and follow in the footsteps of Christ imposed more drastic demands on the slaves than on the free coloreds and blacks.

To make these demands the missionaries appealed precisely to the intellectual and moral qualities the slave system in principle denied its chattels. They provided a new philosophical and organizational framework for the exercise of these capacities and, in the last decade before emancipation, the skills in literacy with which to develop them. They also unwittingly encouraged the slaves to extend the customary rights they enjoyed as independent producers and traders within the organization of plantation production. The slaves' property and marketing rights allowed them to graft church attendance onto the existing weekly routine, thus extending their rights at the expense of their masters'. The political significance of the slaves' action was underlined by the intermittent but persistent antisectarianism of the slave managers, who regarded the mission churches as an outcrop of the party in England that sought their destruction.

The slaves utilized mission teaching in different ways. Some bridged the disparities between their own cultural traditions and the missionaries' message by creating their own Native Baptist sects. These sects, generated initially by the Black Baptists and encouraged by the use of church members in positions of authority, represented different degrees of "independency" from the mission churches in terms of beliefs and practices. All these groups, however, afforded the slaves positions as leaders with authority equivalent to that of the missionaries and an opportunity to develop their ideas among themselves.

Others became convinced mission Christians prepared to remain subordinate to the missionaries while resisting any attempts by their masters to deprive them of their religion. Williams, his supporters on Rural Retreat, and the mission members they represented used their Christianity, as converts had done across the centuries, as the basis for resistance to oppression.

Sam Sharpe, ideologue and organizer of the 1831 rebellion, as a leader in the Baptist church and ruler among the Native Baptists, united the Native Baptist traditions of slave leadership and free thought with the radical Christian tradition of principled resistance. Under his leadership, in the ferment created by economic and political pressures of 1831, members of the mission churches and of the independent sects united to form a key element in the bid for freedom.

The contribution the missionaries made to the development of the slaves' political consciousness can best be measured by the difference between the 1824 Argyle war and the 1831 rebellion. The slaves on both occasions were responding in part to the antislavery agitation in England and the rumor that emancipation had taken place. On both occasions the planters themselves provided one final provocation: the denial of Saturday morning for work on the provision grounds in one case, and the reduction of the Christmas holiday in the other. The slaves in 1824 planned first to "sit down," and if the whites did not agree to given them freedom, they intended, according to the chief informer, "to kill the white people and take the country." Other estates were expected to follow suit. But there was evidently no extensive organization; "they made no bargain," one witness testified, "but like a parcel of sheep, one made a jump and the whole followed." The preparations may have been more extensive than the informers were aware, but it is interesting that even the eloquent chief informer did not weave this element into his narrative.[3]

Seven years later conditions for a large-scale rebellion were, overall, more mature. The standard of living for the plantation slaves had deteriorated to the point where mass grievances against the existing system provided far greater potential for an islandwide explosion. At the same time the freedmen's attainment of civil rights, and the end of the planters' monopoly of political power, demonstrated that political change was possible. These elements were given political direction, however, by men trained, like the missionaries, in the intellectual and organizational traditions of Dissent. Sharpe formulated justifications for action inspired by the ideology that informed the radicals of the English revolution and their descendants in the antislavery movement. He mobilized committed support by the methods the missionaries used. And the missionaries themselves provided an important element in the propaganda; they were projected as the slaves' allies in the cause of freedom and friends of the slaves' friends in England. Within this framework the rebels formulated their demands, which mirrored the demands formulated by the antislavery movement on their behalf, for legally sanctioned achievement of free status.

The missionaries, in turn, were equally serviceable to the antislavery cause. The recurrent harassment of the missionaries became a regular feature of antislavery propaganda in the decade 1823–33. While the missionary magazines lavished praise on the elements among the planters who promoted their work, the antisectarian attack on the St. Ann's Bay mission, the Barbados mission, and the martyrdom of John Smith, Henry Williams, and Sam Swiney were used by the *Anti-Slavery Monthly Reporter* as well as the Baptist and Wesleyan church magazines to mobilize public and parliamentary support for government action on behalf of the slaves and the missionaries.

The missionaries assisted the antislavery movement to demonstrate the nature of the planters' regime. More important, however, was the information they disseminated about the slaves. Their letters, published in the missionary magazines, established an image of the slaves as church-goers: orderly, clean, pious, serious, and responsible, identifiable with their British counterparts. The very success of the missionaries, the lengthening lists of stations and outstations, the tables recording increasing membership, detailed in the missionary societies' annual reports, showed how readily the slaves responded to Christian instruction.

The missionaries also established that the slaves' appetite for Christianity was matched by their appetite for learning in general. The young people they described who dropped the hoe to pick up the pen, and snatched sleep between reading lessons, suggested that the slave population of Jamaica had its leavening of potential entrepreneurs, ready to maximize their opportunities. It was knowledge about the slave population derived from the missionaries that made convincing the emergence of Christian heroes like Henry Williams and Sam Swiney and sharpened the public's condemnation of the slave regime's customary methods of discipline as well as its particular persecutions.

The image of the slave established by the missionaries made abolition a practical as well as a principled demand for Christians to support. The missionaries' converts clearly merited freedom and were capable of handling it. This conviction proved strong enough to survive the slave rebellion. The rebellion involved both armed resistance and strike action, but it was never allowed to serve as anti-abolition propaganda. The slave managers themselves, by claiming that the missionaries fomented it, ensured that much of the ensuing debate in England revolved around their exoneration. And the mission delegates had every opportunity, while exonerating themselves, to justify their converts.

The slaves' appreciation of the role the missionaries played in the developments leading to emancipation was expressed on Emancipation day itself when they flocked in their thousands to the mission churches. Their bitter defeat in the rebellion had left the churches half-empty. "What can church and prayer do fe we again" they asked.[4] Emancipation salvaged their hopes for the future and, with their own leaders dead or exiled, they turned to the missionaries. On August 1, 1834, from one end of the island to the other, people crammed into the chapels long before services started and multitudes gathered outside. "There never, in the recollection of man, was seen such a concourse of negroes in this town at one time," wrote one missionary from Hanover. ". . . There was no dancing, nor music, but the whole body of the negro population seemed to vie with one another who should conduct themselves best." There were special treats for the Sunday school children, who had been given complete freedom under the act. At Spanish Town one missionary worked up great excitement by calling for responses to a series of questions: What month of the year is it? What day of the month is it? What is done today? And the children shouted, "Negroes all made free!" "At this moment several of the little black children involuntarily burst out laughing and throwing their bodies about in every attitude of expressive joy." Months later, in October, 1834, William Knibb, the Baptist missionary, returned to a hero's welcome. The people ran to greet the ship, practically pushing Knibb and his wife into the water in their eagerness to greet them, and cried, "Him come, him come, for true. Who da come for we King, King Knibb, Him fight de battle, him win de crown."[5]

But the missionaries of free Jamaica worked in a society where the people had made their own struggle for freedom, under their own leaders, and had pushed their country into the revolutionary mainstream of the time, the struggle for individual liberty sanctioned by law. The missionaries' most enduring achievement was the contribution they made to the political formation of Sam Sharpe and his supporters.

NOTES

1. Sturge and Harvey, *West Indies in 1837*, p. 226; Dorothy Ryall, "The Organisation of the Missionary Societies, the Recruitment of Missionaries in Britain and the Role of Missionaries in the Diffusion of British Culture in Jamaica during the Period 1834–65" (Ph.D. thesis, University of London, 1959), pp. 133, 141, 151.
2. Philip Wright, *Knibb 'the Notorious': Slaves' Missionary, 1803–1845* (London, 1973), p. 238, quoting Clark, Brown's Town, Sept. 15, 1845,

Extracts from Letters, 1840–46, B.M.S. Archives; Ryall, "Missionary Societies," p. 216, quoting memo by James Stephen on Metcalfe to Russell, Apr. 30, 1840, no. 75, C.O. 137/248.

3. P.P. (Commons) (no. 66), 1825, 25:116–18.

4. Waddell, *Twenty-nine Years in the West Indies*, p. 71.

5. *S.M.R.* 15 (Oct., 1834):445, Watson, Lucea, Aug. 4, 1834; W.M.M.S. Letters, Corlett, Spanish Town, Aug. 13, 1834, f. 61, Box 135; Hinton, *Memoir of William Knibb*, p. 194.

Bibliography

MANUSCRIPTS

London, School of Oriental and African Studies, Methodist Missionary Society Archives.
    Correspondence, West Indies General, Boxes 112–134.
    Correspondence, Outgoing, Box 24.
    Synod Minutes, West Indies, Boxes 148, 149.
    General Minutes of the Committee of the Wesleyan Methodist Society, Box 547.
    Various Papers, Box 588.
    Special Series, notes and transcripts, Box 662.
London, Baptist Missionary Society Archives.
    Boxes W.I./1, W.I./3, W.I. uncatalogued.
    Letters to the Rev. E. Steane, D.D., 1794–1844, bound vol.
London, Moravian Missionary Society Archives.
    Minutes of the Society for the Furtherance of the Gospel, 1796–1831, bound vols. 3–5.
London, British Museum.
    Huskisson Papers, Add. Mss. 38751–57.
London, Public Record Office.
    Original correspondence between the Secretaries of State and the governor of Jamaica, 1808–34, C.O. 137, 138, 854.
Bristol, Baptist College.
    Letters from William Wilberforce to Dr. John Ryland, bound vol.
Oxford, Rhodes House.
    Anti-Slavery Papers, M.S. British Empire 5.20. E2/1–4.

OFFICIAL PUBLICATIONS

Jamaica: *Journals of the House of Assembly, 1802–15.*
    Votes of the House of Assembly, 1816–28.
Great Britain, Parliamentary Papers (Commons):
"Papers relating to the Manumission, Government and Population of Slaves in the West Indies, 1822–24, pt. 7, Copy of all Judicial Proceedings,

relative to the Trial and Punishment of Rebels, or alleged Rebels in the Island of Jamaica, since the 1st of January 1823" (no. 66), 1825, 25.

"Copies of all Dispatches which His Majesty's Government have received from Jamaica, relative to an Attack made on the Wesleyan Missionary Meeting House and the Dwelling of Mr. Ratcliffe the Missionary, at Christmas last" (no. 554), 1826–27, 18.

"Copy of all Communications made to the Colonial Department since 1st January 1826 by the Government of Jamaica, or by the Colonial Organs of the different Religious Societies employing Missionaries in Jamaica, respecting the obstacles alleged to be thrown in the way of their giving religious instruction to the Slaves, and the alleged persecution, imprisonment, or other punishment of Missionaries employed by them in that Island" (no. 672), 1830, 21.

"Jamaica: Copy of any information received from Jamaica respecting an Inquiry into the treatment of a Female Slave, by the Rev. Mr. Bridges, Rector of St. Ann" (no. 231), 1830–31, 16.

"Jamaica: Copies of all Communications relative to the reported Maltreatment of a Slave named Henry Williams in Jamaica" (no. 91), 1830–31, 16.

"West India Colonies: Slave Insurrection, Copies of Despatches and Correspondence between Viscount Goderich and the Governors of the West India Colonies, respecting the recent rebellion amongst Slaves in Jamaica" (no. 285), 1831–32, 47.

"Jamaica: Slave Trials and punishment, no. 1, Copies of all Communications from Jamaica relating to the Trial of George Ancle and Samuel Swiney, Negro Slaves for certain alleged offences relating to Religious worship" (no. 480), 1831–32, 47.

"Jamaica: Slave insurrection. Copies of communications made to the Government relative to Rebellion in Jamaica, received subsequently to those already presented to the House and Return of all Teachers or Preachers and Persons connected with Missionary Establishments in Jamaica who have been arrested this year; the charges against them; and the Proceedings that have occurred thereupon" (no. 482), 1831–32, 47.

"Jamaica: Slave Insurrection. Copy of the Report of a Committee of the House of Assembly of Jamaica, appointed to inquire into the Cause of, and Injury sustained by, the recent Rebellion in that Colony; together with the Examination on Oath, Confessions and other Documents annexed to that Report" (no. 561), 1831–32, 47.

"Jamaica: Copy of all Correspondence relative to the Punishment of Two Female Slaves belonging to Mr. Jackson, Custos of Port Royal, and the Proceedings thereon" (no. 737), 1831–32, 47.

"Report from the Select Committee on the Extinction of Slavery Throughout the British Dominions" (no. 721), 1831–32, 20.

Great Britain, Parliamentary Papers (Lords):
Minutes of Evidence taken before the Select Committee of the House of Lords appointed to inquire into the Laws and Usages of the several West India

Colonies in relation to the Slave Population (no. 127), 1831–32, 306 and 307.

PRINTED PRIMARY SOURCES

Annual Reports of the Society for the Conversion and Religious Instruction of Negro Slaves in the West Indies, 1823–1833.
Anti-Slavery Monthly Reporter, 1825–29, continued as *Anti-Slavery Reporter,* 1829–30.
Address of the Committee of the Church Missionary Society to the members of the Society in the West Indies. London: Committee of the C.M.S., 1833.
Baptist Annual Register, 1793–1802.
Baptist Magazine, 1819–34.
Baptist Missionary Society. *Annual Reports,* 1819–34.
Instructions to Members of Unitas Fratrum who minister in the Gospel among the Heathen. London: Printed for the Brethren's Society, 1794.
Jamaica Journal and Kingston Chronicle, 1823–26.
Letter of Instruction. London: Baptist Missionary Society, n.d.
London Missionary Society. *Report of the Proceedings against the late Rev. J. Smith, of Demerara.* London: F. Westley, 1824.
Miscellaneous regulations, being an appendix to the General Instructions of the Wesleyan Methodist Missionary Committee. London: J. Mason, 1832.
Missionary Herald (London), 1819–34.
Missionary Notices (London), 1816–38.
Periodical Accounts relating to the Missions of the United Brethren, 1818–38.
Royal Gazette (Kingston, Jamaica), 1823–26, 1829–34.
Scottish Missionary and Philanthropic Register, 1823–35.
A Statement of the Plan, Object and Effects of the Wesleyan Missions to the West Indies. London: Council of the Wesleyan Methodist Missionary Society, 1824.
Watchman and Jamaica Free Press, 1830–34.
Wesleyan-Methodist Magazine, 1818–34.
Wesleyan Methodist Missionary Society. *Annual Reports,* 1818–35.

SELECTED SECONDARY SOURCES

Abbott, Thomas F. *A Narrative of certain events connected with the late Disturbances in Jamaica and the charges preferred against the Baptist Missionaries in that Island.* London: Holdsworth and Ball, 1832.
Ajayi, Jacob, F. Ade. *Christian Missions in Nigeria 1841–1891, the Making of a New Elite.* Ibadan History Series. London: Longmans, 1966.
Anstey, Roger T. "Capitalism and Slavery: A Critique." *Economic History Review* 21 (1968):307–20.

_____. "A Re-interpretation of the Abolition of the British Slave Trade, 1806–1807." *English Historical Review* 87 (Apr., 1972):304–32.

_____. *The Atlantic Slave Trade and British Abolition, 1760–1810.* London: MacMillan Press, 1975.

Aptheker, Herbert. *American Negro Slave Revolts.* Studies in History, Economics and Public Law, no. 501. New York: Columbia University Press, 1943.

Ayendele, Emanuel A. *The Missionary Impact on Modern Nigeria 1842–1914.* Ibadan History Series. London: Longmans, 1966.

_____. *Holy Johnson, Pioneer of African Nationalism.* London: Frank Cass, 1970.

Barclay, Alexander. *A Practical View of the Present State of Slavery in the West Indies.* London: Smith, Elder and Co., 1826.

Bascom, William R., and Melville J. Herskovits, eds. *Continuity and Change in African Cultures.* Chicago: University of Chicago Press, 1959.

Beckford, George L. *Persistent Poverty.* New York: Oxford University Press, 1972.

Bennett, J. Harry. *Bondsmen and Bishops: Slavery and Apprenticeship on the Codrington Plantations of Barbados, 1710–1838.* Berkeley: University of California Press, 1958.

Bickell, Richard. *The West Indies as they are; or a real picture of Slavery.* London: J. Hatchard and Son, 1825.

Blassingame, John W. *The Slave Community: Plantation Life in the Antebellum South.* New York: Oxford University Press, 1972.

Bleby, Henry. *Death Struggles of Slavery.* London: Hamilton, Adams and Co., 1835.

Blyth, George. *Reminiscences of a Missionary Life.* Edinburgh and London: Partridge, 1853.

Brathwaite, Edward. *The Development of Creole Society in Jamaica, 1770–1820.* Oxford: Clarendon Press, 1971.

Bridges, George W. *A Voice from Jamaica; in reply to William Wilberforce.* London: Longman and Co., 1823.

_____. *The Annals of Jamaica.* 2 vols. London: John Murray, 1828.

Buchner, J. H. *The Moravians in Jamaica.* London: Longman and Co., 1854.

Bunting, Thomas. *The Life of Jabez Bunting, D.D.* 2 vols. London: Longman and Co., 1859, 1887.

Burchell, William F. *Memoir of Thomas Burchell.* London: B. L. Green, 1849.

Burn, William L. *Emancipation and Apprenticeship in the British West Indies.* London: Jonathan Cape, 1937.

Buxton, Charles, ed. *Memoirs of Sir Thomas Fowell Buxton, Bart.* London: John Murray, 1849.

Caldecott, Alfred. *The Church in the West Indies.* London: Society for Promoting Christian Knowledge, 1898.

Campbell, Mavis C. *The Dynamics of Change in a Slave Society, 1800–1865.* Rutherford, N.J., Fairleigh Dickinson University Press; London: Associated University Presses, 1976.

Carey, Samuel Pearce. *A Life of William Carey, Baptist Missionary*. London: Marshall, Morgan and Scott, 1936.

Carmichael, Mrs. A. C. *Domestic Manners and Social Condition of the White, Coloured and Negro Population of the West Indies*. 2 vols. London: Whittaker, Treacher and Co., 1833.

Childs, Gladwyn M. *Umbundu Kinship and Character*. London: Oxford University Press for the International African Institute and the Witwatersrand University Press, 1949.

Clark, John, Walter Dendy, and James M. Phillippo. *The Voice of Jubilee*. London: John Snow, 1865.

Clarke, John. *Memorials of Baptist Missionaries in Jamaica*. London: Yates and Alexander, 1869.

Clarkson, Thomas. *Thoughts on the Necessity of Improving the Condition of Slaves in the British Colonies, with a view to their ultimate emancipation, and on the practicality, the safety and the advantages of the latter measure*. London: Richard Taylor, 1823.

Coke, Thomas. *A History of the West Indies, containing the Natural, Civil and Ecclesiastical History of each Island*. 3 vols. Liverpool: Nuttall, Fisher and Dixon, 1808–11.

Cooper, Thomas. *Facts illustrative of the Condition of the Negro Slaves in Jamaica*. London: J. Hatchard and Son, 1824.

————. *A Letter to Robert Hibbert Jun. Esq.*. London: J. Hatchard and Son, 1824.

Coupland, Reginald. *Wilberforce*. Oxford: Clarendon Press 1922; reprinted New York: Negro University Press, 1968.

Cox, Francis A. *A History of the Baptist Missionary Society 1792–1842*, 2 vols. London: T. Ward and Co., 1842.

Craton, Michael. "Jamaican Slave Mortality: Fresh Light from Worthy Park, Longville and Tharpe Estates." *Journal of Caribbean History* 3 (Nov., 1971):1–27.

————. *Searching for the Invisible Man*. Cambridge, Mass.: Harvard University Press, 1978.

————. "Proto-Peasant Revolts? The Late Slave Rebellions in the British West Indies 1816–32." *Past and Present* 85 (Nov., 1979):99–125.

Craton, Michael, and James Walvin. *A Jamaican Plantation: The History of Worthy Park, 1670–1970*. London: W. H. Allen, 1970.

Curtin, Philip D. *Two Jamaicas: The Role of Ideas in a Tropical Colony, 1830–65*. Cambridge, Mass.: Harvard University Press, 1958; reprinted, New York: Greenwood Press, 1968.

————. *The Atlantic Slave Trade: A Census*. Madison: University of Wisconsin Press, 1969.

Davidson, Basil. *The African Awakening*. London: Jonathan Cape, 1955.

Davis, David. B. "James Cropper and the British Anti-Slavery Movement 1821–23." *Journal of Negro History* 45 (Oct., 1960):241–58.

————. "James Cropper and the British Anti-Slavery Movement 1823–33." *Journal of Negro History* 46 (Apr., 1961):154–73.

_____. *The Problem of Slavery in Western Culture*. Ithaca, N.Y.: Cornell University Press, 1966.

_____. *The Problem of Slavery in the Age of Revolution, 1770–1823*. Ithaca, N.Y.: Cornell University Press, 1975.

Davis, Henry, W. C. *The Age of Grey and Peel*. Oxford: Clarendon Press, 1929.

De La Beche, Henry T. *Notes on the Present Condition of the Negroes in Jamaica*. London: T. Cadell, 1825.

De Schweinitz, Edmund. *The Moravian Manual*. Philadelphia: Lindsay and Bakiston, 1859.

Douglass, Frederick. *My Bondage and My Freedom*. William L. Katz, gen. ed., *The American Negro: His History and Literature*. New York: Arno Press and *New York Times*, 1969.

Drescher, Seymour. *Econocide: British Slavery in the Era of Abolition*. Pittsburgh: Pittsburgh University Press, 1977.

Drew, Samuel. *The Life of the Rev. Thomas Coke, LLD*. London: Printed by Thomas Cordeaux, Agent, 1817.

Duncan, Peter. *A Narrative of the Wesleyan Mission to Jamaica*. London: Partridge, 1849.

Duncker, Sheila. "The Free Coloured and Their Fight for Civil Rights in Jamaica, 1800–1830." M.A. dissertation, University of London, 1960.

Edwards, Bryan. *The History, Civil and Commercial of the British Colonies in the West Indies*. 3 vols. London: J. Stockdale, 1801.

Ekecki, Felix K. *Missionary Enterprise and Rivalry in Igboland*. Cass Library of African Studies, no. 119. London: Frank Cass, 1971.

Ellis, John B. *The Diocese of Jamaica*. London: Society for the Propagation of Christian Knowledge, 1913.

Ellis, William. *The History of the London Missionary Society*. London: John Snow, 1844.

Eltis, David. "The Traffic in Slaves between the British West India Colonies 1807–1833." *Economic History Review* 25 (1972):55–65.

Findlay, George G., and William W. Holdsworth. *The History of the Wesleyan Missionary Society*. 5 vols. London: Epworth Press, 1921–24.

Fogel, Robert W., and Stanley L. Engerman. *Time on the Cross: The Economics of American Negro Slavery*. London: Wildwood House, 1974.

Foulks, Theodore. *Eighteen months in Jamaica; with recollections of the late Rebellion*. London: Whittaker, Treacher and Arnott, 1833.

Freeman, Thomas W. *Pre-Famine Ireland*. Manchester: Manchester University Press, 1957.

Furley, Oliver W. "Moravian Missionaries and Slaves in the West Indies." *Caribbean Studies* 5 (July, 1965):3–16.

Gardner, William J. *History of Jamaica*. London: E. Stock, 1873.

Genovese, Eugene D. *The Political Economy of Slavery: Studies in the Economy and Society of the Slave South*. New York: Random House, 1965.

_____. *Roll, Jordan, Roll: The World the Slaves Made*. New York: Pantheon Books, 1974.

———. *From Rebellion to Revolution: Afro-American Slave Revolts in the Making of the Modern World.* Baton Rouge: Louisiana State University Press, 1980.

Gluckman, Max. *Order and Rebellion in Tribal Africa.* London: Cohen and West, 1971.

Goveia, Elsa V. *Slave Society in the British Leeward Islands at the End of the Eighteenth Century.* New Haven, Conn.: Yale University Press, 1965.

Goveia, Elsa V., and Douglas Hall, gen. eds. *Chapters in Caribbean History.* Barbados: Caribbean Universities Press, 1970. No. 2: *West Indian Slave Laws of the 18th century,* by Elsa V. Goveia.

Green, Margaret M. *Ibo Village Affairs.* London: Sidgwick and Jackson, 1947.

Hall, Douglas, *Free Jamaica, 1838–65.* New Haven, Conn.: Yale University Press, 1959.

———. "Slaves and Slavery in the British West Indies." *Social and Economic Studies* 11 (1962):305–18.

———. "Absentee-Proprietorship in the British West Indies, to about 1850." *Jamaica Historical Review* 4 (1964):15–34.

———. *A Brief History of the West India Committee.* Barbados: Caribbean Universities Press, 1971.

Hassé, Evelyn R. *The Moravians.* London: National Council of Evangelical Free Churches, 1912.

Herskovits, Melville J. *The Myth of the Negro Past.* New York: Harper and Bros., 1941.

Herskovits, Melville J. and Frances. *Trinidad Village.* New York: Alfred Knopf, 1947.

Heumann, Gad J. "Between Black and White: Brown Men in Jamaican Politics and Society, 1823–1865." Ph.D. thesis, Yale University, 1975.

Higman, Barry W. "The West India 'Interest' in Parliament 1807–33." *Historical Studies* 13 (Oct., 1967):1–19.

———. "Household Structure and Fertility on Jamaican Slave Plantations: A Nineteenth Century Example." *Population Studies* 27 (Nov., 1973):527–49.

———. *Slave Population and Economy in Jamaica 1807–1834.* Cambridge: Cambridge University Press, 1976.

Hinton, John H. *Memoir of William Knibb, Missionary in Jamaica.* London: Houlston and Stoneman, 1847.

Hobsbawm, Eric J. "Methodism and the Threat of Revolution in Britain." *History Today* 7 (Feb., 1957):115–24.

———. *Primitive Rebels.* Manchester: Manchester University Press, 1959.

———. *Bandits.* London: Weidenfeld and Nicolson, 1969.

Hutton, James E. *History of the Moravian Missions.* London: Moravian Publication Office, 1922.

Jackson, George. *A Memoir of the Rev. John Jenkins, late a Wesleyan Missionary in the Island of Jamaica.* London: J. Mason, 1832.

Jackson, Thomas P. *Memoir of the Life and Writings of the Rev. Richard Watson.* 12 vols. London: J. Mason, 1834–37.

Jakobssen, Stiv. *Am I Not a Man and a Brother?* Uppsala: Almquist and Wicksells Boktryckeri, 1972.

Jones, Wilbur D. "Lord Mulgrave's Administration in Jamaica, 1832–33. *Journal of Negro History* 48 (Jan., 1963): 44–56.

Klingberg, Frank J. *The Anti-Slavery Movement in England.* London: Oxford University Press, 1926.

Knaplund, Paul. *James Stephen and the British Colonial System 1813–1847.* Madison: University of Wisconsin Press, 1953.

Latrobe, Christian J. *A Concise Account of the Present state of the Missions of the United Brethren.* London: W. McDougall, 1811.

Le Page, Robert B. *Jamaican Creole.* London: MacMillan, 1960.

"Letters Showing the Rise and Progress of Early Negro Churches in Georgia and the West Indies." *Journal of Negro History* 1 (Jan., 1916):69–92.

Lewis, Matthew G. *Journal of a West Indian Proprietor.* London: J. Murray, 1834.

Lichtheim, George. *A Short History of Socialism.* London: Weidenfeld and Nicolson, 1970; Collins-Fontana, 1977.

Long, Edward. *The History of Jamaica.* 3 vols. London: T. Lowndes, 1774.

Mackerrow, John. *History of the Secession Church.* Glasgow: A. Fullarton, 1841.

Mackichan, Dugald. *The Missionary Ideal in the Scottish Churches.* London: Hodder and Stoughton, 1927.

McNeill, George. *The West Indies, the Story of Our Missions.* Edinburgh: Foreign Mission Committee of the Church of Scotland, 1911.

Madden, Richard R. *A Twelvemonths Residence in the West Indies.* 2 vols. London: James Cochrane and Co., 1835.

Manning, Bernard. L. *The Protestant Dissenting Deputies.* Cambridge: Cambridge University Press, 1952.

Marly; or a Planter's Life in Jamaica. Glasgow: Griffin and Co.; London: Hurst and Co., 1828.

Mathieson, William L. *British Slavery and Its Abolition 1823–1838.* London: Longmans, Green, 1926; reprinted, New York: Octagon Books, 1967.

Mbiti, John S. *New Testament Eschatology in an African Background.* London: Oxford University Press, 1965.

Mellor, George R. *British Imperial Trusteeship, 1783–1850.* London: Faber and Faber, 1951.

Mintz, Sidney W. "Historical Sociology of the Jamaican Church-founded Free Village System." *De West-Indische Gids* 38–39 (Sept., 1958):46–70.

_____. comp. *Papers in Caribbean Anthroplogy,* vol. 47. New Haven, Conn.: Yale University Press, 1960.

Mintz, Sidney W., and Richard Price. *An Anthropological Approach to the Afro-American Past: A Caribbean Perspective.* Philadelphia: Institute for the Study of Human Issues, 1976.

Morison, John. *The Fathers and Founders of the London Missionary Society.* 2 vols. London: Fisher, Son and Co., 1844.

Murray, David J. *The West Indies and the Development of Colonial Government 1801–1834.* Oxford: Clarendon Press, 1965.

Oliver, Roland. *The Missionary Factor in East Africa.* London: Longmans, Green, 1952.

Owen, John. *The History of the Origin and First Ten Years of the British and Foreign Bible Society.* 2 vols. London: Tilling and Hughes, 1816.

Parrinder, Geoffrey. *West African Religion.* London: Epworth Press, 1961.

Patterson, Orlando. *The Sociology of Slavery.* London: MacGibbon and Kee, 1967.

———. "Slavery and Slave Revolts: A Socio-Historical Analysis of the First Maroon War, Jamaica 1655–1740." *Social and Economic Studies* 19 (Sept., 1970):289–325.

———. "Slavery in Human History." *New Left Review* 117 (Sept.–Oct., 1979):31–67.

Penson, Lillian M. *The Colonial Agents of the British West Indies.* London: London University Press, 1924.

Phillippo, James. *Jamaica: Its Past and Present State.* London: J. Snow, 1843.

Phillips, Ulrich B. *American Negro Slavery.* New York: D. Appleton and Co., 1918.

———. *Life and Labour in the Old South.* Boston: Little, Brown, 1929.

———. "A Jamaica Slave Plantation," *American Historical Review* 19 (Apr., 1914):543–58.

Ragatz, Lowell J. *The Fall of the Planter Class in the British Caribbean, 1760–1833.* American Historical Association. New York: Century Co., 1928.

———. "Absentee Landlordism in the British Caribbean 1750–1833." *Agricultural History* 5 (Jan., 1931):7–24.

Ramsay, James. *An Essay on the Treatment and Conversion of African Slaves in the British Sugar Colonies.* London: James Phillips, 1784.

Ranger, Terence O., and Isaria N. Kikambo. *The Historical Study of African Religion.* London: Heinemann and Co., 1972.

Rawick, George B. *From Sundown to Sunup: The Making of the Black Community.* The American Slave: A Composite Autobiography, no. 1. Contributions in Afro-American and African Studies, no. 11. Westport, Conn.: Greenwood Publishing Co., 1972.

Reckord, Mary (née Turner). "The Jamaica Slave Rebellion of 1831." *Past and Present* 40 (July, 1968):108–25.

———. "The Colonial Office and the Abolition of Slavery." *Historical Journal* 14 (Dec., 1971):723–34.

Roby, John. *Members of the Assembly of Jamaica . . . Arranged in Parochial Lists.* Jamaica: A. Holmes, Montego Bay, 1831.

Roughley, Thomas. *The Jamaica Planter's Guide.* London: Longman, Hurst, Rees, Orme and Brown, 1823.

Ryall, Dorothy. "The Organisation of the Missionary Societies, the Recruitment of Missionaries in Britain and the Role of Missionaries in the Diffusion of British Culture in Jamaica during the Period 1834–65." Ph.D. thesis, University of London, 1959.

Samuel, Peter. *The Wesleyan-Methodist Missions in Jamaica and Honduras.* London: Partridge and Oakley, 1850.

Schuler, Monica. "Akan Slave Rebellions in the British Caribbean." *Savacou* 1 (June, 1970):8–31.

[Senior, B. M.] *Jamaica as it was, as it is, and as it may be.* London: T. Hurst, 1835.

Shepperson, George, and Thomas Price. *Independent African.* Edinburgh: Edinburgh University Press, 1958.

Sheridan, Richard. "The West India Sugar Crisis and British Slave Emancipation 1830–33." *Journal of Economic History* 21 (1961):539–51.

_____. "Simon Taylor, Sugar Tycoon of Jamaica, 1740–1813." *Agricultural History* 45 (Oct., 1971):285–96.

Short, K. R. M. "Jamaican Christian Missions and the Great Slave Rebellion of 1831–32." *Journal of Ecclesiastical History* 27 (Jan., 1976):57–72.

Simpson, George E. *Religious Cults in the Caribbean: Jamaica, Trinidad and Haiti.* Rio Piedras: Institute of Caribbean Studies, University of Puerto Rico, 1970.

Sketch of the History and Proceedings of the Deputies appointed to protect the civil rights of the Protestant Dissenters. London: Printed for Samuel Burton, 1814.

Smith, Michael G. "Some Aspects of Social Structure in the British Caribbean about 1820." *Social and Economic Studies* 1 (1953):55–79.

Soloway, Richard A. *Prelates and People: Ecclesiastical Social Thought in England 1783–1852.* Toronto: University of Toronto Press, 1969.

Starobin, Robert S., ed. *Denmark Vesey: The Slave Conspiracy of 1822.* Gerald Emanuel Stearn, gen. ed., *Great Lives Observed.* Englewood Cliffs, N.J.: Prentice–Hall, 1970.

Stephen, George. *Anti-Slavery Recollections: in a series of letters, addressed to Mrs. Beecher Stowe.* London: Thomas Hatchard, 1854.

Stewart, John. *A View of the Past and Present State of the Island of Jamaica.* Edinburgh: Oliver and Boyd, 1823.

Stock, Eugene. *The History of the Church Missionary Society.* 4 vols. London: Church Missionary Society, 1899–1916.

Sturge, Joseph, and Thomas Harvey. *The West Indies in 1837.* London: Hamilton, Adams and Co., 1838.

Sundkler, Bengt G. M. *Bantu Prophets in South Africa.* London: Lutterworth Press, 1948.

Thompson, Augustus, C. *Moravian Missions.* London: Hodder and Stoughton, 1883.

Thompson, Edward P. *The Making of the English Working Class.* London: Victor Gollancz, 1963.

Townsend, William J., Herbert B. Workman, and George Earys, eds. *A New History of Methodism.* 2 vols. London: Hodder and Stoughton, 1909.

Turner, Mary. "The Bishop of Jamaica and Slave Instruction." *Journal of Ecclesiastical History* 26 (Oct., 1975):363–78.

Underhill, Edward Bean. *Life of J. M. Phillippo, Missionary in Jamaica.* London: Yates and Alexander, 1881.

———. *The West Indies: Their Social and Religious Condition.* London: Jackson, Walford & Hodder, 1862.

Waddell, Hope. *Twenty-nine Years in the West Indies and Central Africa 1826–1858.* London: Nelson, 1863.

Wearmouth, Robert F. *Methodism and the Working Class Movements in England, 1800–1850.* London: Epworth Press, 1937.

Wesley, John. *Thoughts on Slavery.* London: John Cruikshank, 1774.

West India Sketch Book. 2 vols. London: Whittaker and Co., 1826.

Whiteley, Henry. *Three months in Jamaica in 1832: comprising a residence of seven weeks on a sugar plantation.* London: J. Hatchard and Son, 1833.

Whitley, William T. *A History of British Baptists.* London: Kingsgate Press, 1932.

Wilberforce, William. *An Appeal to the Religion, Justice, and Humanity of the Inhabitants of the British Empire, in Behalf of the Negro Slaves in the West Indies.* London: J. Hatchard and Son, 1823.

Williams, Cynric R. *A Tour through the Island of Jamaica . . . in the Year 1823.* London: Hurst and Clarke, 1827.

Williams, Eric. *Capitalism and Slavery.* Chapel Hill: University of North Carolina Press, 1944.

Williams, James. *A Narrative of Events since the First of August, 1834.* London: J. Rider, printer, 1837.

Wolf, Eric R. *Peasant Wars.* London: Faber and Faber, 1971.

Wood, Peter H. *Black Majority.* New York: Alfred Knopf, 1974.

Wright, Philip. *Knibb 'the Notorious': Slaves' Missionary 1803–1845.* London: Sidgwick and Jackson, 1973.

Young, Robert. *A View of Slavery in connection with Christianity; being the substance of a discourse delivered in the Wesleyan Chapel, Stony Hill Chapel, Sept. 19, 1824.* London: Smith, Elder and Co., 1825.

Index

A Note on the Author

MARY TURNER was born in Hull, Yorkshire, England, and received an M.A. from Manchester University (1953) and a Ph.D. from King's College, London University (1963). She presently teaches at Dalhousie University in Nova Scotia.

BOOKS IN THE SERIES